HUDSON MOHAWK GATEWAY

Additional Chapters and Timeline Contributed by

P. Thomas Carroll, Lois M. Feister, Denise Scammell,
Diana S. Waite, and Robert G. Waite

Photograph Research and Editing by
Sloane Bullough, Kimberly A. Klem, and Peter D. Shaver

Additional Editorial Assistance by
Kathleen M. Helfrich

American Historical Press
Sun Valley, California

HUDSON MOHAWK

GATEWAY

An Illustrated History

Thomas Phelan & P. Thomas Carroll

Inside Covers: This is a view of Troy from Watervliet in 1877. In the foreground is the sidecut of the Erie Canal. The Rensselaer and Saratoga Railroad Bridge is at the left and the newly completed Congress Street Bridge is at right. Courtesy, New York State Library

p. 135 Mendal, Mesick, Cohen Waite, Hall Architects now known as John G. Waite Associates Architects PLLC

© American Historical Press
All Rights Reserved
Published 2001
Printed in the United States of America

Library of Congress Catalogue Card Number: 2001093544
ISBN: 1-892724-17-0

Bibliography: p. 240
Includes Index

CONTENTS

PREFACE

A short distance below the confluence of the Mohawk with the Hudson River is the first dam on the Hudson, marking the headwater of navigation on this great waterway. Nearby, along both banks of the river, a harmonious grouping of communities developed toward the end of the eighteenth and into the nineteenth centuries. Troy occupies some seven miles of the east bank of the Hudson in this area. Opposite, dotting the west bank from north to south and bordered by the various fingers of the Mohawk's mouth, are the municipalities of Waterford village and town, Cohoes, Green Island, Colonie, and Watervliet.

The themes of commerce and industry, labor and management, business and services prevail here. The establishment of this Gateway area as New York State's first Heritage Area—*Riverspark*—has woven these adjacent communities of the Upper Hudson into a natural grouping, though each has maintained its political separateness, integrity, and special character. The region works together in spite of boundaries reinforced by location in three different counties. Thus, it seemed wise to advance these cities' common cause by preparing a single local history which would focus to a considerable extent on the theme that draws them together: their industrial heritage.

The principal author has been fortunate in enlisting the cooperative service of Lois M. Feister, author of the first chapter; the sixth chapter is the work of Troy native Professor Robert G. Waite of Idaho State University's Department of History; Diana S. Waite is an early collaborator and author of the eighth chapter; and Thomas Carroll, director of the Hudson Mohawk Industrial Gateway, brings the history up to date in chapter 11 and also brings together various other sections of the book. Research material was put together by Caroline A. King; Kathryn A. Larsen saved the principal author from his own hand by perfectly translating his abysmal handwriting onto a word processor. Great gratitude to all.

What you read here is a much shortened version of what was written. Hopefully, it is accurate and will serve the Gateway area well. All of us hope that you understand where we come from and where we are going. It is especially clear that industrialization was the core theme of the last two centuries and that we are riding the crest of the new wave with the word "communications" as key.

May the book kindle your love of this wonderful GATEWAY.

Thomas Phelan
Troy, New York

The Cohoes Falls on the Mohawk River, slightly idealized by the engraver, encumbered travelers in the seventeenth and eighteenth centuries but was an early tourist attraction nonetheless. Courtesy, New York State Library

To my father who loved Troy
and taught me to see what
is here and to my mother
from whom I inherited the
discerning eyes

Prehistoric caribou were hunted by the first inhabitants of New York State, known as Paleo-Indians, using spears with chipped stone projectile points. Courtesy, New York State Museum/The State Education Department

CHAPTER ONE

IN THE BEGINNING

When Henry Hudson sailed into the Hudson-Mohawk Gateway in 1609, he was greeted by people whose arrival predated his by many thousands of years. The native Americans who boarded his ship, the *Half Moon,* were probably Mahicans, members of the Algonkian-speaking family of Indians. The Iroquoian speakers, a separate linguistic group, dwelled in the woodlands farther west up the Mohawk River, with settlements reaching into northern and western New York. In 1609 all of the Gateway's native Indian tribes shared a common way of life at a time characterized by archaeologists as the Late Woodland period— about A.D. 1000 to 1600. They were agriculturists, living in villages, with intricate trading networks stretching far beyond the boundaries of the Hudson-Mohawk region.

The prehistoric Indians left no written records. Only by analyzing artifacts left buried in the earth have archaeologists discovered how the Indian cultures grew and developed in the Gateway area. Even to this day the story remains incomplete. However, recent excavations, along with scholarly research, have resulted in the reconstruction of a useful, though somewhat fragmented, history.

The first inhabitants of the Hudson and Mohawk valleys were Paleo-Indians. They probably arrived around 10,500 B.C., after the retreat of the last glacial ice sheet. Characterized as big game hunters, these Indians followed herds of large animals, such as caribou, and also foraged food from the land. Moving in small bands through vast conifer forests and grassy meadowlands, the Paleo-Indians kept this nomadic way of life until approximately 8000 B.C. Their chipped stone tools have been discovered in the immediate Gateway region.

Few people seem to have occupied the upper Hudson valley from roughly 8000 B.C. to 5000 B.C. During this interlude, known as the Early Archaic period, coniferous forests dominated the area. The environment, according to some prehistorians, did not support plants and animals needed by man, thus the sparse human population. By

5000 B.C., deciduous forests had grown and Indians, following the game, returned. Called "specialists in diversification," they were also gatherers who lived a semi-nomadic lifestyle. They traveled in small bands, setting up fishing stations near the rivers and establishing hunting base camps on the long, low terraces above the alluvial flats so characteristic of the upper Hudson valley.

In the upper Hudson region, archaeologists in recent years have found the remains of small Archaic Indian campsites, mostly dating from after 3000 B.C. The Thompson Collection, acquired by the State Museum in 1914, displays thousands of chipped stone tools from the Archaic period gathered principally from the areas around Lansingburgh, Waterford, and Green Island.

By about A.D. 1000, the Indians were living in semi-permanent villages. They continued to hunt and gather, but also began cultivating crops such as corn, squash, and beans. Agriculture made them a more sedentary group. Woodland sites have been discovered in the upper Hudson area as well. The first Early Woodland site to be unearthed in eastern New York State was recently discovered just south of Watervliet. Three early horticultural

Above: In 1609 English navigator Henry Hudson, sailing on behalf of the Dutch East India Company in his ninety-ton yacht, Half Moon, *traveled 160 miles up the river that now bears his name. From* The Empire State, *by Lossing*

Right: The bones of an Ice Age mastodon were discovered while excavating for an addition to Harmony Mills in 1866. This photograph recorded the important find and eventually the animal was reconstructed at the New York State Museum. Courtesy, Rensselaer County Historical Society

sites in Waterford have also been uncovered since 1976.

Over thousands of years, the early inhabitants of the Gateway region enjoyed the Hudson valley's many advantages. Living at the confluence of two great rivers—the Hudson and the Mohawk—afforded numerous benefits. The area had much the same appeal, in fact, for the Indians as for Europeans who arrived in the early seventeenth century.

Like the aboriginal tribes before them, Europeans soon discovered that the Hudson-Mohawk region held a unique position as a gateway for travel both north to south and east to west. However, from the earliest time, natural barriers blocked the free flow of river traffic. The rifts, or rapids, two miles north of Waterford impeded north to south travel by boat. And the Cohoes Falls obstructed east to west passage. Because travel in these directions was essential for trade and commerce, the Hudson-Mohawk Gateway was where traffic paused. Here men unloaded batteaux and canoes and piled their produce on wagons or on backs to be taken north to Stillwater or west around Cohoes Falls. Once past these barriers, the boats returned to the water.

Above: This detail of a mid-seventeenth-century Dutch map of the Northeast shows what a Mahican Indian village may have looked like. Courtesy, New York State Library

Left: Both mammoth and mastodon were once present in New York State. Courtesy, New York State Museum/The State Education Department

SITE 209
SQUARE S202 W
UNIT 30
FEATURE 21
LEVEL 3
W→   8 1 79

Above: This hearth, from the Woodland stage of Indian occupation, was discovered at the Mechanicville Road site in 1979. Much evidence of prehistoric inhabitation of the Gateway area has been destroyed by over 300 years of development along the riverbanks where many of the Indian encampments and villages were located. Courtesy, Hartgen Archeological Associates

Right: Projectile points unearthed at the Mechanicville Road site in Waterford date from the Late Archaic to the Middle Woodland eras. Courtesy, Hartgen Archeological Associates

Henry Hudson's visit opened the Gateway region to Dutch traders. Establishing their early posts in the Albany area, these European entrepreneurs encouraged the Indians to come to them, which caused territorial disputes among local tribes. The Mahicans, with villages located largely on the east side of the Hudson, were historic rivals of the Mohawks, the nearest tribe of Iroquoian speakers to the west. The Dutch traders soon learned to stay clear of inter-tribal battles, and the Mohawks, with their far-reaching networks to the west and north, eventually took over the fur trade. However the Mahicans remained a local influence in trade and warfare well into the eighteenth century.

Before 1629, when the Dutch established a colonization plan for their New World territories, the Hudson-Mohawk Gateway was a busy area for trade. Beginning in 1630, the new Dutch landowner, or patroon, Kiliaen Van Rensselaer, had his agents purchase large tracts of land from the Indians. A map prepared about 1632 for the patroon demonstrated his claim over territory that stretched south from a Mahican village on Peebles Island to Beeren Island, south of Albany. This was land Van Rensselaer's agents thought most promising for settlement. That the patroon himself had little idea of the vastness of his new

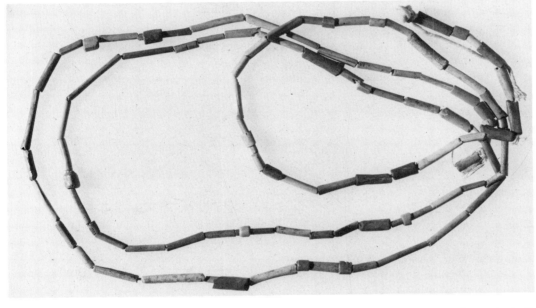

These bone beads (left) and glass and copper beads (below) were traded by the Indians and Dutch. From Prehistoric Archeology, *by Phil Lord, Jr., 1979. Courtesy, New York State Museum/The State Education Department*

holdings is shown by his July 20, 1632 request that some-one pace off the area from Peebles Island to Cohoes Falls and south to Watervliet. However, he readily expressed his faith in the area's potential, writing, "the territory of the Mahicans . . . has altogether over 1,200 morgens of cleared land . . . being not only fat, clayey soil of itself, but yearly enriched by the overflow of high water. . . ."

Lubbert Gijsbertsz, a 1634 arrival, may have been one of Troy's original European settlers, since the early name of the Troy area was Lubbertsland. However the first re-corded European pioneer in the Hudson-Mohawk Gate-way was a carpenter named Thomas Chambers. In 1646 Chambers entered into a five-year agreement with Van Rensselaer to lease land along the river between the Wynantskill and the Poestenkill, part of what is now South Troy. The lease also gave him first preference for constructing a mill on the land. Chambers left his farm in 1654 to become a prominent citizen in the Kingston area. His valuable land was then taken over by mill operator Jan Barentz Wemp.

By 1651 the patroon Van Rensselaer had purchased the Wynantskill area from the Indians and tried to build a mill there. He apparently succeeded by 1656, when water-power on the creek was leased. Two years later Wynant Gerritse van der Poel entered into a partnership, and for thirty years operated a mill on the Wynantskill, which still bears his name.

At this time of early settlement and growing industry in the Troy area, an unusual visit by a sea creature made every Rensselaerswyck resident acutely aware of the rest of the Gateway region. After an especially severe spring flood, a whale somehow found its way up the Hudson and was grounded on an island near Cohoes Falls. This island, thus called Whale Island since 1646, became a hub of great excitement and curiosity. Despite the settlers' best efforts to boil out huge quantities of whale oil, the river was slick for three weeks. An observer described the incident: "As the fish lay rotting, the air was infected with its stench . . . perceptible for two miles to leeward."

By the 1660s Van Rensselaer had leased most of the Gateway region to arriving settlers. Since every farmer was also a trader, attempts to intercept the routes to Al-bany provided ongoing drama and intrigue until the 1730s when Albany lost its legal monopoly on the fur trade. While acquiring title to the property from the pa-troon, however, the new occupants still had to satisfy the claims of the resident Indians.

In 1664 two well-known citizens joined forces in an ef-

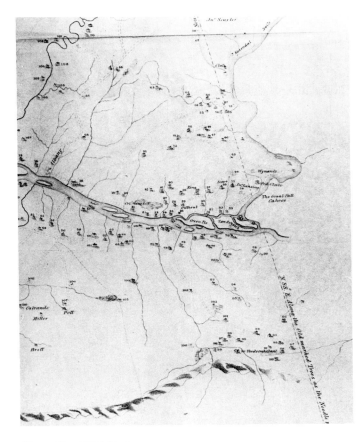

Above: The 1767 Bleeker map identified property owners and Van Rensselaer tenant farmers along the Hudson and Mohawk rivers. Van Schaick and Green Islands still retain a similar configuration to what was shown. Courtesy, New York State Library

Facing page: Among the items traded between the Indians and Dutch in the seventeenth century were (from top to bottom) an Iroquois clay pipe, a Dutch pipe, a stone celt (axe), and an iron axe. From Prehistoric Archeology, *by Phil Lord, Jr., 1979. Courtesy, New York State Museum/ The State Education Department*

fort to gain control of the Half Moon tract. Philip Pietersen Schuyler and Goosen Gerritsz Van Schaick purchased the area from Van Rensselaer, including two islands at the mouth of the Mohawk. In 1674 Schuyler deeded his portion to Van Schaick. But then in 1676 Schuyler purchased Green Island from the Indians. The original deed states that a nearby island was already sown with winter wheat; cultivation had begun even before the sale was completed. Meanwhile settlers were also coming to Troy. A 1663 account of an Indian scare mentions eighteen families there.

As early as 1660 patroon Van Rensselaer contemplated establishing a village at present-day Watervliet, then called the Stone Hook. Instead he leased the land to Bastiaen de Winter, who then set up a farm. After De Winter's death in 1678, Schuyler purchased the property to add to his own farm.

The patroon evidently maintained control of the Cohoes area until the 1690s, when he began to extend leases. But even then he reserved for himself a strip of land on the west side below the falls, no doubt recognizing its value for mill sites. Other settlers farmed areas outside the manor line, choosing the Boght and the Lansingburgh region, known then as Stone Arabia, which was acquired in 1670 by Robert Sanders. The farmland north of the Poestenkill and south of the Piscawenkill (now the heart of Troy) was also deeded throughout this period. By the early eighteenth century, most of this land was acquired by the Van der Heyden family who farmed and operated a ferry across the Hudson.

The power struggle between the French and the British for control of the North American continent which started at the end of the seventeenth century greatly increased the dangers of life on the frontier. Between 1686 and 1763 four wars erupted. During the peaceful interludes, sometimes lasting as long as thirty years, each side expanded its territory until warfare broke out anew. Both the French and the British enlisted the aid of Indian groups, and sudden raids kept the northern frontier in turmoil.

During these years of warfare, the Hudson-Mohawk Gateway region served as a corridor for the transport of military supplies and troops. Albany became a center of military activity. Crews of twenty-five men moved large batteaux carrying supplies from Albany through the Hudson-Mohawk Gateway to points around the falls and rapids. Beginning about 1690 small forts were erected to protect this vital route. One was located at Half Moon

Above: General James Abercrombie led his British troops to horrible defeat against the French garrison at Ticonderoga during the French and Indian War. From Dictionary of American Portraits, *by Cirker, 1967*

Right: This was a map of the Hudson-Mohawk Gateway at the time of the American Revolution. The Van Rensselaer family owned much of the land south of the confluence of the Hudson and Mohawk rivers. Vanderheyden farm occupied the area of present-day Troy. Courtesy, New York State Library

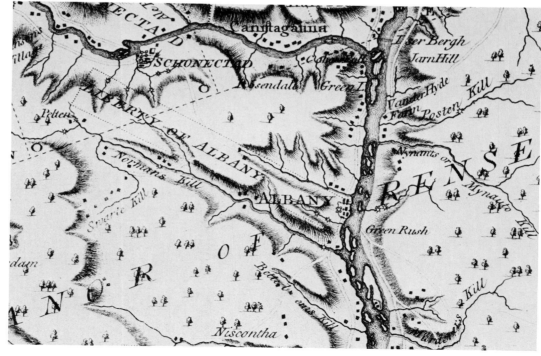

Facing page, top right: Indian commissioner William Johnson was well liked by the Iroquois. In 1755 he led an expedition of British soldiers and Iroquois warriors to victory over the French at Lake George and earned the title of Baronet of the British Empire in New York. From Dictionary of American Portraits, *by Cirker, 1967*

Above: Major General Horatio Gates replaced General Philip Schuyler as commander of the Northern Department of the Continental army. From Dictionary of American Portraits, *by Cirker, 1967*

near the ferry operating just north of Waterford. A military road ran north from Albany along the Hudson, across the islands at the mouth of the Mohawk to Half Moon, and north to Saratoga. These islands—stepping stones as they were—provided fords across the mouth of the Mohawk. Thus during the eighteenth century, Green, Van Schaick, and Peebles islands became centers of military encampments, while Waterford duly received its name.

Between the wars, British settlements expanded north and west of Albany. The Van Schaick house on Van Schaick Island was built in the 1730s during the longest interlude of peace, and other farms were reestablished in the Gateway region. Meanwhile the French were extending their influence southward from Canada. In the 1730s they established Fort St. Frederic at Crown Point in the Champlain valley. This daring French expansion into what the British regarded as their territory eventually led to another outbreak of hostilities. During the two wars

that followed, Fort St. Frederic posed a serious threat to settlers in New England and in the Gateway area. One historian calculated that from 1744 to 1748 as many as twenty-seven raids were launched southward from Fort St. Frederic into British frontier areas. Settlers in the Gateway region were particularly terrified in 1745 when Saratoga was destroyed. Farmers on the east side of the Hudson and north of Albany deserted their farms.

The last of the French and Indian Wars broke out in 1755. During this final conflict large provincial and British armies, under the command of such leaders as William Johnson, James Abercrombie, and Jeffery Amherst, marched through the Hudson-Mohawk Gateway. Finally in 1759, Fort St. Frederic and Quebec fell to the British, bringing peace to the area. The French were defeated and the British added Canada to their burgeoning empire.

Settlers once again pushed into the lands north of Albany, no longer fearful of French and Indian raids. True settlement of Gateway areas away from the rivers and creeks then began in earnest. One early resident of present-day Menands observed: "The settlers . . . set up sawmills on every stream, for the purposes of turning to account the fine timber which they cleared in great quantities off the new lands."

The islands at the mouth of the Mohawk once again became the scene of military encampments and the movement of military supplies in the War for Independence. By 1777 they were strategic points to be defended against the British advance led by General John Burgoyne in his southward march from Canada to Saratoga and Albany. First General Philip Schuyler and General Horatio Gates, in succession, established command headquarters at the old Van Schaick house; their troops camped around the house. Under the direction of Polish engineer Thaddeus Kosciusko, the American army fortified Peebles Island facing north toward Saratoga, protecting the ford across the Mohawk on the road towards Albany. General Burgoyne noted: "Mr. Gates . . . is now strongly posted near the mouth of the Mohawk River, with an army superior to mine." Because Burgoyne was halted at Saratoga, the fortifications were never used in battle.

By 1790 the Hudson-Mohawk Gateway region faced a new era. The population of the area would soon be swelled by new arrivals, the mill creeks utilized in more efficient ways for power, and the barriers on the north-south and east-west transportation corridors eliminated— all contributing to a busy, booming nineteenth century expansion of business and commerce.

This was the first boat through Lock Two of the Waterford flight of the Barge Canal in 1915. Courtesy, Gene Baxter

CHAPTER TWO

WATER: THE KEY TO POWER AND GROWTH

Like most flourishing areas of the young republic, the Hudson-Mohawk Gateway owed its settlement and early growth largely to water. In the early years, water afforded transportation for settlers and goods as well as power for industry. Even today, the abundant water supplies of the Gateway area have continued to serve a multiplicity of needs for businesses and factories, homes, and public institutions.

The Gateway area has been blessed by nature, and enhanced by engineering genius, with generous water resources. It is, first of all, the place where two great rivers meet. The Mohawk rises near the center of New York State and flows east. At Little Falls and "the Noses," the river breaks through mountain barriers into a deep, rocky ravine. Less than a mile from its island-studded mouth at Cohoes, it flows over a perpendicular precipice some seventy feet high and nearly a quarter-mile wide, forming one of the greatest and most powerful waterfalls of the Northeast. About ten miles north of Albany, the Mohawk merges into the mighty Hudson.

The Hudson rises in Tear-of-the-Clouds, a lake nestled among the highest peaks of the Adirondacks, more than 4,000 feet above sea level. Starting as a small stream, the river descends rapidly through narrow gorges, collecting the output of lakes and streams along the way. At the dam between Troy and Green Island, approximately 160 miles from the sea, the roaring river falls into a tidal estuary. From Troy to its mouth, the Hudson is broad, deep, and somewhat sluggish.

The Gateway area has always existed first and foremost as the headwater of navigation on the Hudson. Early Lansingburgh had a landing for sloops as large as ninety tons, but the wharf was functional only during springtime, when the water was running high. A news item appearing in the Lansingburgh *American Spy* on March 8, 1793 suggested that only if dams were erected to the south would there be "sufficient depth of water up to this town to navigate vessels of 40 to 50 tons burden," presumably

Right: The confluence of the Mohawk and Hudson rivers is depicted in this 1843 map. Courtesy, New York State Library

Far right: A typical homestead of the 1760s in the Gateway area was the Douw Fonda house in Cohoes, shown here as it appeared in the late nineteenth century. Courtesy, New York State Library

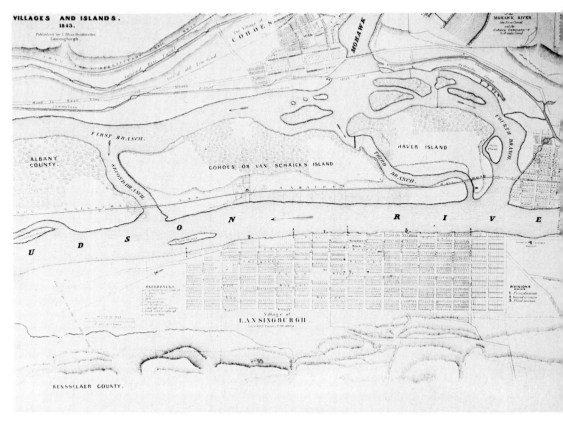

most of the year round. The first dam constructed between Troy and Green Island in 1823 did precisely that; it opened Lansingburgh to sloop navigation in seasons other than spring. Earlier, its cross-river neighbor, Waterford, also offered a sloop dock, but it was submerged when the dam was built.

Troy had no need of dams. Elkanah Watson, in his brief description of what was soon to become Troy, stated unequivocally, "This place is situated precisely at the head of navigation on the Hudson." Watson noted that, even in these early times, "several bold and enterprising adventurers have settled here; a number of capacious warehouses and several dwellings are already erected. It is favorably situated in reference to the important trade of Vermont and Massachusetts."

Lansingburgh had its origins in 1763 when Abraham Jacob Lansing purchased the Stone Arabia patent. He had the land surveyed and a portion of it laid out in building lots. The map was filed in the Albany County Clerk's office on May 11, 1771. A steady stream of immigrants, mainly from New England, began pouring into the settlement. In a short time, a thriving community had sprung up at the head of sloop navigation. Nieuw Stadt, or New

City, was the popular name given the village to distinguish it from Oude Stadt, or Old City, the name by which Albany was first known. Lansingburgh received its first charter on April 5, 1790, and seven men were appointed to act as trustees for one year.

To the south of Lansingburgh, Dirck Van der Heyden purchased, in 1707, the property which became the center of the original city of Troy. The patroon of Rensselaerwyck confirmed this transaction on December 15, 1720. The annual rent was three bushels and three pecks of wheat and three fat hens or capons. By 1786 Dirck's land had been divided into three farms. The owners were Jacob I., Jacob D., and Matthias Van der Heyden.

The Van der Heydens strongly opposed all suggestions that a community be established on any portion of their land. However, with Old City prospering to the south and New City growing by leaps and bounds to the north, the Van der Heydens soon realized that they were passing up an opportunity that might prove more profitable than farming. Jacob I. sold a lot to Benjamin Thurber of Providence, Rhode Island, who had earlier located in Lansingburgh. Thurber set himself up as a merchant and trader at the foot of Hoosick Street under the sign of a bunch of

grapes.

The next applicant was Captain Stephen Ashley of Salisbury, Connecticut, who bought the old residence of Matthias Van der Heyden at the corner of Division and River streets. Ashley opened the house as an inn which became popularly known as Ashley's Tavern. Under the terms of his lease, he also took control of the ferry that operated from the foot of Ferry Street. His monopoly over the only public crossing of the river in the vicinity—Ashley's Ferry—brought him increasing prosperity and influence.

Jacob D. Van der Heyden, the owner of the middle farm and the last holdout of the three, finally succumbed to the influence of friends who advised him to apportion his land in city lots. Subsequently the middle farm was surveyed, and lots for homes and sites for shops were established. This planned area, with squares and rectilinear blocks modeled after Philadelphia, became the very center of Troy.

Jacob D. called the projected village Vanderheyden, but the earlier names of Ashley's Ferry and Ferry Hook continued in popular usage. Benjamin Covell was the first to bargain for a land parcel, selecting lot number five on the

west side of River Street. Dr. Samuel Gale, a physician from Guilford, Connecticut, built a two-story structure on the west side of River Street north of Covell's store. And so the settlers came.

The majority of the new arrivals, being New England Yankees, felt uncomfortable with the Dutch place names that dominated the area. Thus, on January 5, 1789, they met at Ashley's Tavern to rename the village of Vanderheyden. They selected Troy. The new name was not a surprising choice in a young nation modeled after Greek democracy and captivated by classical styles of architecture. The Van der Heydens, however, were not happy with the name change. In fact Jacob D. went as far as to write "Vanderheyden, alias Troy" on all his deeds and leases for many years afterward. But the settlers were clearly satisfied. When the city was incorporated in 1816, the motto attached to the seal read, "Ilium fuit; Troja est." "Ilium is dead; Troy lives." Meanwhile, the first village charter was passed in 1791, and another in 1798.

Waterford, to the north of Troy, had its beginnings in the ancient tract of Half Moon. Named for its shape, it also evoked memories of the ship on which Henry Hudson had first explored the Gateway region. As early as 1664, Philip Pieterse Schuyler and Goosen Gerritse van Schaick received permission to purchase the Half Moon tract. At the time, Half Moon included Half Moon Precinct, Half Moon Point, Half Moon-on-the Hudson, and Half Moon Village. It was Half Moon Point that was destined to become Waterford. A map representing Half Moon Point in 1784 showed two log cabins, two wood houses, and two taverns: the Eagle, haven of the rebels, and the Lion, meeting place of the Tories. Half Moon Point was purchased by the founders of the village in 1784.

Waterford was charter-incorporated by the New York State Legislature on March 25, 1794. Only one of a few villages in the state operating under such a special charter, it is also the oldest incorporated village in the state. At first part of Albany County, it became the southeast anchor of Saratoga County when that county was established in 1791.

Waterford's charter provided for seven trustees, all equal. Fire was a subject of primary concern to the citizens. Freeholders were compelled to equip themselves with fire buckets and tools to extinguish blazes, and fifteen citizens were appointed to care for all fire-fighting tools and instruments. The town of Waterford was formed from Half Moon in 1816.

Waterfordians, of course, were river-oriented. Realizing that the great Cohoes Falls nearby interrupted river trade on the Mohawk, they built a 244-foot pier extending out into the confluence of the Hudson and Mohawk rivers for the landing of goods to be carried overland around the falls. This early engineering achievement was submerged by the construction of the Troy-Green Island Dam in 1823.

In 1795 the first bridge across the Mohawk was erected between Waterford and neighboring Cohoes. In describing the bridge, Count Rochefoucauld Liancourt wrote: "It is constructed of timber and rests on stone pillars about 25 or 30 feet distant from each other. The masonry is not remarkable for solidity or neatness; but the carpenter's work is exceedingly well done." With its weak piers, the bridge, located west of the present railroad bridge, was soon damaged by ice. On April 4, 1806, the Cohoes Bridge Company was incorporated to rebuild it. Stock was sold, higher tolls were charged, and a second bridge was erected, opening the area to further development.

The falls, however, were the true key to Cohoes' growth. In 1811 the Cohoes Manufacturing Company was incorporated. With wise forethought, the founders pur-

chased sixty acres of river bank, along with rights to the water. After building a wing dam the new company turned to manufacturing screws. Development slowed for lack of capital, however, and in 1815 the screw factory burned. Two brothers from New York City then bought a large share of stock in the company and built a cotton factory. Despite their efforts development again came to a standstill. Then construction began on the Erie and Champlain canals, and everything changed. The waterways brought attention and people to Cohoes and renewed life and vitality in the entire area. The southern section of modern Cohoes, the place where the two canals merged on their way to Albany, became a lively, bustling junction frequented by merchants, travelers, traders, and seamen.

The first successful design for the systematic and complete utilization of the Cohoes Falls' waterpower was developed by Canvass White of Waterford, one of the chief engineers of the Erie Canal. White got financial backing from the patroon Stephen van Rensselaer, and from the firm of Peter Remsen and Company of New York City. With others, they incorporated in 1826 as the Cohoes Company. The Cohoes Company acquired all water rights a half-mile above and below the falls. It also gained permission to dam the Mohawk above the falls, construct a system of power canals, and lease and sell waterpower as well as land.

The dam was built in 1831 and, although destroyed by ice the following winter, it was soon replaced. The first power canal was completed in 1834, and the company began selling land privileges in 1836. Thus the Cohoes Company's activities grew, and at the same time, so did the surrounding community. In 1848 Cohoes was formally established as a village. Just twenty years later, it became a city.

Slightly to the south of Cohoes, the town of Watervliet was formed in 1788. It included the entire west district of the sprawling manor of Rensselaerswyck, exclusive of Albany. In the nineteenth century Watervliet was the most populous town in the state. The village of Gibbonsville in the town of Watervliet, opposite Congress and Ferry streets in Troy, was incorporated in 1823. It stood at the beginning of what was to become the present city of Watervliet. To the south arose two other settlements known as Washington and Port Schuyler.

On June 18, 1812, Congress declared war against Great Britain. The United States Army Ordnance Department was little more than a month old, and Decius Wadsworth,

Above: Although a major obstacle to the early transportation network of the Gateway, the harnessing of the Cohoes Falls of the Mohawk River in the 1830s led to the development of Cohoes as a major textile manufacturing center. Photo by Robert Chase

its commanding officer, set out to select suitable sites for military arsenals. It was decided to establish one arsenal somewhere in upstate New York so that material could be easily shipped either north or west to meet an anticipated British attack via Lake Champlain and/or from the Niagara frontier. Colonel Wadsworth discovered an appropriate location in what was soon to be the incorporated village of Gibbonsville.

After purchasing a twelve-acre tract of land from James Gibbons, the Ordnance Department was ready to build. At first, the new establishment was known vaguely as the arsenal "at Gibbonsville" or "near Troy," but by 1817, people began to call it the "Arsenal at Watervliet."

Some years later, in 1836, the hamlets of Gibbonsville, Washington, and Port Schuyler were incorporated as the village of West Troy. Some residents, however, preferred the name Watervliet, a word of Dutch origin meaning "floodtide" or "rolling water." In 1897 West Troy was incorporated as a city and its name changed to Watervliet.

Green Island, the southernmost island in the mouth of the Mohawk River, chose not to join West Troy and was incorporated as an independent village in 1853. This event coincided with another major benchmark in Green Island's history: the arrival of the car works of Eaton, Gilbert and Company in the same year.

As the Gateway area began to grow and prosper, the need arose to provide easy access between the municipalities developing on opposite banks of the rivers. Ferry boats were the earliest means of linking such neighboring communities. As early as 1786, a stagecoach line, running between New City and Old City, Lansingburgh and Albany, stopped at Ashley's Tavern and took a ferry across the Hudson.

The ferry boats used in the eighteenth century were large, flat-bottomed scows, propelled by poles. At the dawn of the nineteenth century, the vessels were attached to ropes stretched across the river and driven "by force of the current from one landing to the other." Still later, horses were employed to turn paddle wheels extending below the deck. The first steam-propelled boat was introduced in 1826.

One of the earliest ferries, eventually known as the upper ferry, connected Troy with what was to become Watervliet. In 1798 Mahlon Taylor, a Poestenkill Gorge manufacturer, started a lower ferry. It left from the foot of Washington Street in Troy and connected with the west bank at an area soon to be occupied by the Watervliet Arsenal. Two ferry lines linking Troy and Green Island were established in 1823 and 1854, respectively. The 1854 ferry sustained a major disaster in its first year of operation. On Friday morning, October 13, 1854, as the vessel was crossing to Green Island from Troy, the steamer *Alice* passed. The swell raised in the steamer's wake caused passengers in the rear of the ferry to stand up to avoid getting wet. This action, plus the crowding of the ferry and the inexperience of its captain, caused the vessel to capsize, drowning eleven of the seventeen passengers.

Another ferry, operated by Harmon Leversie, was said to have been in use as early as 1685, connecting what was to become Lansingburgh and Waterford. First known as the Half Moon Ferry, it later was called the Upper Lansing Ferry. It continued to operate until 1805, a year after

Above: The waterfalls of the Poestenkill look untouched in this late-nineteenth-century view, but above and below the gorge the stream was channeled to provide power for several mills. Courtesy, Rensselaer County Historical Society

Left: The Troy-Watervliet Bridge was constructed in 1970. Upon completion of the new bridge, the Congress Street Bridge to the north was removed. Photo by Gene Baxter

the Union Bridge was constructed.

Bridges eventually replaced the ferry boats. They became dramatic silhouettes in an area so punctuated by great rivers and numerous streams. The first important bridge in the Gateway area linked Waterford and Cohoes. The second, the Union Bridge, connected Lansingburgh and Waterford. Constructed in 1804 by the Union Bridge Company, it employed the Burr Arch Truss, a wooden bridge system named after its inventor, Theodore Burr. This was the first bridge to span the Hudson north of New York City. It burned in 1909 and was replaced by the predecessors of the current bridge which was constructed on top of some of the original 105-year-old piers.

A wooden railroad bridge, 1,600 feet in length, built by the Rensselaer and Saratoga Railroad in 1835, crossed the Hudson River between Troy and Green Island. At the Troy end it had a draw of sixty feet to allow boats to pass through. This bridge, ignited by a spark from a passing engine, burned on May 10, 1862. The fire, fanned by a strong wind from the west and north, spread to engulf seventy-five acres in the heart of Troy's business section. It was replaced first by a wooden bridge, and then by a steel one, the western section being completed in 1876 and the eastern section in 1884. The steel bridge was constructed on 1834 piers, but, on March 15, 1977, one of the piers gave way during high water. The bridge collapsed, leading to the construction of the current Green Island Bridge which opened in 1981.

Bridges abound in the Gateway area. The Lansingburgh-Cohoes Bridge, also known as the 112th Street Bridge, was completed in 1923, replacing two earlier bridges on the same site. The Troy-Menands Bridge was dedicated in 1933, and the current Troy-Watervliet Bridge, which opened in 1971, replaced two earlier Congress Street Bridges, built in 1874 and 1917, respectively. One of the most recent bridges in the area, the Collar City Bridge, is a high-level span connecting Troy and Green Island and leading by a limited access highway, from Hoosick Street in Troy to the Northway, Interstate Route 87.

Waterfalls are among the natural wonders and resources of the Gateway region. Along the Hudson, cascades of water as high as 225 feet fall from the upper level to the alluvial plane below. The roar and majesty of the Cohoes Falls on the Mohawk have inspired awe in onlookers from the earliest times to the present.

Besides drawing visitors, the area's waterfalls were also destined to attract industry to the Gateway region. First,

though, a way had to be found to go around the falls, which in the case of the Cohoes Falls presented a natural obstruction to the westward movement of travelers and goods. Getting around the falls was the challenge; the opening of the Erie Canal met this challenge successfully.

In 1810 Jonas Platt, an avid supporter of a canal that would cut through the barriers of the Appalachian Chain to the Midwest, enlisted the support of DeWitt Clinton, then mayor of New York City. Although Clinton had previously demonstrated little interest in a canal, he soon emerged as the driving force toward its construction. This advocacy helped to catapult him to the governorship of what would soon be dubbed "the Empire State."

The Erie Canal was one of the longest locked canals ever built, running 363 miles through an unfriendly, untamed wilderness marked by hilly terrain and turbulent streams. The builders had to accommodate a water-level difference of 568 feet between its two terminals at Albany and Buffalo. It presented a mammoth engineering challenge.

On April 15, 1817, the New York State Legislature passed the Canal Law, creating a fund to build the canal. Ground was broken on July 4 that year, at Rome, New York, and the canal was constructed east and west from the center of the state. The portion that ran through the Gateway area was ready in 1823, and the entire, completed canal opened on October 26, 1825.

During the opening day ceremonies, Governor Clinton's barge had barely passed by the Watervliet "cut" when merchants from Troy locked the barge, *Trojan Trader,* into the waterway. The vessel laden with Trojan goods was the first barge bound west for Rochester. No time for celebrations for the enterprising Trojans!

The original Erie Canal was forty feet wide and four feet deep, accommodating horse- or mule-towed boats of about thirty tons capacity. It had eighty-three locks, each of which was ninety feet long and fifteen feet wide. The Champlain Canal, constructed at the same time, had identical dimensions. The two canals met at the junction in Cohoes and traveled through Watervliet to the basin north of the center of Albany.

In the folklore of the Erie and Champlain canals, the Watervliet "cut" into the Hudson opposite Troy developed a rowdy and lawless reputation. At one point it hosted twenty-nine saloons bearing suggestive names like "Black Rag" and "Tub of Blood," and it is said to have witnessed "a hundred fights a day, and a body a week in the canal." Today's settlement of Maplewood was the loca-

These barges were waiting for the early spring opening of the Erie division of the New York State Barge Canal at Waterford circa 1920. The United Shirt & Collar Company and Lansingburgh are in the background. Use of the Barge Canal for recreational purposes has increased recently; pleasure boats can travel from New York City through Waterford west to the Great Lakes or north to the St. Lawrence River. Courtesy, Gene Baxter

Canal boats are tied up in the Hudson River at West Troy waiting for the Erie Canal to open in the spring. Courtesy, Rensselaer County Historical Society

tion of one of the four weighlocks which determined passage fees for barges. The toll post was a flat-roofed, columned building now commemorated with a historical marker.

The canal was such a success that it soon needed to be widened and deepened. Enlargement began in 1836 and was completed only in 1862, making the Erie seventy feet wide and seven feet deep to handle boats of 240 tons' capacity. Tonnage climbed rapidly, peaking at 6,673,730 tons in 1872. But the railroads chipped away at the canal's monopoly. At mid-century seven independent railroads stretching across New York State were united as the New York Central Railroad. Much faster than barges traveling through the canal, the trains quickly stole canal passengers and began to make inroads into canal freight. The first significant decline in canal tonnage occurred during the 1870s, coinciding with a tripling of rail freight. The New York-to-Buffalo run which took ten days by canal took only eleven hours by rail in 1875.

Eager to rescue the canal from its precipitous decline, the New York State Legislature approved the Barge Canal Referendum Bill in 1903, and construction of a new barge

canal system began in 1905. Completed in 1918, the updated waterway used river and lake channels wherever possible and connected these by man-made aqueducts. During this period the so-called Waterford flight of locks was built, raising boats from the Hudson River, around Cohoes Falls, to the Mohawk River above the falls. Five proximate locks lifted boats 170 feet, making them the highest set of lift locks in the world.

Canvas White had developed a satisfactory hydraulic (Portland) cement for "waterproofing" the Erie Canal. In the process, he built stronger retaining walls and tighter locks and aqueducts. Despite this and other improvements throughout the nineteenth and into the twentieth century, tonnage continually declined on the Erie Canal. The waterway is now host mainly to recreational boats, and its management has been transferred to the New York State Thruway Authority, which has aggressively promoted it as a heritage attraction. For well over a century, the Erie and Champlain canals made the Gateway a booming commercial area and, with the advent of the railroads, one of the greatest crossroads of commerce in nineteenth-century America.

Water, besides spurring the Gateway's commercial

growth, was also the key to its industrial development. Up to the time when a usable steam engine was available in America in 1806—and well beyond—running, falling water was the main energy source for industry. Power canal systems were constructed to take advantage of this natural energy resource.

The first and greatest power canal system was built in Cohoes. Canvass White designed the original system but died before it got underway. His brother, Hugh, directed the building of the dam and the first channels. More or less parallel canals were designed to bring water to successive levels, culminating in the return of the water to the river below the falls. By 1880 seven levels had been built. The fall between levels provided power for factories constructed between the channels.

Troy also had a successful power canal system. Benjamin Marshall created a reservoir in 1840 by damming the Poestenkill immediately above the falls at the eastern end of the gorge. An intake was then constructed on the north side of the reservoir not far behind the dam, and a 600-foot tunnel was cut through the rock of Mount Ida to bring water to a succession of mills built on the hillside, one of which was Marshall's cotton mill. In later years, a turbine connected to an electric generator at the lower end of the system added a new form of power to the mechanically generated power above.

This particular system meant power in the Gateway area until 1962, when Marshall's creation finally went off line. Water had been used to operate a mill at the mouth of the Poestenkill gorge at least as early as 1667, marking a 300-year history of waterpower in that locale. It is interesting to note that a new hydroelectric power system has been recently built, using some of the 1840 system.

Water, which originally caused the Gateway to develop,

Right: The Waterford sidecut of the old Champlain Canal was photographed at the time of the opening of the Barge Canal. This set of locks is a reminder of the significance of the Gateway as a major crossroads for commerce in the nineteenth century. Photo by George Michon. Courtesy, Paul E. Grattan

Below: A weigh lock for determining tolls on the Erie Canal was located just above where the sidecut entered the Hudson River opposite Troy, in present-day Maplewood. Courtesy, Rensselaer County Historical Society

is still a vital area asset. In recent years, Rensselaer Polytechnic Institute has tried to focus local attention on the rivers as a valuable regional asset. The Hudson River Celebration features creative and inexpensive boats which cross the river from near the Cluett Peabody Factory and return to the Troy side near the new City Hall. The Capt. J.P. Cruise Line in Troy offers tours and dinner passages, using the area's waterways for education and recreation. Troy's new Riverfront Park, with its ethnic festivals, represents another attempt to reconnect people with the river and with their past—and hopefully their future.

Electric street railways connected all of the Gateway communities until before World War II.

CHAPTER THREE

CREATING A TRANSPORTATION NETWORK

The Hudson-Mohawk Gateway is an area traversed and crisscrossed by numerous waterways. From the earliest times, the inhabitants used boats to transport themselves and their products from one locale to another. The Indians plied the rivers and streams in their canoes. The early settlers used scows and sailing vessels. By the end of the eighteenth century the sloop was the mainstay of travel and commerce in the Gateway region. And commercial sloops, as well as schooners, could still be seen sailing the Hudson at least fifty years after the first steamboat was introduced.

Colonial Lansingburgh and Waterford had sloop docks. Troy was an even more important port. As early as 1788 the sixty-ton schooner *Flora* carried wheat and other cargo from Vanderheyden to New York "and to different points along the New England coast." By 1830 eighty sloops were conducting commerce between Troy and New York City.

Travel by sloop, however, was slow and tiring. In Troy's *One Hundred Years,* historian Arthur J. Wiese says some interesting things about sloop travel in the 1820s:

A voyage to New York from Troy in a sloop, although pleasurable and inexpensive, was sometimes long and tedious. Contrary winds and calm weather not infrequently lengthened the time beyond a week .... Fourteen hours were considered to be the time of a short passage to the city. A sloop making a voyage down and back in four days was exceedingly fortunate .... Sailing with a "white-ash breeze," when there was no wind, implied the use of long, white-ash oars or sweeps, as they were usually called, to advance the progress of the vessel. Fourteen miles a day was the distance commonly accomplished by rowing and floating with the tide. Kedging was a more tiresome and slower way of moving a sloop in calm weather. A boat carrying a line from the sloop having been rowed to

Right: Matton shipyard of Cohoes was originally located in Waterford along the old Champlain Canal. The last three wooden canal boats built there are ready for launching in this circa 1915 photo. Photo by George Michon. Courtesy, Paul E. Grattan

an island in advance of it, where a small anchor called a kedge having been sunk into the ground, the vessel was hauled forward by means of the line fastened to the kedges. Ten to fourteen passengers were the number which could be accommodated conveniently with berths on a sloop.

Travel by sloop could indeed be wearisome. It is no wonder, then, that the advent of the steamboat was welcomed with such enthusiasm. As early as 1798 Robert R. Livingston was promised a steamboat monopoly over New York's waterways, provided he could produce a vessel of the required size and speed within one year. He did

not, but the time limit was extended. Livingston then met Robert Fulton, an artist turned engineer and inventor, and they became collaborators. Their steam-propelled invention marked the beginning of a new era in American navigation. On August 22, 1807, Fulton left New York City aboard the *North River Steamboat of Clermont,* which became famous as simply the *Clermont.* The initial trip to Albany and back won Fulton and Livingston a twenty-year monopoly over steamboat operation on New York State waters. On September 4 the *Clermont* formally entered commercial service and ran to Albany in 28 hours, 45 minutes. The much slower sloops could not compete. After being rebuilt and enlarged, the *Clermont*

*Facing page, top: The City of
Troy steamboat is seen docked at
the Citizens' Steamboat Company
in Troy in the late nineteenth
century. This steamboat made
daily trips between Troy and New
York City from 1876 to 1907. An
excursion ticket in 1898 was $2.50.
Courtesy, Frances D. Broderick*

*Right: This certificate was for ten
shares of stock in the Troy Steamboat Company in 1825, the year
the company was chartered. Courtesy, Rensselaer County Historical
Society*

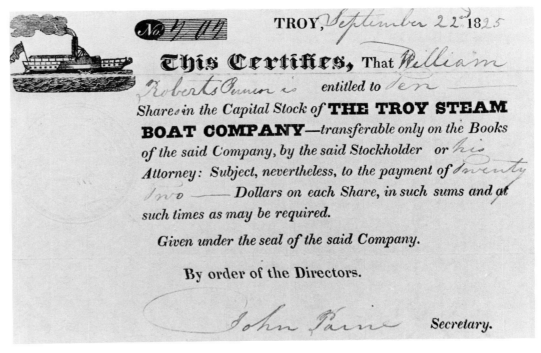

continued to operate on the Hudson until 1814. In the meantime, Livingston and Fulton added other steamboats to their fleet, including the *Firefly* in 1812 which traveled between Troy and Albany.

In 1824 the United States Supreme Court declared Livingston and Fulton's monopoly unconstitutional: steam on the Hudson was open to all. Troy immediately began to make the move from sailpower to steam. The Troy Steamboat Company was chartered in 1825. Its first steamboat, the *Chief Justice Marshall,* was named for the Supreme Court judge who had opened the river to competition. This 314-ton ship plied the Hudson from March 31, 1825, until April 22, 1830, when her boiler burst shortly after departing from Newburgh. Eight persons died, and five were seriously injured.

During this early period of steamboat travel, the Troy Public Shipyard launched three experimental steamers: the *Star,* the *Helen,* and the *Diamond.* The *Star* initially set sail in 1827. She was designed by William Annesley, a naval architect who was then living in Troy. Annesley designed his boats with crisscrossing layers of wood, much like modern plywood. The lamination strengthened the boat so that it did not require structural members. The hull had a channel extending through the middle from front to back, and the paddle was housed in this channel. A band of planking around the hull above the waterline served to tighten and strengthen that part of the ship.

The next experimental steamboat was built by Henry Burden, an inventor and iron manufacturer from South Troy. Burden designed an early steam catamaran, the *Helen,* named for his wife and sometimes referred to as the "Cigar Boat." The vessel had two wrought-iron cylindrical pontoons or hulls, 300 feet in length and eight feet in diameter. A deck was built on top of the twin hulls, and a large center paddle wheel was inserted with the steam engine located on deck.

Burden theorized that his "floating island" would draw only four feet of water and travel at twenty-five miles per hour. But he did not understand the surface tension problem caused by so much exposed hull. On July 7, 1834, in a race from New York City to Albany, the *Helen* arrived two hours after her competitor, a conventional steamboat. Worse yet, on August 2, the *Helen,* "with a full head of steam, ran on the Castleton dam," breaking up in the process.

Burden at first planned to rebuild the *Helen,* but he eventually gave up the notion. Nonetheless, he did construct the *Diamond* with a more conventional hull and sidewheels. Launched in 1837, this ship ran on the Albany-to-New York City route for eleven years. She was distinguished by the truss system of latticework Burden used to strengthen the shallow hull. The lattices formed diamonds, giving the ship its name. Although they strengthened the shallow hull, the small diamond openings on

both sides of the ship impeded the movement of passengers and goods. No other Hudson River steamboat employed this truss system.

But there was yet to be a 100-year history of steamboats out of Troy. The *Troy* and the *Empire* were built by the Troy Steamboat Company in 1840 and 1843, respectively. These ships started out as "day boats," that is, vessels making the trips between Troy and New York City during daylight rather than nighttime hours. Night boats soon followed.

While the *Troy* and the *Empire* continued as day boats, the *Albany* and the *Swallow,* of the Peoples' Line, ran between Troy, Albany, and New York City at night. Lighthouses had not yet been built along the Hudson to warn navigators of treacherous shoals. Thus, on the night of April 7, 1845, the *Swallow,* not long out of Troy, struck a rocky islet off Athens during a snow squall. Her hull broke open, the stern sank back into the river, and fifteen lives were lost. It was one of the worst steamboat disasters in Troy's history.

The *Troy* and the *Empire* continued to operate until the early 1850s, but after 1848, they ran as night vessels. In 1854 the Troy Night Line was established, and every night for nearly three decades it ran steamboats along the

Hudson.

In 1872 the Citizens' Steamboat Company was organized, launching the *City of Troy* in 1876 and the *Saratoga* in 1877. These beautiful, stately vessels took over the Troy-to-New York City run. In 1906 the *Saratoga* was rammed by another steamboat off Cougers Island, carrying away the port boiler. She later sank. The following year the *City of Troy* caught fire on the way up the river, put in at Dobbs Ferry, and burned to the water's edge.

In 1909 the Hudson Navigation Company launched the *Trojan* and the *Rensselaer* which did the night run out of Troy until the eve of World War II. It was in 1937 that the last of the night-line steamers, the *Trojan* and the *Berkshire,* made their final runs. The age of steam on the Hudson out of Troy had ended.

At the same time that Gateway residents were developing better and faster methods of traveling over water, they were also creating finer and more efficient modes of journeying over land. Before the coming of the railroads, stagecoach lines carried settlers between neighboring villages and hamlets. An early stage connected Lansingburgh and Albany, crossing the river at Ashley's Ferry. There also were coaches serving Schenectady, Saratoga Springs,

and even more distant places like Boston and Montreal. The coming of the railroad, however, rendered the stagecoach obsolete.

A group of Troy businessmen proposed to build a railroad from Troy to Ballston Spa. In 1832 the Rensselaer and Saratoga Railroad (the R&S), was chartered and granted an exclusive franchise to construct railroad bridges between the two points. The citizens of Albany at first failed to recognize the threat implicit in this exclusive Trojan franchise. As a result, they spent nearly thirty years in court seeking permission to build a railroad bridge at Albany, crossing the Hudson at their city, rather than at Troy.

The R&S line was surveyed and built, and a railroad bridge constructed between Troy and Green Island. On October 6, 1835, the first train arrived at the western end of the bridge. The locomotive was detached, and the cars drawn across the bridge by horse—assuring that the wooden structure would not be set afire by a spark from an engine. The line passed through Green Island, and across bridges connecting the islands at the mouth of the Mohawk, to Waterford. This part of the line to Waterford was maintained until 1982 when it was abandoned and the track taken up.

At the Ballston Springs terminus of the railroad, passengers bound for Saratoga had to take a stage or wait for a Schenectady and Saratoga Railroad train to take them to their destination. However, about 1840, Troy merchants purchased a large number of shares thus outwitting Albany interests—and bringing the Schenectady and Saratoga under R&S control. So the R&S, chartered to go only as far as Ballston Springs, was extended to Saratoga Springs, a city fast becoming an important resort.

In 1836 the Schenectady and Troy Railroad was chartered, opening up the route to the west. The first train passed over the line in 1842. The railroad employed a novel means of getting its cars from Cohoes to the Green Island side of the R&S railroad bridge. All passengers were loaded in a single car, the car was given a push, and was then propelled by gravity downhill to the Green Island Bridge. From there it was towed by horses to the Troy side of the river. An account in the *Buffalo Gazette* had this to say about the line's importance in its heyday:

The Trojans are proverbial for their enterprise and public spirit. Everything which they take hold of "goes ahead." For two or three years past, they have been endeavoring to compete with Albany for the Western travel to New

Right: The W.H. Frear, *named after the wealthy Trojan dry goods merchant, was a connecting boat between Albany and Troy. Courtesy, Rensselaer County Historical Society*

Middle: The night boat Trojan *is seen docked at Congress Street in Troy a few years before its last run in 1937. Courtesy, Rensselaer County Historical Society*

Bottom: By the 1830s Troy had several large hotels such as the Troy House on the corner of First and River streets. Stagecoaches stopped at the hotels which provided overnight accommodations for the passengers. Courtesy, Rensselaer County Historical Society

Facing page, top: This is a broadside for the stagecoach line running between Troy and Saratoga in 1834. This particular line was short-lived because a year later the Rensselaer & Saratoga Railroad began operation. Courtesy, Rensselaer County Historical Society

Bottom: The Rensselaer & Saratoga Railroad ran this newspaper ad in 1836. Courtesy, Rensselaer County Historical Society

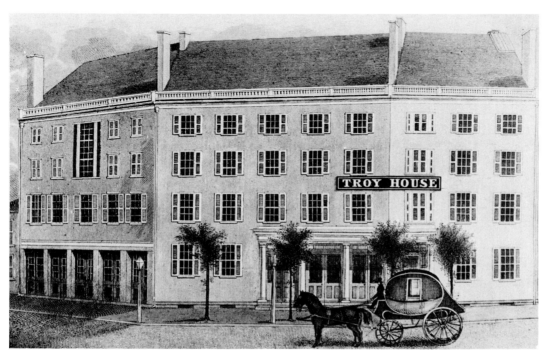

TROY, BALLSTON
AND
SARATOGA,

DAILY LINE OF COACHES.

This line will commence running on the first day of July, leaving each place at half past 8 A. M. every day. Passengers wishing to travel from Saratoga to Lebanon Springs, will find this line not only the most expeditious but cheapest.

Passengers for Pittsfield, Northampton and Hartford by taking this line will dine at Troy, lodge at Pittsfield, and arrive at Hartford early the next day. The road is now put in the best order, and all that is now wanting is that liberality which the establishment merits.

☞ Seats taken at G. W. Wilcox's, York House, *Saratoga*, and at all the Principal Houses in Troy.

L. V. & J. B. REED, Proprietors.

J. S. KEELER, *Agent*, Troy.
S. DEXTER, *Agent*, Saratoga.

TROY, JUNE 25. 1834.

N. B. On the arrival of the ERIE or CHAMPLAIN, Parties can be accommodated with coaches to Saratoga or Ballston the same evening.

TROY, BALLSTON AND SARATOGA RAIL-ROAD.

UNTIL further notice the Cars will leave Troy,
At 9 3-4 o'clock, A. M.
2 do. P. M.
3 1-2 do. do.

Passengers going north of the Springs, should take the 9 3-4 o'clock train from Troy. Immediately after the arrival of the train at Saratoga, stages leave for Fort Edward, Glen's Falls and Sandy Hill. From Fort Edward they are conveyed in the fast packet boat *Red Bird* to Whitehall. Also, a daily line of stages from Saratoga to Lake George.

From Whitehall, the packet boat *Red Bird* will convey passengers to Fort Edward, and from thence to Saratoga by stages, where rail road cars will be in readiness for Troy, Schenectady and Albany by steam power.

JOS. S. DUTTON, Superintendent.
H. GREEN, Agent, Albany—office at Exchange Coffee House, opposite Eagle Tavern.
sept 1 A. REED, Agent, Whitehall.

TROY AND ALBANY.

York and the East. For this purpose, a railroad has been constructed to Schenectady which intercepts the Great Western Line at that point, and upon the river, a line of most splendid steamers has been put. . . . The railroad is one of the best constructed in the United States . . . This with the gentlemanly attention of those in charge of the cars—which by the way are superb . . . renders it a trip of pleasantness and comfort.

The Trojans had always been eager to provide uninterrupted train service between Troy and Boston. Their dream was realized with the construction of the Hoosac Tunnel. That five-mile underground passage, the longest railroad tunnel in the United States, was one of the great engineering feats of the nineteenth century. A start on the tunnel was made between 1855 and 1858, but the enormous undertaking was not completed until 1875. Not long afterward train travel between Troy and Boston took as little as five hours.

Troy's location at the terminus of four major railroads made it necessary to have an adequate railroad station. In 1853 the rail companies joined together to form the Troy Union Railroad Company. This fledgling firm then purchased a block on Sixth Avenue as the site for the proposed depot.

The Troy station, completed in 1854, was a huge brick structure, 400 feet long, that encompassed the entire city block. Its barreled roof was supported at each end by a great oak arch. Five hundred state legislators and dignitaries, most of whom had come to Troy by train, attended the opening banquet in the Union Depot on February 22, 1854.

With its bridge across the Hudson and its enormous depot, Troy became a prominent railroad center. In this new era of budding self-confidence, engines were finally permitted to cross the wooden bridge connecting Troy and Green Island. That proved to be a tragic misjudgment. On May 10, 1862, sparks from a passing locomotive ignited the bridge, creating a fire which destroyed much of central Troy, including the railway station. The edifice was rebuilt, this time with a roof supported by iron arches and without the high central tower that had distinguished the original building. Its life span was less than forty years, however; the Trojans then decided to construct a new Union Depot. It was a handsome red brick building with neo-classic elements and underground passages to each track. This third and last station was razed in 1958-59 after railroading in Troy had almost completely disap-

The Troy and Lansingburgh
horse railway, the first in the
Gateway, began operation in 1861.
By the 1880s, 100 horsecars carry-
ing five million people annually
connected area communities.
Courtesy, Rensselaer County
Historical Society

peared.

In 1862 the Rensselaer and Saratoga (R&S), Troy's first line, carried 556,000 passengers, 310,000 tons of freight. Less than a decade later in 1871, the R&S and its lines were leased to the Delaware and Hudson Railroad, creating one of the larger—and still independent—railroads in the country. A year later, construction was completed on the R&S locomotive repair shops in Green Island. The Green Island shops continued building and refurbishing freight cars until the late 1930s when this work was transferred to the Colonie yards, near Watervliet. The round house of the Green Island shops was thought to be one of the earliest such structures still standing in the United

States. Unfortunately, it was recently razed by the present owner, who continues to use the locomotive and car shops for his business.

The only railroading to remain in the Gateway area are Conrail's freight line over the old Troy and Greenbush line and the freight line of the D & H passing through Watervliet, Cohoes, and Waterford. Unhappily, no passenger train stops or even passes through the Gateway region today. There is, however, an outside chance that railroading could enjoy a renewed burst of life in the area. At this writing, officials from Quebec, Vermont, and New York have commissioned a study for a high-speed train connecting Montreal and New York City, possibly passing through the Gateway.

In the mid-1800s, while steam on rails was successfully providing transportation over long distances, rails also began to be used for short-distance travel within and between cities. The vehicles originally used for short-haul traffic were drawn by horses, while later models relied on electricity. Improved transportation facilitated the growth of cities, the concentration of central business districts, and the beginning of suburbs. With the arrival of the horse car, the worker, who had always walked to and

Above: Troy's last Union Depot is seen here circa 1915. When it closed in the late 1950s there was an unsuccessful attempt to convert it into a new city hall. Courtesy, Rensselaer County Historical Society

Left: The James M. Marvin locomotive of the Rensselaer & Saratoga Railroad was built in 1867 by the Schenectady Locomotive Works. This view was taken at the Fulton Street end of Union Depot in Troy as the train prepares for a northern trip. Courtesy, Rensselaer County Historical Society

The Fifth Avenue Bus Company, running between downtown Troy and Lansingburgh, provided an alternative to streetcars. Courtesy, Gene Baxter

from the factory, could live farther away from it. Residents no longer were constrained by the location of the neighborhood store and could travel quite easily to the center of town to do their shopping.

The earliest form of public intra-urban transportation was the omnibus, a horse-drawn wagon which picked up passengers and deposited them at, or nearer to, their destination. Cohoes enjoyed an early omnibus as did Troy.

The first horse railway in the Gateway joined Lansingburgh and Troy. The line opened in 1861 and was extended north through Lansingburgh to the Waterford Bridge the following year. In its first year of operation, the line made eighty trips daily, a tribute to its popularity. The railway became known as the "Red Line" because of the color its cars were painted.

The "White Line" from Troy to Cohoes opened in 1863, followed by a route connecting Troy and Albia. The steep climb up Congress Street along this track often made it necessary for passengers to get off and push.

A "Blue Line" linked Lansingburgh and Cohoes in 1880, and Waterford and Cohoes were joined by a "Green Line" in 1884. By 1885 the local street railways had 468 horses, car barns, and stables, and carried more than five million passengers per year.

One of the persistent problems posed by horse railways was the collection and disposal of manure. Another was the great "Epozooic" of 1872 in which thousands of horses died of equine encephilitis. During that period, men replaced horses to keep the street railways running. These problems spurred the search for an alternative to horse-

power. The first acceptable solution was an underground cable to which a car could be attached and detached by a gripper. The cost of installation, however, was usually prohibitive.

Finally, the electrically motorized car provided a solution. Thomas Davenport of Vermont produced a model railroad using a battery-powered rotary engine, first exhibited at the Rensselaer Institute in 1835. In 1885 Leo Daft, an Englishman, designed a small truck, placed on the roof of the car, which "trolled" on an overhead wire, and was attached by another wire to the motor inside the streetcar.

Frank Sprague, a former assistant to Thomas Edison, built the first successful electric street railway in Richmond, Virginia in 1888. In less than two years, Sprague's system was operating in Troy. In 1896 a transfer ticket program was adopted: patrons could transfer and ride to any point served by the line—for five cents.

In 1900 the street railway system of the Gateway area and Albany combined to form the United Traction Company. Shortly before this, the area witnessed the rapid growth of interurbans. The interurbans employed cars, each equipped with its own electric motor, to carry passengers from one city to another. Henry Averill opened the Troy and New England Railway, which connected Troy to Averill Park in 1895. The United Traction Company ran its first interurban to Schenectady in 1903. These electric cars were inexpensive to run and thus provided enormous competition for the steam railways. The giant railroads counterattacked by buying the street rail-

In the early twentieth century Franklin Square was an important center for Troy's business and transportation. Here the streetcar lines on Fourth and River streets intersected and, with the railroad tracks, crossed the Green Island Bridge. Courtesy, Rensselaer County Historical Society

ways. The United Traction Company, the last holdout in this area, was purchased by the Delaware and Hudson Railroad in 1905.

This purchase was not a happy development for area residents. By 1921 the Troy *Record,* while opposing an impending fare increase, went on to criticize the company's inferior service as follows:

Trojans always can count on the Traction Company doing everything in its power to unpopularize itself and make life disagreeable for those who from necessity are compelled to ride on its ill-smelling, flat-wheeled cars. The courteous grants of six and seven cent fares were followed by no appreciable addition in service in spite of promises, implied and actual.

Buses provided the first serious competition for the trolleys. After a long court battle, the first bus company was created in Troy in 1915 "so long as the routes were well removed from the trolley routes." As time passed, United Traction trolleys inevitably gave way to United Traction buses.

Meanwhile, strikes by motormen and conductors were a volatile part of the trolley scene. A motormen's strike occurred in 1900, another in 1901 over new schedules, and yet another over wages in 1905. Most of these strikes were short, and the motormen usually won their demands.

Trolley service was totally disrupted, however, by the great strike of 1921 when both motormen and conductors walked off their jobs for almost a year. The issues included an impending fare raise, possible discontinuation of the transfer system, and the reduction of motormen's wages from sixty to forty-five cents per hour. The Gateway area was accustomed to labor disputes, but this was the first strike to inconvenience a broad spectrum of people on a day-to-day basis over a long period of time. The strike finally ended, but its effects were deep and long-lasting. Both the union and the area lost. Merchants were hurt; recovery was sluggish. For the trolleys, it was the end of an era.

Trolleys continued to run in the Gateway until the 1930s. The last streetcar made its final run on February 4, 1932. Then trolleys disappeared into history—relics of a retreating past. A new epoch was dawning in the Gateway and in America as a whole: the age of the automobile. The invention of the internal combustion engine revolutionized travel and transportation. As increasing numbers of cars gave greater speed and mobility to more and more Americans, life was never again to be quite the same as it had been before. But public transportation is still important. Shortly after the failure of the United Traction Company in 1967, the Capital District Transportation Authority (CDTA) took over public transportation within the Gateway area.

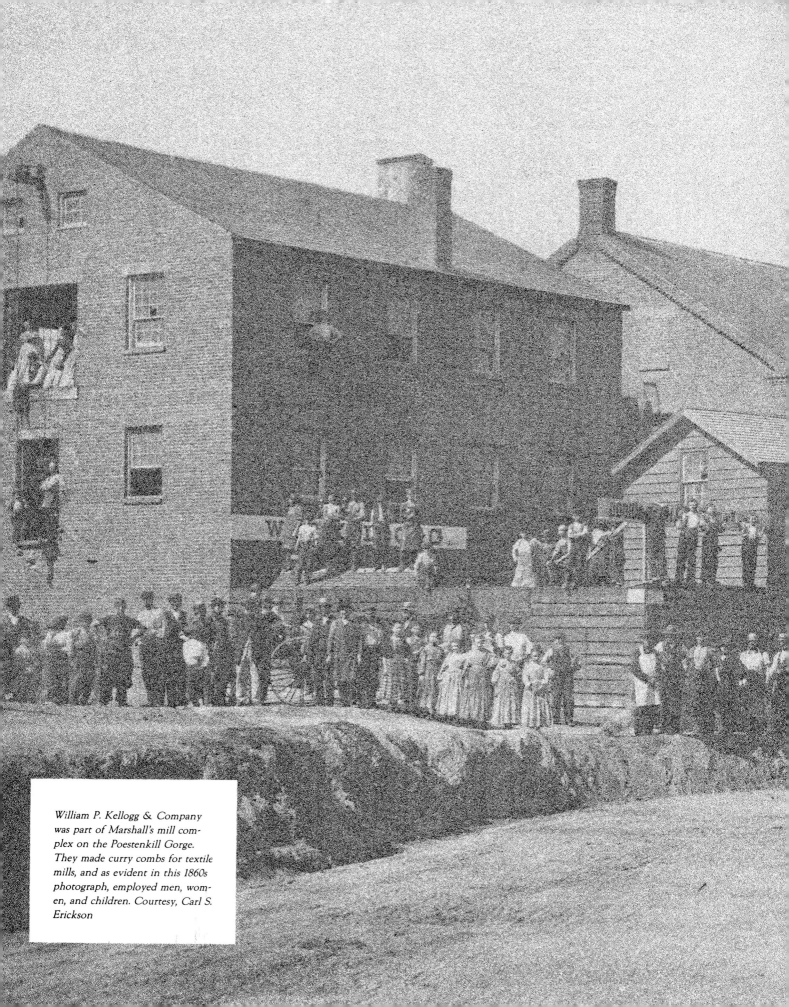

William P. Kellogg & Company was part of Marshall's mill complex on the Poestenkill Gorge. They made curry combs for textile mills, and as evident in this 1860s photograph, employed men, women, and children. Courtesy, Carl S. Erickson

CHAPTER FOUR

A BIRTHPLACE OF AMERICA'S INDUSTRIAL REVOLUTION

Change and innovation were characteristic of the Industrial Revolution. And, in a responsive social climate where each new invention inspired a dozen more, the process was accelerated, building on its own momentum. It is difficult to ascribe definitive dates to what is called the Industrial Revolution. However, a dramatic increase in inventions could be cited as an indication of the beginning of the period. If that is the case, then industrial history took a radical turn in Britain in the mid-1700s. In the United States rapid industrial growth began when Americans started borrowing freely from European technology and building on it. Imported ideas were quickly complemented by native ingenuity to launch America into its own Industrial Revolution.

The new nation's first Secretary of the Treasury, Alexander Hamilton, envisioned his country as a great industrial power. In 1791 he penned a "Report on Manufactures," a landmark document, which called for stimulating inventions, easing the movement of cash payments around the country, and encouraging the import and prohibiting the export of raw materials needed in manufacturing. Hamilton's statement aimed at making the United States independent in the manufacturing realm. It was not so much the cause of industrialization as an indicator of a process ready to begin.

Already in 1790 a young Englishman, Samuel Slater, arrived in Rhode Island to confer with Moses Brown, the owner of a spinning mill in Pawtucket. Slater agreed to reproduce British machinery in a new plant that Brown would finance. In 1793 Eli Whitney, who was working as a private tutor on an estate in Georgia, invented the cotton gin to remove seeds from the plant's fibers. The Industrial Revolution, announced by Hamilton, was underway.

The Gateway area possessed all the basic ingredients for becoming a great industrial center. It had abundant water-

Right: One of the earliest photographs of Troy was taken in 1860 by James Irving looking east on Congress Street which was the main thoroughfare between the Hudson River and the east. In seven blocks it accommodated over fifty businesses including clothiers, confectioners, hatters, four hotels, and an oyster dealer. The Tibbits mansion is at the head of Congress and on the hill is the short-lived Troy University which closed in 1862. Courtesy, Carl S. Erickson

Far right: A group of iron workers pose with their tools and castings outside Marshall Foundry in Troy circa 1870. Courtesy, Rensselaer County Historical Society

The Griswold wire works complex, along the Poestenkill Gorge, was photographed in the late nineteenth century. This mill and the others on the hillside were powered by Marshall's 600-foot tunnel which harnessed the power of the Poestenkill Falls. Courtesy, Rensselaer County Historical Society

being operated by Isaac Merritt by 1818. There also was a cotton factory, as well as a mill which produced augers and screws. The last plant on this location was the Griswold wire works, established in 1879, and dissolved in 1911.

Further development of the gorge took place in 1840 when the cotton manufacturer, Benjamin Marshall, undertook construction of the still existing underground/overground power canal system. Marshall moved up the hill and built a factory that specialized in making fine cotton goods. These fabrics were sent downriver near Hudson where they were printed into calicoes. Other industrialists subsequently erected factories near Marshall's mill, leasing land and purchasing waterpower from him. In 1846 the Tompkins machine works began turning out knitting machinery. Charles Kellogg built a factory at mid-century for the production of curry combs and other hardware. By the 1860s, the mills on the north slope of the gorge were manufacturing a wide variety of goods—from cotton cloth to rivets. Paper was an especially important product.

The original paper mill developed by Mahlon Taylor was purchased on December 29, 1792, by new owners, who bought the plant for 400 pounds sterling. To supply the factory with raw materials, they advertised in area newspapers that they would pay "three pence per pound for white, blue brown and check rags, and a proportionate price for other kinds." By the end of the eighteenth century, a second paper mill was built in Troy on the Wynantskill. It became known as A.&W. Orr in 1837,

power, excellent transportation, and ample raw materials, available locally or easily brought in by ship. The work force grew as New Englanders moved west and immigrants came up river from New York City. Successive waves of manufactures, strong inventive spirit, and wide mercantile interests allowed the Gateway to claim the title as one of the birthplaces of America's Industrial Revolution.

The Poestenkill Gorge developed rapidly in the nineteenth century. As early as 1667, there is mention of a mill at the mouth of the gorge in Troy. The mill appears again on a map dated 1720. By 1792 Mahlon Taylor, a New Jersey millwright, had purchased the site of the old mill, rebuilt the dam, and was constructing a sawmill, a flour mill, and the first paper mill established in northeastern New York.

Upstream at the foot of the falls, another flour mill was

when Alexander Orr joined his brother, William, in the business of printing fine wallpapers. The brothers were said to have introduced the first cylindrical printing machine. With this new equipment, they could produce 1,000 nine-yard-long rolls of wallpaper in three colors each day. The Orrs also claimed to have been the first to manufacture mercantile printing paper with wood fibers in it. Meanwhile, R.T. Smart erected the Gold Leaf Mill and the Troy City Paper-Mill on the Wynantskill. There he made "an excellent quality of straw wrapping paper."

An important paper company that operated up to 1962 on the north slope of the Poestenkill Gorge in Troy was the one founded in 1846 by William H. Manning, Gardner Howland, and Alvin Williams. From the beginning the founders of the Mount Ida Mill manufactured manila paper. In 1855 the firm was reorganized and became known as Manning and Peckham. This company, now part of Hammermill Paper Company, has operated on Green Island since 1962.

Another early paper mill, the Enterprise Paper Company, was founded in Waterford some time after 1829. Today the firm is still in business and is known as the Mohawk Paper Company.

During this period, Troy became an important center of iron- and metal-related industries. Its growth was assisted by the fact that the Gateway area was surrounded on three sides by rich iron ore deposits. Limestone for flux in the smelting process was quarried in the Hudson valley, and vast tracts of nearby forestland supplied raw material for the charcoal industry. Coal, which eventually replaced charcoal as fuel in the conversion process, was brought to the area from eastern Pennsylvania.

The Wynantskill stream in south Troy was the first site of the area's iron industry. In 1807, on the north side of the lower falls of that stream, John Brinckerhoff and Company of Albany built a mill to convert bar iron into hoop iron and nail rods. In 1849 this firm, then owned by Erastus Corning, built the first steam-powered rolling mill in the area, a plant which still stands today to the west of the Troy approach to the Menands Bridge.

In 1809 the Troy Iron and Nail Factory opened on the south side of the Wynantskill's upper falls. Scottish-born and trained engineer Henry Burden was to bring the firm to prominence. Having been named superintendent in 1822, this ambitious immigrant subsequently purchased the plant himself. Burden's inventive genius was responsible for the creation of many innovative machines such as the rotary concentric squeezer that mechanized the manufacture of wrought iron. The invention which brought Henry Burden his greatest success and wealth, however, was a machine for making horseshoes. He improved the original 1835 invention twice so that, by 1857, it could produce these items in a single movement and at the rate of one each second.

In its early days, Burden's factory employed five small waterwheels; yet, as production increased, the need for a

The Burden Iron Works was a major supplier of horseshoes to the Union army during the Civil War. Later improvements in horseshoe machines enabled the company to produce several million annually. Courtesy, Rensselaer County Historical Society

Left: Henry Burden's great over-shot waterwheel was photographed circa 1900, a few years after its abandonment. It powered Burden's horseshoe factory on the Wynantskill from 1851 to 1896. Courtesy, Rensselaer County Historical Society

Julius Hanks, the Gateway's first bell founder, distributed this business card with an illustration of his foundry in the 1820s. The foundry was located at what now is the intersection of Fifth Avenue and Fulton Street. Courtesy, Rensselaer County Historical Society

larger prime mover became evident. Construction of a great wheel commenced in 1838 and continued for thirteen years. The result was distinguished by its huge size—sixty feet in diameter and twenty-two feet wide—and its detailed design. Burden's enormous creation became known as "the Niagara of Waterwheels," the overall largest waterwheel in the world, never surpassed by any other in either capacity or massiveness.

Iron goods manufactured in the Gateway were by no means exclusive to Troy. In 1832 David Wilkinson established an iron foundry in Cohoes. Under the direction of H.D. Fuller and Robert Safely, a new factory was built in 1867 to produce heavy castings and a wide variety of industrial machinery. George and Thomas Brooks rented a portion of the new Fuller and Safely factory and, using ten presses, manufactured wrought-iron nuts. Nevertheless it was Daniel Simmons who first produced axes, the iron product for which Cohoes became famous. By 1847, Simmons employed 200 men who turned out 600 axes a day. Thirty years later, after new owners had taken over Simmons' factory, production more than doubled.

In 1854 Jonas Simmons built a rolling mill in Cohoes. The firm produced shafting, axe poles, bar and band iron, and trestle work for buildings and bridges. The company employed 200 hands and consumed 1,200 tons of iron ore a year.

The Hudson-Mohawk Gateway was also renowned for

the quality of its bells and high-precision engineering instruments. The first bell manufacturer in the area was Julius Hanks who brought a foundry from Connecticut to Gibbonsville and then to Troy in 1825. Hanks was "prepared to execute any orders . . . (for) church bells, with improved cast iron yokes, also town clocks, copper and brass castings, (and) surveyors' instruments of the most improved construction." Julius' brother bought out the firm in 1830, but continued to make similar products. They were "prepared to furnish church bells from 100 to 3,000 pounds."

The greatest name in Gateway bells was undoubtedly that of Andrew Meneely. At seventeen he was apprenticed to Julius Hanks and even married one of Hanks' daughters. In 1826 he founded his own firm in Gibbonsville. Meneely is credited with the invention of the "conical rotary yoke," later catalogued as "the most desirable and perfect rotary yoke in the world." His firm remained a family-held, single-product business for well over a century, casting some of the most important bells, pads, and chains used in this country and abroad.

Like the Meneely Bell Company, the W. & L.E. Gurley Company made products that were celebrated for their high quality. The firm's owners, William and Leland Gurley, became world-famous makers of high-precision instruments. Their products were widely distributed nationally and abroad, causing Troy historian Arthur J. Weise to comment that the company was an "enterprising firm (that) makes annually more engineering and surveying instruments than any other three mathematical and philosophical instrument manufactures in the United States, and widely distributes them in all parts of the world."

The Gateway area, especially Troy, along with Albany, was the premier stove-manufacturing center of the United States during the nineteenth century. In 1821 Charles and Nathaniel Starbuck and Ephraim Gurley were the first to regularly manufacture heating stoves in the region. By 1853, seven Trojan foundries employed 670 men to cast 75,000 stoves, collectively valued at one million dollars.

Above: This carillon was made by Meneely & Company in Watervliet in the early 1930s. Courtesy, Rensselaer County Historical Society

Left: These men were casting a bell at the Meneely Bell Foundry in the late 1930s. Courtesy, Rensselaer County Historical Society

In his *History of Rensselaer County,* Nathaniel Bartlett Sylvester says, "There is seldom an improvement in a stove that cannot be traced to the inventive skill of a Troy manufacturer." Indeed, patents for various components were granted to a number of local inventors. Cooking, for example, was a fireplace chore made difficult by bending and the unevenness of the heat. Benjamin Franklin had invented a cooking stove which was available in Troy as early as 1814, but it was Philo P. Stewart, an adopted Trojan, who created and patented the "Large Oven and Air-Tight Cooking Stove" which became the most popular in the nation. Stewart's invention was first manufactured by Starbuck and Company, and later by Fuller and Warren. Filling orders for Stewart's stove caused a mammoth production boom in the Hudson Mohawk Gateway.

High quality cloth was also produced in the Gateway, and Cohoes, while respected for its iron goods, was renowned for cotton textiles. The firm that contributed most to this fame was the Harmony Mills Company, incorporated by Peter Harmony and twenty-one others in 1836. One year later, the company erected its first mill, a four-story brick building capped with a slate roof, measuring 165 feet long and fifty feet wide. An adjacent picking

Left: Workers assemble kitchen ranges at Fuller & Warren Company's Clinton Stove Works in South Troy in the early twentieth century. Courtesy, The Times Record

Facing page, far right: This advertisement for P.P. Stewart's famous cooking stove, manufactured at Fuller & Warren Company, ran in the 1860 Troy city directory. Courtesy, Rensselaer County Historical Society

room and repair shop extended the plant's length to 213 feet. In addition, three double brick structures were built to house the superintendent and the workers. The mill began operation with 5,000 spindles. Within thirteen years there were 7,000.

In 1850 Garner and Wild bought Harmony Mills. Only two years later, the new firm built Harmony Mill #1 with a capacity of 30,000 spindles and a labor force of 750 operators. This plant was so successful that Mill #2 was completed in 1857.

In 1855 the Mohawk Mill, of which Joshua Bailey was president, was reported to be the largest knitting factory in America. It employed 600 workers and introduced a new laundry machine that could wash 1,200 pairs of drawers a day.

Troy was also known for producing high-quality cotton textiles. It was, however, the invention of the detachable collar that really launched the Trojans into their curious, yet rapidly growing, position in the industry.

The new-fangled collar was apparently invented by Hannah Montague who tired of washing her husband's voluminous shirts. It is said that the fastidious Orlando Montague changed shirts two or three times a day. Some time in the late 1820s, Hannah cut the collars off Orlando's shirts and insisted that he keep his shirt on while she washed the collar. Retired preacher Ebenezer Brown was intrigued by Hannah's idea. With a true entrepreneurial spirit, he hired women to make "freestanding" shirt collars. He sold them in his dry goods store and peddled them door to door.

Orlando Montague and Austin Granger organized the process in 1834, opening the first firm to manufacture linen collars and "shirt bosoms," also called dickeys or shams. A year later, Independence Starks got into the business and soon added a laundry to his manufacturing operation.

Troy's textile industry gained further momentum with the invention of the detachable linen cuff in 1845 and the introduction of sewing machines in 1852. The firm of Bennett and Edison was the first to operate these machines by steampower. Trojan women had by this time become so skilled at this new employment that, when other cities tried to launch into this rapidly growing industry, they failed because of the less experienced nature of their labor force. It was not long before a single woman could stitch forty to eighty dozen collars a day, while an-

Abram Haney of Morrison & Morrison in Troy was issued a patent for this coal-burning stove in 1849. Courtesy, Rensselaer County Historical Society

other could sew thirty to forty dozen cuffs, bringing total sales of some five million dollars annually.

During this period, for the first time in history, women in large numbers left their homes to join the conventional work force. At the factories, females labored long hours—a fourteen-hour day was not uncommon—doing tedious work for low pay. Women thus became an integral part of the Industrial Revolution and later a voice in rising demands for shorter hours, better wages, and more humane working conditions.

Troy was also known for making distinguished coaches and carriages. Orsamus Eaton opened a factory in 1820, and Charles Veazie set up his factory several years later. By 1830 the two coach builders together employed about sixty men and turned out 150 carriages annually at a sale value of $50,000. As early as 1831, the Troy *Budget* remarked that "Eaton and Veazie have rendered Trojan carriages almost as noted as the wooden horse of old Troy." Stagecoaches made in Troy were renowned throughout the country. From Georgia to Ohio, the nation's stage lines clamored for coaches "of the best Troy manufacture."

In 1831 Eaton took on a partner, Uri Gilbert, who had earlier been apprenticed to him. Charles Veazie went out of business in 1836. Soon the only coach maker in the Gateway area, Eaton, Gilbert and Company, focused on manufacturing railroad passenger cars. Every order filled won the coach builders greater acclaim. In 1850 the firm employed 150 workers to build omnibuses, thirty-one passenger cars and 150 freight cars. After a disastrous fire

Right: Starbuck Iron Works was located on Center Island south of the Rensselaer & Saratoga Railroad Bridge (Green Island Bridge). Starbuck specialized in the manufacture of columns, window caps, plows, and bark mills. The foundry complex featured a row of worker housing to the right of the main building. Courtesy, Rensselaer County Historical Society

Below: This is an advertisement for the Pembroke collar, made by George P. Ide & Co. of Troy in the early twentieth century. Courtesy, Rensselaer County Historical Society

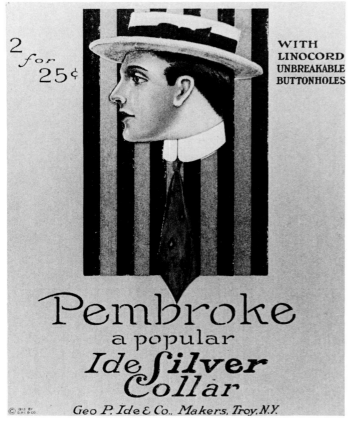

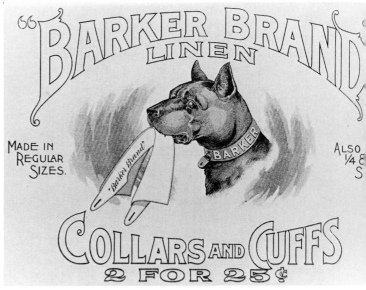

Above: William Barker & Co. used this ad in the early 1900s. Founded in Troy, the company built a modern factory in Watervliet in 1898 south of the Congress Street Bridge. They had salesrooms in New York City, Chicago, and Boston. Courtesy, Rensselaer County Historical Society

leveled the factory in 1852, the business moved to Green Island where it grew to huge proportions. Various Gateway artists worked for Eaton, Gilbert as muralists.

In 1817 William Powers of Lansingburgh, a former teacher, began to manufacture floor cloths, the forerunner of linoleum. The business was small, but, with his wife Deborah as an active partner, he found himself "realizing a handsome profit." Powers plowed this profit back into the business by building a large factory in 1828. The following year a vat of heated varnish caught fire. Powers was badly burned in the resulting blaze and died within a few hours.

Deborah, undaunted, carried on the business. When her son Nathaniel joined her as a partner in 1847, the firm was incorporated as D. Powers and Sons.

There is no doubt that Deborah Powers provided the force and drive that made the floor cloth business a huge success. She soon opened a factory in Newburgh and a warehouse in New York City. She, herself, sailed a sloop up and down the Hudson in pursuit of business.

It was a bold breed of men and women who initiated the Gateway's industrial boom. And, simultaneously, equally inventive and enterprising residents arose to become the area's leaders and business tycoons. Active in civic and community affairs, these dynamic entrepreneurs left their mark on the Gateway. Some arrived with financial means; others came equipped only with ideas and energy. All were characterized by limitless drive and burning ambition—and achieved extraordinary success.

One such man was George Tibbits who, at age twenty-

Above: Eaton, Gilbert & Company, located at what is now Sixth Avenue and Broadway, ran this ad in the city directory in 1850. In addition to making stagecoaches, they built passenger and freight cars. Courtesy, Rensselaer County Historical Society

Right: Gilbert & Bush Co. of Green Island manufactured this parlor car circa 1880. Courtesy, Rensselaer County Historical Society

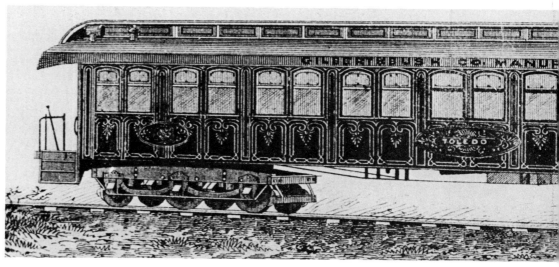

Below right: Richard P. Hart was involved in many area businesses including banks, real estate, and railroads. From History of Rensselaer County, *by Nathaniel Sylvester, 1880*

Above: "Mount Ida," the Gothic Revival mansion of the Warren family on a promontory overlooking Troy, was purchased by the city in 1903 and became Prospect Park. The house was used as a museum until the 1930s. Courtesy, Rensselaer County Historical Society

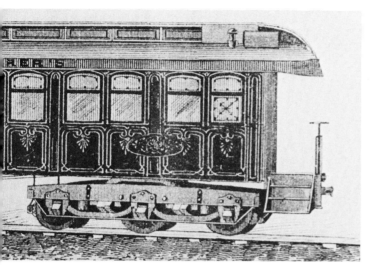

one, set up a mercantile business in Lansingburgh, which he later moved to Troy. The young merchant was so prosperous that he was soon able to retire and build himself a house on the slopes of Mount Ida.

George Tibbits then devoted himself to civic and political affairs. Eminently successful in politics, he was elected to office at the local, state, and national levels. Also active in banking, he became a charter founder of Troy's first commercial institution and also displayed a special flair for transportation as a director of numerous Trojan railroad, steamboat, and turnpike companies. Active well past seventy, Tibbits was one of the dynamos of his—or any age.

Another outstanding civic and business leader was Richard P. Hart, who started his career in Troy as a clerk in his uncles' store. He soon set up his own business and made his fortune supplying military needs during the War of 1812. Hart was the prototypical business tycoon. He was involved in banks, roads, steamboats, real estate, and utilities, and was a founding member of almost every railroad that originated in Troy. Hart also was a trustee on the original board of Emma Willard's Female Seminary and served the Rensselaer Institute in the same capacity.

Around the turn of the century, Eliakim Warren, a member of one of New England's oldest families, arrived in Troy aboard his ship, the *Three Brothers*, named in honor of his three sons. Thus was established in Troy a dynasty that for well over 100 years contributed leadership and capital to the city's development. Eliakim's sons and grandsons helped establish turnpikes, steamboats, and railroads. Four became presidents of Troy's financial institutions. And three Warrens—a son, a grandson, and a

great grandson of Eliakim—served as mayors of Troy.

At the tender age of twelve, Russell Sage began working in his brother's store in Troy. By the time he was twenty-one, he was owner of a thriving wholesale grocery business. Sage was eventually drawn into politics, and was elected to Congress; however, it was as a businessman and a wily investor in America's railroads that he realized his greatest success.

By 1863 Sage had outgrown both politics and Troy. He moved to New York City and proceeded to amass one of America's first great fortunes. After his death, his widow financed the building of the modern Rensselaer Polytechnic Institute, built the current Emma Willard School, and established the old campus as a college named for her husband.

It was during this exciting period of industrial beginnings that Troy became the home of the man who was to give America its symbolic representation as "Uncle Sam." In the early 1790s, two brothers, Samuel and Ebenezer Wilson, left New Hampshire and migrated west to Troy. There they began manufacturing bricks made from the blue clay of Mount Ida.

During the War of 1812, Samuel Wilson became a meat packer and supplier of beef and pork to the United States Army stationed outside of Greenbush. One tale has it that Elbert Anderson, a contractor who furnished beef to the army, visited Troy to inspect Wilson's operation. The barrels in which the meat was shipped were marked "US-EA." A workman asked what the letters meant and was told facetiously, that they obviously stood for Uncle Sam's and Elbert Anderson's initials. "Uncle Sam" was Samuel Wilson's nickname. The joke caught on and spread among workers and soldiers, who laughed and bantered about packing and eating Uncle Sam's meat. Another version says that soldiers misread the letters as "Uncle Sam" instead of United States.

One way or the other, the story first appeared in print in 1830 in the New York *Gazette* when it reported Elbert Anderson's death. The times were beginning to be prosperous, and the new nation was full of hope. An appropriate symbol was needed, and Uncle Sam captured the public imagination. The actual tall, lean, bearded figure, dressed in red, white, and blue, evolved in later years as the work of political cartoonists, especially Thomas Nast. In 1961 a resolution of Congress finally and officially acknowledged Samuel Wilson's role in the creation of the symbol. The original Uncle Sam was one of the Gateway's many gifts to the nation.

Major General Joseph B. Carr and staff of the New York National Guard led a parade on Second Street in Troy in the 1880s. During this time Carr served as secretary of state under governors Alonzo Cornell and Grover Cleveland. Courtesy, Rensselaer County Historical Society

CHAPTER FIVE

THE CIVIL WAR AND INDUSTRY

One does not think of the Civil War resulting in the triumph of industrial capitalism, yet this may have been its principal outcome. Although the war freed black Americans from the bonds of slavery, it certainly did not fulfill a promise of equality. It did, however, thoroughly liberate industrial capitalism, spurring mechanized production, expanding productivity, and increasing national income. American wages subsequently became the highest on earth. It is no wonder, then, that the Hudson-Mohawk Gateway, already mature as an industrial center, supported the war enthusiastically.

The 2nd Regiment of New York State Volunteers was organized in the spring of 1861. Some 900 strong, its soldiers came from the Gateway area and beyond. After gathering at Rensselaer Park in Lansingburgh, the volunteers marched to the courthouse in Troy. The 2nd Regiment received its flag, boarded barges at the steamboat dock, and six days later became the first volunteer unit to encamp in Virginia. As part of the Army of the Potomac, the 2nd Regiment fought valiantly at Fredericksburg and Chancellorsville. When the soldiers' two-year enlistments ended in 1863, only 300 were alive and well enough to return to the Gateway and receive hometown welcomes.

The 22nd Regiment, which had been organized at Albany in the spring of 1861 and included Company A composed of men from Waterford and Cohoes, returned in 1863. Out of 825 men, only 500 came home. About the same time, survivors of the 34th, including a Company A with men from West Troy, returned. The Gateway area was sacrificing some of its best young men to the Union cause.

In 1862 the 125th Regiment set off from Troy with George Willard in command. These men fought in twenty-one battles and confronted General Lee's troops at Gettysburg. That same year, 900 volunteers from Rensselaer and Washington counties arrived in Virginia. As members of the 169th Regiment, they fought against Lee at Richmond, participated in the siege of Fort Sumter, and

Right: The Troy City Artillery at Washington (Monument Square) probably was preparing for Abraham Lincoln's visit in February 1861. Soon afterward the artillery became Company F of the 2nd Regiment of New York State Volunteers. Courtesy, Rensselaer County Historical Society

Below: The return of the 2nd Regiment to Troy from service in the Civil War was celebrated on May 14, 1863. An arch was erected on Second Street and speeches were made at Washington (now Monument) Square. Courtesy, Rensselaer County Historical Society

formed part of General Grant's left flank in the battles of Cold Harbor and Petersburg. When Lee surrendered on March 12, 1865, the 169th returned home with fewer than 120 of its original 900 men.

Troy also contributed several high-ranking officers to the war effort. John Ellis Wool, for example, had distinguished himself during the Mexican War by leading a force of 3,000 men some 900 miles from San Antonio to Saltillo. Although already seventy-seven years of age at the outbreak of the Civil War, he was given a command and promoted to the rank of major general. Many of Wool's military accoutrements, including a great sword awarded him for his services in the Mexican War, are on display at the Rensselaer County Historical Society.

Joseph Bradford Carr set off from Troy in the Civil War as commanding officer of the 2nd Regiment. When his horse was shot out from under him at the Bristol Station, he mounted the horse of an orderly, and at the head of his men, charged the enemy. Known as the "Hero of Bristoe," Carr was later brevetted a major general.

William Badger Tibbits was another Trojan soldier who marched off in 1861 as a captain in the 2nd Regiment and was soon promoted to major. At the head of a cavalry unit, he fought in most of the battles waged in Virginia. When he left the army after the war, Tibbits was raised to the rank of full brigadier and brevet major general.

Alonzo Alden, a descendant of John Alden of the *Mayflower*, entered the army as a private. While convalescing at home in Troy from a bout with typhoid fever, he was appointed a major in the newly formed 169th, and soon assumed command of the unit. Wounded at Suffolk, Virginia, Alden was shot in the head at Cold Harbor while planting the regimental colors upon the parapet. At Fort Fisher, he was thrown some thirty feet, buried by falling debris from a wrecked magazine, and left mangled and apparently dead. His obituary was published, but despite partial paralysis of his right side, Alden recovered and even rejoined his regiment. Shortly after 1865 he was appointed full brigadier general in the New York State National Guard.

Above: Colonel Joseph Bradford Carr was the commanding officer of the 2nd Regiment of the New York State Volunteers during the Civil War. Courtesy, Rensselaer County Historical Society

Left: The Soldiers and Sailors Monument was erected in Washington Square in Troy in 1890-91 to honor Rensselaer County soldiers and sailors who served in the Civil War. Courtesy, Rensselaer County Historical Society

Besides supplying men, the Gateway made another major contribution to the war effort: the building of the *Monitor.* This vessel, a milestone in naval annals and in the history of warfare, was made possible by a combination of ingenuity, money, and determination. While the Confederacy was assembling an ironclad ship in Virginia, Cornelius Bushnell of New Haven, Connecticut won a contract to build such a vessel, the *Galena,* for the Union navy.

Bushnell then met with two Gateway iron manufacturers: John F. Winslow and John A. Griswold of Troy. The three men initially discussed the building of Bushnell's ship, but ended up looking at a model of the *Monitor,* designed by Swedish-born engineer and inventor, Captain John Ericsson. Winslow became the spokesman for all of the principals in an effort to obtain a Navy contract to build the *Monitor.*

On October 4, 1861, the contract for "a floating battery" was signed. Ericsson rushed to New York City to prepare the plans, Winslow and Griswold to Troy to gear up their iron works, and Bushnell to New Haven to build the ironclad *Galena* for which he had earlier won a contract. The agreement read that they would produce the vessel in 100 days.

Exactly 101 working days later the completed vessel slid off the ways in Brooklyn. The Navy accepted and manned the *Monitor* on February 20, 1862. In March the former U.S. Navy steam frigate *Merrimack,* rechristened the *Virginia* by the Confederacy, was wreaking havoc in Hampton Roads. Towed to Virginia waters, the *Monitor*

arrived in time to confront the Confederate ironclad on March 8, 1862. Although the ensuing battle is usually considered a stalemate, the *Virginia* never again ventured out to harass Union ships.

During this same period, opposition to the draft arose in the Northeast and exploded in Troy in the riots of July 1863. Though not as serious as similar draft riots in New York City, they were nevertheless the most serious civil outbreaks to date in that city. The white working class, especially Irish immigrants, opposed the inequity of a law that allowed men to escape conscription by hiring a substitute or paying the government $300. They considered it grossly unfair that rich men could use their money to buy poor men's blood. Opponents of the draft also harbored strong feelings of resentment against members of the black community, viewing them as a major cause of the war.

So, on July 15, 400 workers assembled at Burden's works in South Troy and marched north through the city. As other sympathizers joined them along the way, the mood became more and more hostile. Some marchers brandished clubs. Merchants and manufacturers prudently closed their shops. At Mount Olympus the mob turned south and swarmed into the Troy *Daily Times* building on River Street, pillaging and destroying machinery and generally venting its anger on the paper which had supported the draft in its editorials.

Above: Liberty Street Presbyterian Church was located on the north side of Liberty Street between Third and Fourth streets in Troy. As early as the 1830s it served the black community and narrowly escaped being burned by an anti-black mob during the draft riots of 1863. Courtesy, Rensselaer County Historical Society

Right: This plaque appears on the Soldiers and Sailors Monument in Monument Square in Troy. It depicts the famous battle between the Monitor (right side) and the Virginia (Merrimac), and a quotation from Troy's General Wool thanking the iron-maker Griswold for his efforts in building the ship. Courtesy, Rensselaer County Historical Society

Proclamation!

In view of the present state of affairs in the City, Breaches of the Peace having occurred, by which the peace and quiet of our citizens is greatly disturbed, I do hereby call upon all peaceably disposed citizens to enroll themselves, at my office, as Special Policemen or Militia. And I do further order that all disorderly assemblages of people and processions do immediately disperse and repair to their several homes and occupations.

W. L. VAN ALSTYNE, MAYOR.

Troy, July 16, 1863.

The mayor of Troy issued this broadside in 1863 in an attempt to put an end to the draft riots. Courtesy, Rensselaer County Historical Society

The enraged multitude then proceeded to unleash its wrath on black residents, stoning any blacks it happened upon, and headed toward the black Liberty Street Presbyterian Church intent on detroying it. A white clergyman, the Reverend Peter Havermans, persuaded them to spare the building. The draft was suspended, but that evening the rioters entered and ravaged the house of Martin I. Townsend, a vocal supporter of the war effort. To restore order, the mayor called up four military companies, and a loaded six-pound howitzer was trained on the rioters. The crowd disbursed. When the draft was resumed in September, two regiments of infantry and one of artillery arrived in Troy to preserve the peace.

Across the Hudson in West Troy, the Watervliet Arsenal started gearing up for the war as early as 1859. As its contribution to the Union cause, the arsenal produced ammunition, making as many as 33,000 bullets a day. Gas lighting was installed so that employees could work around the clock. At that time, the arsenal employed 2,000 workers, one-quarter of whom were children—girls as well as boys.

For a time, the mobilization effort induced by the war offered prosperity to mill owners and upward mobility to mill workers. On the other hand, the era was also marred by two depressions and great labor unrest. Also threatening Gateway industry was growing competition from western industries which had the advantage of cheaper labor, more available natural resources, and locations closer to expanding markets. At home, the immigrant labor

population exerted further pressure on local institutions as the newcomers began feeling their strength and started organizing to control the workplace, as well as the area's political apparatus.

As early as 1842 there was a brief strike in Cohoes by Harmony Mills Company workers who were protesting a 20 percent wage reduction. In 1849 Ogden Mill employees struck against a 15 percent pay cut, but they returned three weeks later when the company threatened to bring in workers from the outside. During the depression of 1857 woolen plants shut down altogether while cotton mills went on part-time schedules. Harmony later reinstated full employment, but reduced wages by 25 percent. The following winter the unemployed and the underpaid sought relief in a soup house and a bread line. By late February the workers began to fear that the owners were trying to nationalize lower wages. Female employees threatened to strike unless the 25 percent wage reduction was eliminated. The next morning, wages were increased by 10 percent, but production speedups were initiated as well; thus, 800 women went on strike for three weeks, returning only when a 12.5 percent increase was offered.

Labor activity in Troy was not as intense during this pre-Civil War period. In 1857 workers from twenty-three stove foundries formed the International Iron Molders Local #2. When in mid-March 1859 the foundries opened at the previous fall's wages, molders from the Clinton and Washington foundries walked out. This stimulated workmen to join the union. After a few weeks the owners made a concession far more important than increased wages: they gave their employees power to regulate the work force. By 1860 the Troy local, numbering 400 men, was the largest in the country. This same union was disbanded during the Civil War on a conspiracy charge of forming a secret and unfair combination. But it soon was revived and regained its former membership strength within two years.

By the mid-1850s commercial laundry had become a relatively large-scale industry in Troy with a complex division of labor that included washing, starching, and ironing. Six hundred women, mainly unskilled Irish immigrants, labored strenuously on eleven- to fourteen-hour daily shifts. They were confined to small shops with temperatures hitting ninety degrees in winter and unimaginable heights in summer. Many of the laborers also contracted consumption. Despite these grueling conditions, laundry work was nevertheless more prestigious than one alternative, domestic service.

RALLY FOR CASH!

GREAT MEETING

AT

LANSINGBURGH,

☞ TO-NIGHT. ☜

The Journeymen and Workmen employed in the BRUSH FACTORIES of Lansingburgh are requested to attend a Public Meeting to be held

This, Saturday Evening, April 23d,

AT MORRIS HALL, Luke Read's Hotel,

To adopt such measures as may be deemed necessary to abolish the present system of Store-Pay, and establish a Cash system in its place.

Good Speakers will be in attendence.   The Meeting will commence at half-past 7 o'clock.   Come one! Come all!   Now is the time or never.

W. BARTLETT,
J. McDONALD,
THOS. CURRAN, Jr.,   *Committee*
E. PLUCKROSE,

Above: Labor unrest in the nineteenth century is evident in this broadside which indicates that many laborers were forced to buy provisions from company-owned stores. Courtesy, Warren Broderick

Right: This was the collar dampening department at Cluett-Peabody in the early 1920s. Courtesy, Rensselaer County Historical Society

In a time of growing union activity, the laundries were fertile ground for organizing. The ironers did band together to form the Collar Laundry Union. Kate Mullaney, the organization's president, was said to head the "only bona fide female union in the country." She won wage increases up to $10-$12 a week while other women were earning only $7, and men $13.50. She also lent financial support to Trojan molders and offered to send laundry union members to New York City to help organize women there.

But if unions were gaining strength through organization, so was management. A three-month strike of the Laundry Workers Union in 1869, for example, forged a bond between collar manufacturers and laundry owners. The former refused to send their collars and cuffs to unionized laundries and began recruiting and training new hands. They also convinced collar manufacturers in other cities to join their boycott. Meanwhile, the laundry owners offered a wage increase—provided workers quit the union. Most employees refused and instead set up a cooperative collar and cuff manufacturing company, as

well as a cooperative laundry. Neither survived for very long.

A regional trades assembly was formed in 1864, at first with fourteen, and later twenty, unions participating. That year, 2,000 workers marched in a labor solidarity parade and 5,000 attended the picnic that followed. Profits were used to form a working men's free reading room and library, a cooperative grocery, a working men's clothing store, a debating society, and a labor newspaper, the *Saturday Evening Herald*.

Meanwhile, the Wool Spinners Association #1 of Cohoes set up a committee to work for the election of an Albany molder as a state assemblyman. The following year a "Working Men's Eight Hour League" was established in Troy to lobby for legislation for an eight-hour work day. Labor leader William Sylvis told the 1866 New York State Trades Assembly Convention: "Troy is the banner city of Americans upon the trades union sentiment, and everything concerning the welfare of working men," with "excellence . . . in the thoroughness of its organization" and "second to none in rendering . . . substantial aid."

The union movement by then had gathered so much strength that iron foundry owners from various industrial cities met in Albany to consider ways to eliminate the molders' union. This gathering led to the creation of a national trade association. Of the thirty-three companies that joined the organization, fourteen were from Troy, and Trojan Charles Eddy was elected president. The molders demanded equal wages among area foundries to be set at the highest prevailing salary level. They also sought a 25 percent wage increase, salary by the day rather than piece work, application for jobs to the shop committee rather than the foreman, and the ratio of one apprentice to ten molders. Foundry owners countered by posting notices which outlawed shop committees and emphasized management control over apprentices. More than 700 molders were locked out, and Sylvis instructed other locals to duplicate Troy's demands. He vowed to start a cooperative foundry as well. The owners responded that molders could keep their jobs if apprentices could be employed when molders were unavailable. The molders accepted this proposal, but because there was no wage equalization, they stayed out. Finally, the owners capitulated, and the molders established the first of three successful cooperative foundries.

The owners' need to economize became more urgent in the early 1870s, owing to the combined forces of western competition and a severe depression. Daniel Walkowitz in his book *Worker City, Company Town* notes that the options available to owners were: lower wages, further mechanization, intensification of labor, dilution of well-paid skills, increased working hours, and the assertion of discipline. Cohoes, a company town, periodically enforced wage reductions and speedups. However, management's paternalistic approach stabilized the textile industry of the era, largely at the expense of adolescent, female workers who become dependent on their company.

In Troy the immigrant Irish labor force was beginning to show that numerical strength can sway elections. Control of the police force and the 1871 inauguration of Thomas B. Carroll, Troy's first Irish mayor, were both signs of rising ethnic voting power. In 1865 the Troy police force had been legislated out of existence by the establishment of a Capital Police District, embracing Albany, the Gateway area, and surrounding towns. This body lasted only five years. By 1871 the locally controlled Irish police force was inevitably sympathetic to its kin in their struggles with management.

Strikes and disruptions also affected Troy's iron and steel industry during this period. Late in 1874 workers at the Bessemer steel plant were told that their wages would henceforth be based not on hours but on tonnage. Although they accepted without protest, the iron workers were not so docile. When a 22 percent wage decrease was announced, blast furnace "puddlers" went out on strike with the "heaters" soon following their lead. Both the iron and steel mills were forced to close. Iron factory owners recruited scabs from New York City and Philadelphia, and private police, or "specials," were hired to guard the non-union workers during the reign of terror that followed. The local police force was, of course, unsympathetic to the scabs and, after a long seige, drove them out of Troy.

In the fall of 1877 there was talk of Gateway companies moving to non-union cities in the West. At the same time, the stove foundries were negotiating contracts to use prison labor in lieu of local workers. Another reign of terror followed, complete with ambushes and shootings.

The 1880s were marked by the emergence of strong national employee organizations like the Knights of Labor. Gateway workers joined out of fear for their job future. The Knights' attempt to submerge local trade union identity led to a revolt which resulted in the creation of the American Federation of Labor. Edward Murphy, then mayor of Troy, met with delegates in the spring of 1882 to establish a Workingmen's Trades Assembly. This group changed its name several times, always trying to distinguish itself from the Knights of Labor. As these competing Trojan labor organizations frustrated union solidarity during the 1880s, only one union retained its prominence, the molders.

On November 1, 1882, iron manufacturers asked the molders to approve a 30 percent wage cut because of declining prices and fewer orders. The union refused, and the foundries shut down. Six weeks later the owners offered to reopen with a 15 percent reduction. Their offer was again rejected. When most of the foundries finally opened at old rates, the Malleable Iron Company posted broadsides stating that workers must give two weeks' notice before quitting or forfeit the equivalent pay. Because the molders rejected this new rule, Malleable locked them out and shut down. The firm opened one week later with scab molders, and the lockout lasted sixteen months. Violence ensued. Local Republicans pushed a new Troy police bill through the state legislature, but Democratic Mayor Murphy managed to neutralize its effect. The Republican police commissioners then elected one-half of an alternate police force and asked the governor to impeach Murphy. The governor refused; however, Murphy had already made up his mind: he declined to seek reelection. Having served as mayor for seven years, he was eyeing a seat in the U.S. Senate, a position he subsequently won.

In the meantime, veteran Trojan police officers locked themselves in their stations, awaiting a court decision about the legal status of personnel changes within the department. While the old police were self-imprisoned, their replacements rushed to defend scabs against the assaults of union workers. The court finally ruled that the new officers were legally in power, leaving the workers without law enforcement allies. Assaults and shootings then became a daily occurrence.

By this time, stove manufacturers had started to exit Troy. Although the union finally agreed to a 20 percent wage reduction, high labor costs, expanding western mar-

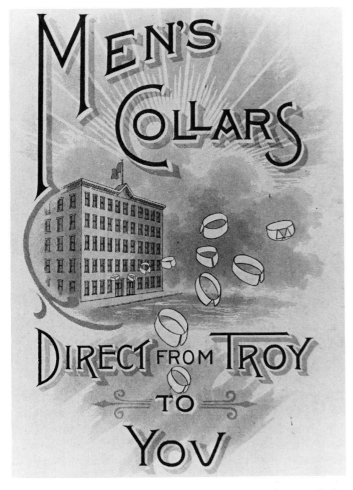

kets, and relatively poor access to raw materials caused the area's entire iron and steel industry to stagnate.

However, during the 1880s there was growing worker self-confidence in Cohoes. The French Canadians, who had arrived earlier and competed with Irish workers for jobs, had adapted so well to their new surroundings that one of their members, Samuel Sault, emerged as a labor leader. There also was considerable labor activity among women. On February 1, 1880, female weavers struck at Harmony Mill #1. The following day the walkout turned into a general strike with some 5,000 men, women, and children walking off the job. The women weavers had demanded a 10 percent pay increase, a longer lunch break, and an end to docking wages for imperfectly woven cloth. Children, a large part of the work force at that time, paraded through the streets, raggedly dressed, carrying banners which read: "Pity Our Hard Fate" and "No Time to Play in God's Sunshine."

After only nine days the strike ended successfully for

Above left: This was a typical advertisement for Troy collars. Most of the collar factories located in Troy had branch factories or outlets in larger U.S. cities. Courtesy, Rensselaer County Historical Society

Above right: This advertisement for collars made by Corliss, Coom & Co. was circulated circa 1915. The company began in Troy in 1838 and moved to Van Schaick Island in 1905. It remained in business until World War II. Courtesy, Rensselaer County Historical Society

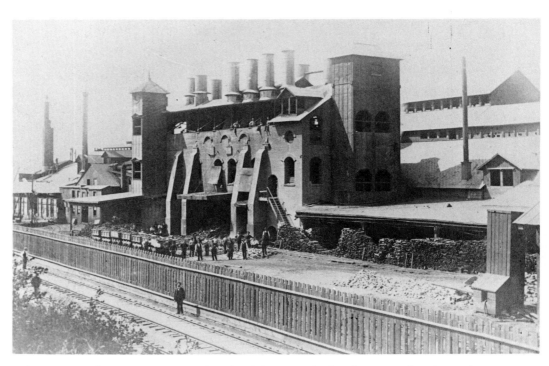

the workers, but also won them the enmity of management. Petty firings followed, ultimately causing mule spinners, then weavers, and finally section heads to strike. Management responded by giving the spinners thirty days' notice to vacate their tenements. In addition, no food was served in the company-owned boarding houses. Strikers were docked two weeks' pay for refusing to give notice. A detachment of police patrolled the mills and non-union French Canadian workers were recruited. A seasoned union man, J.P. McDonald, arrived from New Jersey to direct the strike and urged workers to ease their demand that overseers be dismissed. When workers went to court to sue for back pay, management finally received a joint committee of spinners and weavers. They came to an agreement whereby no trade union would be recognized by management, though mill operators would not interfere with the unions or blacklist workers. The workers regained their no-notice wages, but two impertinent weavers were not rehired.

In 1881 Harmony reduced wages by 10 percent, resulting in a four-month strike. After just two months destitution was so prevalent that the workers offered to compromise. Management responded by importing Swedish strike breakers. Although the company tried to intimidate non-striking relatives still working in the mills, the workers remained united and mostly non-violent. But hunger and poverty led to the dissolution of neighbor-hood solidarity and after four months, the strikers returned to work, having accepted the wage reduction.

During the second half of the nineteenth century, the Gateway's iron and steel industries experienced serious declines. However, metal-related manufacturing enjoyed a brief, renewed injection of vigor after 1860 when the men who built the *Monitor* brought about yet another industrial coup. In 1862 Alexander L. Holley, who became a partner with John F. Winslow and John A. Griswold, visited England and investigated Henry Bessemer's process for transforming pig iron into steel. Returning to Troy, he convinced Winslow and Griswold to join him in purchasing the American rights to this new steel-making process. The three men erected a plant on the banks of the Hudson in Troy, just north of the Menands Bridge. Here, the first Bessemer conversion of iron into steel on this side of the Atlantic took place on February 16, 1865. The works were enlarged several times and other Bessemer plants were built. In the early years of the twentieth century, however, the movement of the steel industry to the coal regions caused the last plant to go out of business.

While steel was declining, the textile industry was expanding. The second half of the nineteenth century was the great age of cotton in Cohoes. The Harmony Mills complex grew by leaps and bounds as higher speed turbines replaced lumbering waterwheels. In 1864 Harmony acquired the Strong Mill and installed a turbine there.

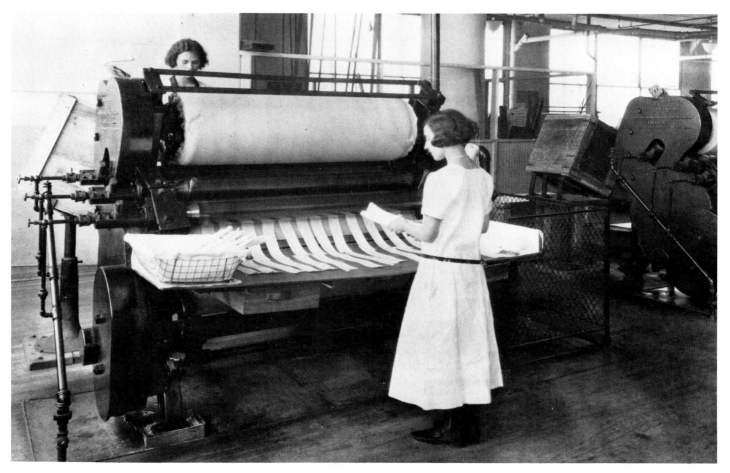

During 1866 Harmony Mill #2 was enlarged, with a Mansard roof on the top floor and turbines placed in the old wheel pit. The Mohawk Mill was purchased and French Canadian immigrant workers hired. The Harmony Company then announced that it was going to build the largest cotton mill in America, Mill #3. Ground was broken, and 700 feet of the 1,200-foot length mill were completed in that same year, 1866. The remaining 500 feet were added five to six years later.

Harmony Mills, in the late 1860s, employed 3,000 workers, ran 220,000 spindles, and in one year produced more than twenty-three million yards of cotton cloth. One hundred new tenements were constructed by John Land, the builder of Harmony Mill #3, who was so rushed that he substituted wood when he ran out of brick.

Child labor, particularly the employment of youngsters under ten, became an issue in Massachusetts in 1869. Cohoes children, however, continued to work as pickers, contributing to the inexorable growth of the Harmony complex. Then the depression of 1873 brought all indus-

trial growth to a sudden halt. Although the cotton textile industry was not so badly hit, from that time on, the mills were plagued by intermittent strikes. Skilled workers started moving out—to other plants in the area as well as to factories in the South whose competition would, before long, reduce northeast operations to a mere shadow of their nineteenth-century prosperity.

Overall, the era was a curious one. After 1850 the Gateway's once prosperous iron and steel industry began a steady decline. The area's textile industry peaked in Cohoes during the same period. However, the nation's industry, like its population, was inexorably moving to the West, and to some extent, the South. There was an urgent need for the consolidation of industry on a larger scale than was possible in the smaller Gateway cities. Continuing labor-management conflicts also exacted a toll from workers and employers alike. In the midst of apparent prosperity, then, the stage was set for a gradual downturn that would soon result in the eclipse of the Gateway as an important industrial center.

Rensselaer County's first court-house and jail, at the southeast corner of Congress and Second streets, is depicted in this late-nineteenth-century print. From History of the City of Troy, *by A.J. Weise, 1876*

CHAPTER SIX

GOVERNMENTS OF THE PEOPLE

S ince the first communities were established in the Hudson-Mohawk Gateway area in the late 1700s, the political life of this area has reflected its growth and changing character. New England merchants and professionals, mostly young and ambitious, were the first to settle here permanently. These optimistic, transposed New Englanders expected this part of the Empire State to prosper, and this confidence was reflected in their politics.

The era of the New England mayors lasted well into the nineteenth century when, as Troy's industrial works attracted a large number of immigrants, political life changed. Increasingly, machine politics—a well-organized system of patronage and support—came to dominate. Challenges to the machine system came shortly after the First World War, and new leadership appeared in the Gateway area. Only in the last two decades has political and economic revival returned as each community again looks to the future.

After the Revolutionary War, a steady wave of merchants from New England came into the Gateway area. Already on January 1, 1771, the residents of Lansingburgh, which was known as New City, agreed to the "Proposals," a document which regulated political life. To the New England businessmen this seemed to guarantee stability, and it attracted additional immigrants. "Whereas ... a considerable number of houses are already erected and occupied by merchants, mechanics, and others," the April 5, 1790 legislative act read, Lansingburgh was incorporated as a village. It was governed by trustees, mostly merchants who, with a vision of the village's promising future, dominated political life.

The entire area benefitted from Lansingburgh's growing economic importance and political organization. The settlement of Waterford was laid out in May 1783, on the former site of Half Moon Point. A charter granted by the state legislature on March 25, 1794 authorized freeholders and residents to make those rules and regulations necessary to maintain "the common streets and highways" as well as to prepare for "the extinguishing of fires." One of

Democrat William Marcy was elected governor of New York in 1832 and reelected in 1834 and 1836. From Dictionary of American Portraits, *by Cirker, 1967*

only a few villages operating under a special charter, Waterford is the oldest incorporated village in New York State.

Already in the 1780s some merchants from Lansingburgh, recognizing the limitations of ship travel that far north on the Hudson, moved southward onto land owned by three Dutch farmers. In 1786, after years of bargaining, the settlers bought building lots from the farmers, and at a meeting held on January 5, 1789, the merchants adopted the name "Troy" for their settlement. This action demon-

strated their community spirit, their democratic ideals, and their dislike of the original Dutch name.

Troy grew rapidly and an act of the legislature incorporated it as a village on February 6, 1798. Within two years Troy's population reached the 1,801 mark, and a local newspaper boasted that "a population so rapid has, we believe, but seldom been witnessed in the United States." And several years later an English visitor described Troy as "a well built town," and he predicted that it would "rival Albany" as an important center of trade.

With its growing population, Troy's political organization continued to evolve. In 1801 and 1803 the trustees gained additional rights for governing from the legislature. Political life became more intense and an English observer maintained that after arriving here he "soon perceived people divided into two parties, the Federalists and the Democrats, and that both were equally violent in their political altercations." By 1815, Troy's population had risen to 4,200, and a year later on April 12, the legislature incorporated the "City of Troy."

Troy's incorporation further defined the local governing body's responsibilities to the electorate. The Board of Magistrates was charged with organizing relief for the poor, who did not have the right to vote, and with establishing an almshouse. The mayor, who until 1840 was appointed by the governor, issued permits for the sale of alcoholic beverages and licensed butchers. The Common Council maintained the streets, bridges, and wharves. Officials were also responsible for keeping the peace and sending "disorderly persons or paupers" out of town. In addition, the city government had the responsibility to raise taxes for street lights and the operation of a night watch. On January 30, 1816, residents voted "with great unanimity" to generate funds for a local school through a new tax.

Until the 1870s the mayors of Troy retained strong connections to the merchant and professional class which had settled this area. The first mayor, Colonel Albert Pawling, operated a successful business in Lansingburgh and Troy before entering politics. The Troy Common Council later noted that Pawling "served his fellow citizens with a marked devotion, usefulness and acceptance."

Most of those who followed Pawling were guided by much the same commitment; most were transplanted New Englanders who had gained success and recognition from their commercial ventures. They reflected their constituency and its aspiring ambitions. Some of Troy's early political leaders ascended to higher office. William Marcy, for example, served as a United States Senator and became governor of New York State in 1833. An ally of Martin Van Buren, Marcy coined the expression "to the victor belong the spoils."

Throughout these years the Gateway area prospered and a strong sense of community emerged. As a correspondent from the *New York Commercial Advertiser* wrote on September 18, 1835:

There is something in the character of the people. No matter where they come from, or what have been their previous habits, the moment they become residents of this place, they are Trojans. They not only look well to their own individual interests, but imbibe the same spirit of enterprise which they find prevailing and unite as one man in sustaining the interests and advancing prosperity of Troy. They know and feel that their interests are identified with those of the city, and in whatever way the latter is benefitted, they readily perceive their own general advantage.

A strong spirit of enterprise and commitment was found in other Gateway communities. Until the early 1800s, only a handful of farmers had settled at Cohoes. After the establishment of the Cohoes Manufacturing Company in 1811, the community grew moderately. By the 1840s, sentiment emerged for a more formal and better organized local government. As the *Cohoes Advertiser* wrote in 1843:

Now for a village charter—for the water works—three or four good engines—clean streets—and a law limiting the number of dogs in each family to two, a law prohibiting swine running at large and we are a made community.

Cohoes received a charter from the Court of Sessions on June 5, 1848. In the 1860s, discussion about the incorporation of Cohoes opened again. Opponents, according to the local paper, feared that government, as in Troy, would "fall into the hands of a political rabble, and that the better class of citizens would have little or no voice in the management of affairs." Proponents insisted that local economic life would benefit and a strong sense of local pride would emerge, and this, in fact, occurred after Cohoes became an incorporated city in 1870.

The local government of the Gateway communities also established fire departments, police forces, schools, and maintained a reliable water supply. From the beginning, fire protection was a major consideration and reponsibility. Already in June 1796, Troy established its first fire department and two years later, fire wardens, who controlled the firemen and directed the fire fighting, were appointed. In addition, the communities required homeowners to keep two buckets on hand at all times. When-

Fires have always plagued the Gateway. Here, in 1868, the well-known Cannon Place in Troy sustained its first of three fires. Courtesy, Rensselaer County Historical Society

Right: The great fire of 1862 in Troy started when sparks from a locomotive ignited the wooden Green Island Bridge. The fire spread into the city and much of downtown was destroyed. From History of the City of Troy, *by A.J. Weise, 1876*

Facing page: The Arba Read steam fire engine, acquired by the Arba Read fire company in Troy in 1860, was housed in the station at the northwest corner of Third and State streets. Courtesy, Rensselaer County Historical Society

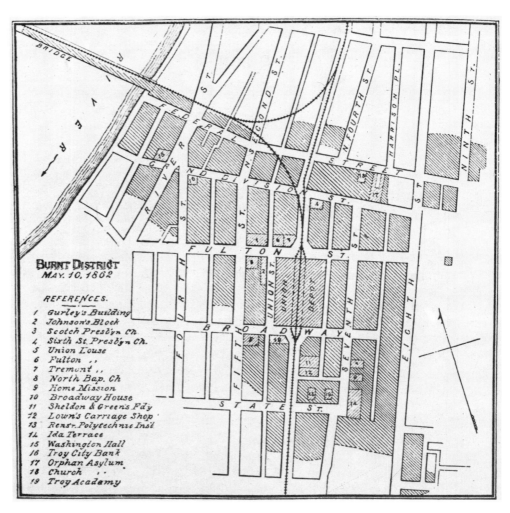

BURNT DISTRICT
MAY. 10, 1862

REFERENCES.

1   Gurley's Building
2   Johnson's Block
3   Scotch Presb'yn Ch.
4   Sixth St. Presb'yn Ch.
5   Union House
6   Fulton ,,
7   Tremont ,,
8   North Bap. Ch.
9   Home Mission
10   Broadway House
11   Sheldon & Green's Fdy
12   Lown's Carriage Shop
13   Rensr. Polytechnic Inst
14   Ida Terrace
15   Washington Hall
16   Troy City Bank
17   Orphan Asylum.
18   Church ,,
19   Troy Academy

ever a fire broke out they were to run to the scene with the buckets and aid the fire wardens.

These measures were essential. A serious fire which struck Troy on December 8, 1797, prompted local authorities to purchase an engine. Another disastrous fire hit Troy in June 1820, destroying more than $370,000 in property. Even though Troy continued to update its equipment and personnel, a fire which started on May 10, 1862, destroyed more than 500 buildings and caused more than three million dollars in damage. Afterwards, Troy's fire department continued to improve and an early historian, Arthur Weise, called it "unexcelled in the United States."

Other Gateway communities faced similar problems. Fearing comparable property damage, measures were taken. Green Island relied on the Troy Fire Department until the 1850s, and Cohoes established a fire deparment in 1847. Unfortunately, the city's old Excelsior No. 1 en-

gine proved inadequate for the several major blazes that occurred that same year. Cohoes purchased some additional equipment and organized two fire brigades.

Besides providing fire protection, local governments were charged with maintaining public order. Already in 1786, Troy established a nightwatch of four men who patrolled the streets, checking for fires and controlling unruly behavior. In 1816, this protection cost the city $764.81. A ward system—a neighborhood based police—was introduced in 1833. But four years later a riot involving several hundred young Irish, who were responding to a hung effigy of St. Patrick, hit the city. When the police could not control the disturbance the mayor called out the Citizen's Corps.

In an effort to tighten control over the police, the Common Council in 1838 began appointing all watchmen on an annual basis. Several other measures helped increase police efficiency, and these reforms were put to a

severe test in 1863. On July 15, a public meeting opposing the conscription of soldiers into the Union Army sparked what a local newspaper described as "a rebellious demonstration."

The state government attempted local police reform when on April 22, 1865, "An Act to Establish a Capital Police District and to Provide for the Government thereof" was passed. The law provided for a new district which included Albany, Watervliet, West Troy, Green Island, Cohoes, Lansingburgh, North Greenbush, and even a part of Schenectady. The district was, however, abolished in the spring of 1870.

Another serious threat to public order came in 1882 when Troy had two rival police forces. It began as a political squabble when the Democratic members of the Board of Police Commissioners walked out of the sessions and the Republican members appointed a new force. After a brief confrontation between the opposing two police

forces, the courts provided a compromise.

Broad social changes had already begun before the Civil War as large numbers of Irish and Canadian immigrants moved into the Gateway area. These new arrivals, coming to work in the iron or cotton mills, had by the 1870s caused political life to change. While the French Canadians in Cohoes were accommodated by the old political order, the Irish in Troy gradually gained control over local political affairs. As they became more settled in Troy, the Irish demanded a greater role in politics. Hard work, commercial and professional success, and the emergence of a political machine using patronage and block voting aided the Irish of Troy to gain and hold power. The new majority used some established methods in dominating political life.

In 1871, Troy's first Irish mayor, Thomas B. Carroll, took office. Three years later, Edward Murphy, another Democrat and also Irish, began an eight-year tenure as

Edward Murphy, Jr. served as Troy's mayor from 1875 to 1882 and as U.S. senator from 1892 to 1899. From Landmarks of Rensselaer County, *by George B. Anderson, 1897*

Cornelius F. Burns was mayor of Troy for eight terms, from 1912 to 1920 and from 1928 to 1936. From Troy and Rensselaer County, New York, *by Rutherford Hayner, 1925*

mayor. From Troy, Murphy went on to become an important political force in state and national Democratic Party affairs. Murphy was followed in office by Edmund Fitzgerald, an independent Democrat who, while remaining loyal to the Democratic Party and his working class constituents, often sided with the city's business leaders.

By the 1880s, a sizable Irish professional and entrepreneurial class had emerged in Troy, and Mayor Fitzgerald depended heavily on its support. The mayor represented these interests as well. He recognized that good business and prosperity demanded social order and industrial harmony. The Democratic Party in Troy clearly was maturing.

During the middle decades of the nineteenth century changes in the political life of other Gateway district communities were occurring. West Troy, originally called Gibbonsville, had its own post office already in 1817. The

state legislature, acknowledging the growth of this community, incorporated it on April 23, 1823. And in 1836, further legislation incorporated "the village of West Troy," which was made up of Gibbonsville and Port Schuyler.

Green Island, earlier known as Tibbits Island, received its articles of incorporation on April 5, 1853, and a strong sense of community began to appear. By the end of the century (and continuing through today), Green Island's political development has been strongly influenced by the McNulty family. Jack McNulty, one of seven candidates for the position, was elected tax collector in 1890. After the First World War, he won election to the Board of Supervisors and he became chairman in 1923. A year later, Governor Alfred E. Smith appointed McNulty superintendent of buildings for the state, a position which gave him control over most of the state's construction proj-

City Hall in Cohoes was constructed in 1895. Photo by Robert Thayer

ects. McNulty held this position through the terms of three governors and thereby gained a powerful political base.

In Troy the Democratic Party remained strong until after 1918 when the machine started losing some of its power. The new strength of the Republican Party came from its reorganization introduced by Dean P. Taylor and a group of young reformers. While Republicans held the mayor's office from 1924 to 1928, the Democrats regained that office and controlled it for the next two decades. Af-

ter the November 1934 election victory, local Democrats were jubilant and the party chairman insisted that:

This indicates conclusively that the people of Renssalaer County have heartily endorsed the program of President Roosevelt and Governor Lehman and that they fully recognize the ability and character of the leadership of the Democratic organization in Renssalaer County, headed by Joseph Murphy.

After 1944, the Republicans again gained control of local government. Mayor Edward Fitzgerald, who held the post for six years, emerged as a powerful mayor, and prominent Trojans increasingly viewed the mayoralty form of government as outdated. They feared that the concentration of so much power in the hands of one leader was a source of potential abuse. In 1958, Congressman Dean Taylor stated that "Troy is reaching a dangerous degree of stagnation," and he led the drive for adoption of the city manager type of government.

A revised charter took effect on January 1, 1964, and Robert Stierer became Troy's first city manager. Over the next decade, four other city managers directed local affairs. Political battles with the city council became increasingly common and acrimonious. Some observers wondered how any governing was done.

Leaders in Troy recognized the need for an economic revival, and they set up the Troy Urban Renewal Agency in 1966. Funded by President Johnson's Great Society programs, this "first-of-its-kind revitalization project for the city's entire shopping district," as the *Times Record* described it, was launched with a fourteen-million-dollar grant. But as the economy slowed, the project stalled, and it was abandoned in the mid-1970s. Local builder Carl Grimm soon came forward and built a two-level mall in downtown Troy, thereby providing some economic relief.

Residents of Cohoes inaugurated far-reaching changes and reforms when in 1967, they voted the local political machine out of office. Civic pride blossomed and Cohoes was identified as an "All America City," and was selected as one of 150 municipalities to receive special funding under the federal government's highly competitive Model Cities Program.

In recent years, the communities of the Gateway district have witnessed a modest economic and political revival. After some hard times the residents are again showing their determination to work together for the benefit of the area, much as the first settlers had done long ago.

The Laureate Boat Club was located at the foot of Glen Avenue in Troy just above the present Federal Dam. This view was taken circa 1910. Courtesy, Gene Baxter

CHAPTER SEVEN

THE SOCIAL AND CULTURAL ENVIRONMENT

As a commercial center the Gateway area from its earliest days offered room and board to weary travelers. Near the ferry landing in Troy were Ashley's Tavern and Moulton's Coffee House. Troy's Washington Square was a central location for many long-lasting establishments. The Mansion House, which opened in 1822, operated until 1926 when it was replaced by the Hendrick Hudson Hotel. On the corner of River and First streets stood Platt Titus' Eagle Tavern, later replaced by the Troy Hotel. Next door, the site of the Cannon Building in the square earlier hosted a tavern built in 1806 known variously as the Bull's Head, the Indian Queen, and the Rensselaer House. The Eldorado Hotel, dating back to the late nineteenth century, once gave shelter to William McKinley, as well as John Philip Sousa's band and Victor Herbert's orchestra. Theatrical troupes playing at the old Griswold Theater and at Proctor's also sought respite there.

Lansingburgh had an early inn on what is now Second Avenue at 116th Street. It burned in 1834, and a new hotel rising from the ashes was named, quite appropriately, the Phoenix. It still stands as a sole survivor of the thirty-five inns that once dotted nineteenth-century Lansingburgh. Across the river in Waterford, at 87 Broad Street, was the City Hotel, also called the "Foxes," which dated from 1784.

Cohoes boasted a famous resort hotel, the Cataract House, built in 1860 on the bluff overlooking the falls. A broadside issued by manager William H. Glynn noted that "the scenery from the many windows in the large Billiard Room is surprisingly beautiful, and a spacious Ball Room for the accommodation of Sleighing Parties is attached to the house." Cohoes is also the home of the area's most famous restaurant, Smith's, currently owned by Eunice Antonucci, but earlier run by Michael T. Smith, chairman of the Democratic Party and host to Albany's political

Right: This was the Phoenix Hotel on Second Avenue (formerly State Street) in Lansingburgh as it look-ed circa 1880. Courtesy, Lansing-burgh Historical Society

Below right: The bar room in the Eldorado Hotel on Fourth Street in Troy has been restored to its 1890s appearance. Photo by Robert Thayer

machine. Smith, an enormous man, was usually pictured wearing a stark white suit and ten-gallon hat surrounded by ward leaders of lesser physical stature dressed in darker, more somber tones. In addition, there was the Elliot Hotel, now the Park Hotel, in Green Island, which opened its doors more than a century ago. Innumerable small hotels also dotted Gibbonsville and, later, West Troy.

While inns, hotels, and restaurants eagerly welcomed travelers, a multiplicity of Gateway churches willingly accepted worshipers. If sheer numbers are any indicator, nineteenth-century religion flourished. By 1900 Troy alone had seventy-two churches, more than one for every 1,000 residents. The Protestant Dutch Reformed Church, whose members follow the teachings of John Calvin, was the first church in the area. One such congregation was organized in Lansingburgh as early as 1784. Its life span was short, however, due to the influx of many Presbyterians, another Calvinist-inspired tradition, from New England.

An old Dutch church was established in Waterford in 1799. Originally standing on the site of the Grand Union warehouses on the Mechanicville road into the village, it became the "Mother Church" of Waterford Protestantism. In 1838 a Dutch Reformed community was organized within the current limits of Cohoes. Earlier, local Dutch farmers worshiped at the Reformed Dutch Church of the Boght, formed in 1784. Dutch Reformed communities were begun in Watervliet in 1814, 1840, and 1844. In fact, Watervliet has the distinction of housing Christ Church— the only Reformed congregation still flourishing in the Gateway area.

The Scots/Northern Ireland Calvinist tradition of Presbyterianism made its regional debut in Troy when a congregation was organized in 1791. Initially meeting at Ashley's Tavern, its members quickly constructed their first church edifice. There, the minister, Reverend Jonas Coe, just as hastily stirred controversy by introducing into the church building a stove, carpeting, and soon thereafter, a bass viol and other musical instruments. These creature comforts were more than some Calvinist souls could bear. Presbyterian congregations prospered in many other Gateway cities as well, and, over the years, as many as fourteen such churches were established in Troy alone. Baptist congregations flourished as well, including a church founded in Troy in 1793, and others in Lansingburgh, Waterford, Watervliet, and Cohoes shortly thereafter.

The Methodist church was also active. Freeborn Garrettson, the great apostle of Methodism in the Hudson valley, visited Lansingburgh in 1788, while Thankful and Zadok King conducted Methodist prayer services in their home in Waterford. Circuit riders, the early Methodist traveling preachers, visited both Lansingburgh and Waterford in the late eighteenth century, and congregations were soon organized throughout the area.

Episcopal churches were also founded in the Gateway with the original parishes of St. Paul's and Trinity being established in Troy and Lansingburgh in 1804. A Quaker community was created in Troy as early as 1803, but began to decline after 1840.

Roman Catholicism grew rapidly in the Gateway as immigrants arrived first from Ireland and French Canada and later from southern and eastern Europe. The premier Catholic parish was St. Peter's in Troy, established in

The Mansion House was a landmark in Troy for over 100 years. This view shows the hotel and Washington Square in 1870. Courtesy, Rensselaer County Historical Society

Right: St. Bernard's Church, on Ontario Street in Cohoes, is shown here at the turn of the century. Completed in 1866 to serve the growing mill community, it still has the original stained glass windows donated by the iron works, cotton mills, woolen mills, and citizens of Cohoes. Courtesy, New York State Library

Facing page, left: The Reverend Henry Highland Garnet, pastor of the Liberty Street Presbyterian Church in Troy in the 1840s, became a national figure upon his delivery of a discourse against slavery at the House of Representatives in 1865. From A Memorial Discourse, *by H.H. Garnet, 1865*

Right: The Reverend Peter Havermans worked to establish numerous schools, orphanages, and hospitals in the Gateway area. From Landmarks of Rensselaer County, *by George B. Anderson, 1897*

1824. The potato famine in the late 1830s brought a great influx of Irish immigrants, spurring the creation of many additional parishes in other Gateway cities.

Lutherans were not organized in the Gateway until 1870 when Troy's Trinity Church was established. However, the Gilead Evangelical Lutheran Church of Center Brunswick, formed in 1742 by Germans from the Palatinate, served area Lutherans before that time.

Trojan Jews first organized a Reformed congregation, B'rith Sholom, in 1866. Its members built a temple four years later. Still in use, the structure is the oldest Reformed Jewish synagogue in New York State. The current Orthodox congregation, Beth Tephilah, is the result of the union of Beth Israel Bikor Sholom, which gathered before 1870; congregation Chai Adam, dating from 1890; Sharah Tephilah, organized in 1873 by Polish and Russian Jews; and Beth Jacob of Cohoes. It is located in Troy. The Conservative congregation Beth El is also headquartered in Troy.

The abundance of churches and synagogues in the Gateway was due primarily to an early lack of public transportation. Before the advent of street railways in the 1860s, the poorer classes were confined to an area which could easily be traversed on foot. Occasionally, doctrinal disputes, and more often ethnic and class distinctions, led to the formation of new congregations. In some instances, well-to-do worshipers erected memorials as monuments.

In an age of better transportation and declining religious affiliation, a multitude of small denominations, each supporting its own clergy and building, became harder to justify. Since World War II, then, the trend has been toward merger and, in some instances, closure of many congregations. However, the arrival of newer fundamentalist Christian bodies has been cause for the reuse of some old structures and the erection of many simpler religious buildings.

Another major influx of Eastern Europeans and Asians brought the orthodox Christian churches of Greece, Russia, and the Ukraine, as well as the early Christian Church of Armenia. If religion today is not the force that it was in the nineteenth-century Gateway, worship is certainly more diverse and varied.

During the nineteenth century the area witnessed the ministry of some towering religious figures. Nathan Beman, "haughty, cold, overbearing, and tyrannical," was the most controversial. Arriving from Georgia in 1822,

Beman became pastor of the First Presbyterian Church of Troy. Denouncing both liquor and slavery, which was still very much alive in the upper Hudson valley, he was usually embroiled in controversy with his congregation. Nevertheless, he served as pastor for some forty years.

Henry Highland Garnet was also a Presbyterian divine and a major black leader of national stature in America's emancipation movement. The grandson of a Mandiggo warrior chieftain and the son of slaves, he escaped with his family to Troy when his slaveowner died in 1824. He served as pastor of the black Liberty Street Presbyterian Church in Troy from 1840 to 1848, and then moved to New York City to become minister of the Shiloh Presbyterian Church. During his lifetime, Garnet became a distinguished writer, newspaper publisher, and preacher with enormous influence not only in Troy but throughout the country. "Let your motto be resistance" was his cry. In 1881 he became U.S. minister to Liberia and died there the following year.

Peter Havermans, a Dutch native of Flemish lineage, arrived in Troy in 1841 and subsequently served as pastor of St. Mary's Roman Catholic Church for more than fifty-two years. When he died in 1897 at age ninety-one, he was the oldest Catholic priest in America, having served in the priesthood for sixty-seven years. As part of his ministry, he helped to establish other Roman Catholic churches in the area, as well as innumerable schools, orphanages, homes for the aged poor, and hospitals to serve the social needs of working-class Catholics. Havermans was ecumenical at a time when ecumenism was hardly the rule, and he was a prime mover in winning acceptance for Roman Catholics and their church in an alien environment.

Another towering nineteenth-century religious figure was John Ireland Tucker, first, and for fifty years, rector of Troy's Holy Cross Episcopal Church. Tucker's greatest fame resulted from his talents as a musician. In 1870 he completed the *Parish Hymnal,* and two years later, brought out the *Church Musical Hymnal,* which was said to have "raised the standard of psalmody from Atlantic to Pacific."

One twentieth-century religious figure, recently deceased, stands out above others. William M. Slavin was the first resident Catholic chaplain at Rensselaer Polytechnic Institute and later served as pastor of Our Lady of Victory Church in Troy. In the pre-World War II period, when America first broke out of its isolationalist bonds, Slavin broadcast a nationally acclaimed Sunday radio program called "News of the Week from a Catholic Viewpoint." When he entered the U.S. Navy as a chaplain in 1943, a glowing editorial in the Troy newspaper acknowledged his contribution toward expanding and broadening Americans' view of the world. Active in a variety of community affairs, Slavin was instrumental in founding the Troy Human Rights Commission, for which Roy Wilkins, long the guiding spirit of the NAACP, bestowed on him honorary life membership. Undoubtedly his greatest contribution, however, was his ecumenical spirit.

In an age when government had not yet assumed responsibility for human services, churches filled the need. For example, during the past 150 years, four out of five orphanages established in the Gateway were church-related.

In the nineteenth century industrial accidents were not a rarity: when one working parent was killed or incapacitated, the surviving spouse assumed the responsibility of sole breadwinner. The children were often placed in institutional care. The earliest orphanage, the Troy Orphan Asylum, privately founded in 1833, still operates today in Wynantskill as Vanderheyden Hall. Four other orphanages were created by the Roman Catholic Church. Of these, however, only St. Colman's Home, located outside Watervliet in the town of Colonie, is still functioning.

Aged, sick, infirm, and destitute residents are still looked after by the Church Home of Troy, founded in 1854; the Little Sisters of the Poor (now moved to Latham); and the Presbyterian Home Associates of the City of Troy. The privately-endowed Deborah Powers Home for Old Ladies went out of existence a few years

ago. Much of the former work performed by these institutions has been taken over by county affiliates and private nursing homes. And for the active elderly, senior citizen centers abound.

Youngsters were once cared for by the Mount Magdalen School of Industry, the Reformatory of the Good Shepherd, and the Guardian Angels Home and Industrial School for young women. This institution survived under the latter title until the 1960s. Martha Memorial House, adjacent to St. Paul's Episcopal Church in Troy, was founded in 1881 to promote missionary work among working women. There also existed Seton House for Working Girls in Troy, as well as a Bethesda Home for homeless and friendless girls and women, which after several moves, survives today in Lansingburgh.

Perhaps no organizations epitomized the Gateway's spirit of social service better than the Mary Warren Free School of Troy and the Harmony Hill Union Sunday School of Cohoes. In 1839 Mary Warren initiated a charity day school for the daughters of the working class at St. Paul's Episcopal Church. As part of the music curriculum, the girls became members of the choir, a move which was apparently unacceptable to some parishioners. So Mary Warren founded the Church of the Holy Cross as "a house of prayer for all people, without money and without price." The Warren Free Institute of the City of Troy was incorporated in 1846 "for the instruction of in-

The Society of Friends meeting-house was located at the southwest corner of Fourth and State streets in Troy in the early nineteenth century. St. Anthony's Roman Catholic Church now occupies the site. Courtesy, Rensselaer County Historical Society

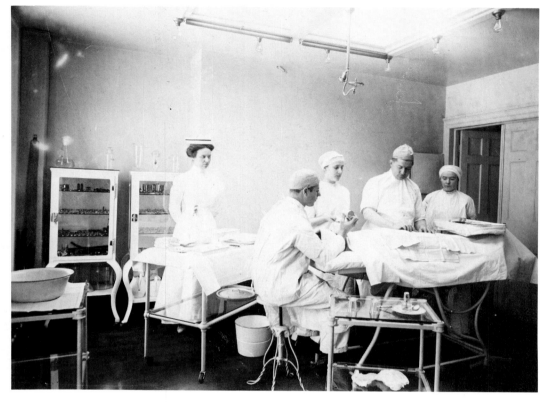

The operating room at Leonard Hospital in Lansingburgh is seen here at the turn of the century. Courtesy, Warren Broderick

digent female children" and a building adjacent to the church housed the school.

The Harmony Hill Union Sunday School was shorter lived but flourished under the aegis of David J. Johnston, whose family managed the Harmony Mills. Founded in the winter of 1853-54, the school maintained ties to the Baptist Church, but was nondenominational. It probably offered the bulk of formal education received by mill children. The number of pupils attending the school grew from eleven in 1854 to 1,124 in 1877. Supported by the mills, it offered "artistically" decorated rooms, pictures, maps, blackboards, an excellent organ, and a library of over 1,000 volumes. In December, yuletide festivities were held in Harmony Hall where the children unwrapped Christmas presents. A spring strawberry festival and a summer picnic were other annual highlights. However, by 1890 attendance was down to 540 students. One year after David J. Johnston died in 1894, the school closed its doors.

Hospitals also sprang up in the Gateway to serve the health needs of local residents. The oldest such institution, the Troy Hospital, was opened in 1850 by the Roman Catholic Church under the guidance of Father Peter Havermans. That building proved inadequate to meet the needs of the community and the rapid medical and nursing advances made during the Civil War. A new structure on Eighth Street at the head of Grand Street was subsequently opened in 1871. In 1914 the hospital moved to its present location on Oakwood Avenue, and at midcentury was formally renamed St. Mary's Hospital.

An early hospital for the insane was the private venture of Benjamin Marshall, the entrepreneur known for developing the third and greatest water power system in the Poestenkill Gorge in Troy. The Marshall Infirmary and Rensselaer County Lunatic Asylum was built in 1850 on a bluff to the south of the gorge. One of the patients was Marshall's son, who suffered from severe emotional illness. Eventually, as New York State took over the care of the mentally ill, the number of patients declined. Marshall's sanitarium was razed about twenty years ago.

The Cohoes Hospital had its origins in 1891 when the city appointed a commission to purchase a suitable site. In the 1950s the hospital board purchased twenty-three acres on Columbia Street and after two major fund drives opened the modern Cohoes Hospital in 1960.

Lansingburgh's hospital owed its existence to the beneficence of Dr. Frederick B. Leonard who left his home to be used as a hospital. New wings were added in 1926 and

1933, and in 1972 a completely new 159-bed facility was opened. Now closed, it was once the only hospital-based, certified Home Health Care Agency in Rensselaer County.

The largest hospital in the Gateway area, offering 300 beds, is the Samaritan Hospital of Troy, now a part of the larger Northeast Health. It is equipped with a medical office building, a mental health division, and a detoxification unit. The Eddy Geriatric Center, also associated with Northeast Health, has constructed nearby apartments with "assistive living services" to provide maximum independence for the elderly.

The Howard and Bush Foundation, serving the needs of residents in the Hartford, Connecticut and Troy areas, has contributed funding to numerous hospitals and all forms of social and community services. In fact, there are monuments to the extraordinary generosity of Edith Mason Howard and her niece, Julia Howard Bush, in almost every community service institution in the area.

The Gateway has long provided a wide variety of social and service clubs for its residents. In 1900 the Troy Chamber of Commerce developed out of a group calling itself the Commercial Travelers' Association. The chamber initiated a Troy Week some eight years later. Former Trojan sons and daughters returned home to a seven-day celebration of Troy's industrial and business greatness. Chamber members have enjoyed a long tradition of active involvement in community affairs. In 1924, for example, after determining that there were fifty-two private, nonchurch-related welfare organizations in Troy, the members helped to form a Community Social Welfare Chest which developed into today's Mohawk-Hudson Area United Way. In more recent years, the Chamber enlarged its scope to encompass most of the Gateway.

Area women have long been meeting to pursue personal, social, and political concerns. The Women's Improvement Society of Troy, which first met in 1906, later became the Women's Civic League. Members sought basic reforms which are now taken for granted, such as food inspection, health regulations, and garbage disposal. The Troy Women's Club, founded in 1920, has had as many as 500 members and continues to attract a significant number of women, and the Junior League actively satisfies its community service goals.

Service clubs such as Rotary, Kiwanis, and Lions draw area business people together in a combined spirit of camaraderie and humanitarianism. And fraternal organizations, especially the Masons, have flourished in almost all Gateway communities from their earliest days. Apollo Lodge No. 49 first met in Troy's Moulton's Coffee House in 1796, and Troy Masonry still boasts three lodges and eight coordinate bodies housed in the former Robison Mansion on Brunswick Road. Odd Fellows have had lodges in Troy, Watervliet, Green Island, and Cohoes, and the Elks boast very active chapters in Troy and Watervliet. The Knights of Columbus have councils in all Gateway communities. At various times, the Order of Druids, Knights of Pythias, Maccabees, Red Men, Owls, Moose, Knights of Malta, and Royal Arcanum have also attracted followings in the region.

Ethnic organizations have also thrived in the Gateway. Danes were once served by a Danish brotherhood in Lansingburgh. Germania Hall continues to flourish in the same section of the city of Troy. Clubs for Poles and Ukranians have found homes in Troy, and Ukranian-American Citizens Clubs, in both Watervliet and Cohoes. A Federation of Armenians Picnic Grounds once flourished in North Greenbush, while French Canadian interests are still very much alive in Cohoes. Church-sponsored activities continue to meet the needs of other ethnic groups like the Greeks. Troy has a community center for Italians housed in an old mansion on Washington Park. Green Island has a modern, circular center for its Italian Fraternal Society. Irish residents in Troy and Watervliet enjoy very active chapters of the Ancient Order of Hibernians. And each year on the feast of St. Patrick, the Friendly Sons of St. Patrick, a society which welcomes persons of all ethnic origins, holds a gala black tie dinner.

Troy's black residents have played a significant role in that city's history. In the 1840s regional, state, and national meetings of blacks working toward abolition were

Sojourner Truth attended an abolitionist meeting in Troy in the 1840s. Courtesy, National Portrait Gallery, Smithsonian Institution, Washington, D.C.

held in Troy. The last of these sessions was attended by Frederick Douglass, Harriet Tubman, and Sojourner Truth. The NAACP has long been active in Troy as well.

Troy was also an important station for runaway slaves on the Underground Railway to Canada. While Harriet Tubman was visiting the city in 1860, an escaped slave, Charles Nalle, was arrested on a warrant from Virginia. As he was being taken away, an angry crowd gathered and someone raised a cry. Nalle escaped during the ensuing melee. Later Uri Gilbert, Nalle's employer, raised $650 from the Trojan community to purchase Nalle's freedom. This is not to say that blacks have always been treated well in Troy. During the nineteenth century black residents were forced to attend separate and less-than-equal schools, confined to work in lower-paying positions,

"Uncle Sam," by sculptor George Kratina, stands at the entrance to Riverfront Park in Troy. Photo by Robert Chase

and denied participation in the industrialization process. Because their freedom was seen as a threat to immigrant job security, blacks were also harassed by white workers during the Civil War. Between 1829 and 1856 the names of black families were italicized in city directories. After World War II the Gateway's black population increased substantially as many black southerners migrated north from South Carolina to Troy.

The arts have always enjoyed a receptive atmosphere in

the Gateway. During the nineteenth century the region was the home of several significant painters and a host of lesser artists. One outstanding painter was Abel Buell Moore, who arrived in Troy in 1823 to paint portraits, an important art form in the era before photography. Moore soon became the portraitist for many of Troy's wealthiest citizens. William Richardson Tyler came to Troy in 1841 to work as a railroad car muralist for the highly respected firm of Eaton and Gilbert. He later opened his own studio and painted landscapes and seascapes after the manner of the Hudson River School.

Like Tyler, Green Island's David Cunningham Lithgow started out as a muralist for the Gilbert car works, but later opened his own studio in Albany. He became a familiar figure on Gateway streets, fashionably dressed in an elegant outfit that was accented by a black derby and pince-nez glasses.

The area's music lovers have enjoyed a justifiable pride in the Troy Music Hall. One of America's acoustically greatest musical spaces, it opened on April 19, 1875, with a concert by American composer Edward A. MacDowell. Great performers including such notables as Ignace Paderewski and Sergei Rachmaninoff have given concerts there, as have the world's greatest symphony orchestras.

One of the area's most famous and longest-lived musical organizations was Dorings Band founded as the Troy Band in 1846. During the Civil War most of its members joined the Union forces to entertain the soldiers of the 2nd Regiment, and some years later, in 1898, the performers again enlisted to play for the troops in the Spanish-American War. The band subsequently served on the Mexican border in 1916 and again in World War I. The musicians, led for nearly eighty-five years by Charles Doring and then by his son, George, have recently faded from the local scene. However, Robert Weiss of Lansingburgh, the band's last leader, still retains the music and the uniforms. If called upon, he could still reunite a group of musicians under the old name.

In the realm of literature the Benet siblings, William Rose, Stephen Vincent, and Laura, as well as Herman Melville, placed the Gateway on the literary map. The Benets' father served as commandant of the Watervliet Arsenal between 1919 and 1921. His talented offspring wrote fiction, poetry, and criticism. Herman Melville resided in Lansingburgh during nine of the most eventful years of his early manhood. In fact, his first published piece of fiction, "Fragments from a Writing Desk," appeared in the *Democratic Press and Lansingburgh Advertiser* on May 4,

This is the interior of Rand's Opera House at Third and Congress streets in Troy as it appeared after remodeling in 1872. The hall seated 1,450 people. Courtesy, Rensselaer County Historical Society

1837. His ties to Lansingburgh ended, however, with his 1847 marriage to Boston-born Elizabeth Shaw.

Vaudeville flourished in the Gateway from the 1890s to the 1930s. Cohoes, in fact, was the hometown of that era's greatest star, Eva Tanguay. Eva came from a poor French Canadian family that had taken up residence in Cobble Alley. She was short and plump with an engaging personality, but a most unexceptional singing voice. To make up for this deficiency, she appeared as an outrageously

dressed, tousle-haired, bleached blonde, warbling her favorite tune, "I Don't Care." In her heyday in 1918 she was paid up to $3,000 a week, an enormous sum for that time.

Theater was very much a part of Troy's entertainment scene. The first performance of "Uncle Tom's Cabin" took place in Peale's Troy Museum, and the city also boasted such great palaces as Rand's, Shea's, Griswold's, and the Troy Opera House. Legendary vaudevillians such as Lillian Russell, Eddie Cantor, and Al Jolson brought live diversion to the common Trojan, bequeathing one of vaudeville's greatest gifts.

The Cohoes Music Hall carried on into the early years of the twentieth century, hosting celebrities like Buffalo Bill Cody, John Philip Sousa, Sarah Bernhardt, and Harry Houdini. After changing hands several times, the building was perfectly restored with the help of federal, state, and local aid. It reopened in 1975, headlining the same play it

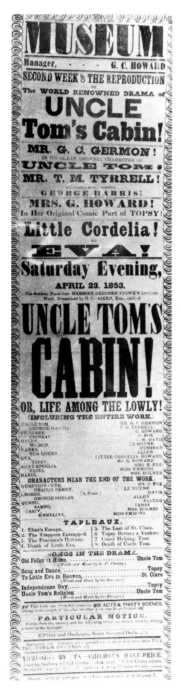

Above: This broadside advertised an 1853 performance of "Uncle Tom's Cabin" which had its debut in Troy the year before. Courtesy, New York State Library

had featured nearly 100 years earlier, "London Assurance."

Sports have formed a lively part of the Gateway's recreational activities. The area produced three world heavyweight boxing champions: John Morrissey, Paddy Ryan, and John Carroll Heenan. John Morrissey of Troy was by far the most colorful. During his lifetime, he was a bartender, saloon-brothel bouncer, riverboat deckhand, gang leader, ward heeler, Tammany leader and opponent, bigtime gambler, an owner of the Saratoga Race Track, friend of the socially and financially elite, state senator, and congressman. He was also heavyweight champion of the world. One story particularly illustrates his fiery temperament. To celebrate his success, Morrissey decided to build himself a splendid mansion in his hometown. However, Troy's business and financial elite successfully stymied his plans by blocking the purchase of the property, so Morrissey built a soap factory downwind from the city's residential district. Daily, the fumes of the industrial process wafted slowly over the elegant homes of Troy's leading citizens. The resulting stench was Morrissey's revenge.

In 1866 a newly-organized baseball team, the Haymakers of Lansingburgh, played the Mutuals of New York on the home green. They defeated the visitors by a lopsided score reported to be 150 to 32. Five years later the Haymakers came in third in the first season of professional baseball organized under the National Association, which was succeeded by the National League. In 1882 six of the players, including Buck Ewing, one of early baseball's greatest catchers, went to New York City to form the nucleus of the New York Giants. It was John J. Evers, however, who became the area's greatest contribution to professional baseball. Traded to the Chicago Nationals in 1902, Johnny Evers was touted for his deft fielding, mighty batting, and brilliant mastery of the "inside play." In 1914 he joined the Boston Braves as a member of the "miracle team" which won both the National League championship and the World Series.

Facing page, top right: The Lansingburgh Historical Society, at First Avenue and 114th Street, occupies what was once the residence of Herman Melville. He wrote Typee *and* Omoo, *his first two novels, in this house. Frances D. Broderick painted this watercolor. From the artist's collection.*

Bottom: This is a view of the Troy Music Hall in the Troy Savings Bank building circa 1890. From Troy Illustrated, *1891*

Journalism formed another dynamic part of the Gateway's tradition. The early municipalities published a multiplicity of newspapers. In Waterford, for example, during a century and a quarter, some ten newspapers were produced. However, these early publications were not particularly *news* papers. The front sheet was usually consumed by short advertisements, while the inner sheets contained acts of Congress, a little federal news, essays, and lugubrious obituaries written in verse. The articles focusing on local personages would most certainly be considered libelous today. Local news coverage did improve as the nineteenth century progressed but Gateway publications had more than their share of lengthy, often pointless, editorials.

Watervliet had the *West Advocate* from 1834 to 1865. The *Watervliet Journal,* founded in 1860, subsequently changed its name to the *Watervliet Journal and Democrat.* Cohoes' earliest paper, the *Cohoes Advertiser,* was created in 1847, soon becoming the *Journal* and the *Cataract.*

The number and variety of general and special interest papers published in the Gateway since 1787 is testimony to the fact that national magazines, radio, and television have only recently arrived on the scene as mass communication vehicles. One local paper of particular interest was the *Northern Budget,* founded in Lansingburgh in 1797. Colonel Charles L. MacArthur joined another great Troy newspaperman, John M. Francis, to purchase the *Budget* in 1867, transforming it into one of the foremost Sunday journals in New York State. The paper continued to be published by MacArthur's heirs until 1917, when it was finally sold out of the family.

John M. Francis, Colonel MacArthur's partner in the 1847 purchase of the *Budget,* was only twenty-two years old at the time. He left the *Budget* in 1849, and two years later established the *Troy Daily Times* which, under his management, soon grew to be one of the most powerful newspapers in the state.

One other Trojan newspaperman stands out in the history of Gateway journalism. Dwight Marvin, a lawyer, became editor of the *Troy Morning Record and the Evening Record* in 1915. He remained in that post for forty-three years until his retirement in 1958. His career was a distinguished one. His excellence and influence as a journalist were recognized not only in Troy, but throughout the state and the nation at large. During his editorship, the *Record* merged with the *Troy Daily Times* to form the *Troy Times Record,* now simply named *The Record,* creating the sole daily newspaper remaining in the Gateway area today.

This Pawling Avenue villa featured a wrap-around porch, a picket fence, and a landscaped yard. The house still stands but is devoid of some of its whimsical decoration. Courtesy, Carl S. Erickson

CHAPTER *EIGHT*

THE ARCHITECTURAL ENVIRONMENT

Buildings define and distinguish each of the communities of the Hudson-Mohawk Gateway and daily provide tangible evidence of their history. These buildings and the streetscapes they form testify not only to the skills of architects and contractors but also to the aesthetic standards and civic-mindedness of their clients. While much has been lost to fire, neglect, or deliberate demolition, each Gateway community retains scores of notable structures, and Troy boasts some of the finest architecture to be found in any small city in America.

The earliest remaining buildings reflect the Dutch settlement of the Hudson Valley. The Van Schaick House, situated on Van Schaick Island, is believed to have been built about 1735. Its Dutch origins are evident in the gambrel roof (a distinctive form with a broad, steep lower slope topped with a narrower, flatter upper slope), sturdy walls of local brick, chimneys inside each end wall, and a central doorway. Just across the Hudson in Lansingburgh, the dwelling at 580 First Avenue (c. 1770) has an additional half-story tucked beneath a gambrel roof, which is supported by walls laid up in English bond—alternating rows of stretchers (the broad sides of the brick) and headers (the narrow ends). Two blocks south, the two-story house at 524 First Avenue, built a few years later, is significantly larger in size as well as scale.

These two Lansingburgh houses stand near the western boundary of the town plan laid out by 1771 at the direction of trader Abraham Jacob Lansing. Delineating the area between the river and what is now 111th and 114th streets and Seventh Avenue, the plan had as its centerpiece a rectangular village green "reserved to Public use" and framed by a grid of streets and alleys which formed building lots measuring 120 feet by 50 feet. The Lansingburgh plan is a notable example of pre-Revolutionary town planning in upstate New York, and the green is still a public space.

The close of the Revolution brought waves of immigrants from New England who settled in Lansingburgh

The Hart-Cluett mansion, at 59 Second Street in Troy, was built in 1827 by William Howard of New York City as a wedding gift for Richard P. and Betsey Hart. Courtesy, Rensselaer County Historical Society

and the newer villages of Troy and Waterford. Dwellings of this period are typically two-stories with window trim nearly flush with exterior walls and hipped or gabled roofs. Smaller houses of this era have a stair hall along one end wall, while larger houses have a center hall plan. Important survivors are the substantial four-square, brick Janes House at the foot of 116th Street and the block of row houses at 612-616 Third Avenue, whose doorways are framed by brick archways. The Lansingburgh Academy (1820), whose function is signaled primarily by an eight-sided, louvred lantern rising from a truncated tower, is only slightly larger in scale than its residential counterparts. Two handsome brick houses attest to Waterford's contemporaneous growth—the Nathaniel Doe House at 60 Third Street and the Isaac Eddy House at 37 Middle Street. Both have elegantly detailed doorways and brick walls laid up in Flemish bond, where headers and stretch-

ers alternate in every course.

In 1793 Troy became the seat of Rensselaer County, demonstrating its increasing vigor and predominance over Lansingburgh. Two remarkable residences were harbingers of Troy's economic growth, as well. The Vail House (1818) at the corner of First and Congress streets has a Flemish bond facade enriched with carved stone trim and iron grilles; the interior has a spectacular, circular three-story stairway and finely detailed wooden trim with decorative painting dating from 1875. The Hart-Cluett Mansion at 59 Second Street is architecturally an equal of prominent houses in New York City. Completed in 1827, it has a white marble facade, elaborate wrought- and cast-iron railings, plaster cornices with egg and dart moldings, and a cantilevered stairway.

Captivated by accounts of the Greek war for independence, Americans during the 1830s looked to antiquity for its building forms and details and adapted them into a truly American architectural style: the Greek Revival. Fortuitously, this fervor for the Greek Revival coincided with a period of economic growth in the Gateway region and resulted in the construction of outstanding examples of high style and vernacular Greek Revival buildings for civic, commercial, religious, industrial, and domestic purposes. Three building forms predominated. The fully developed temple front has a gable and freestanding columns boldly facing the street; examples include houses at 713 and 819 Third Avenue in Lansingburgh, the First Baptist Church in Troy, and the White Homestead in Waterford. In other buildings the portico was compressed to form subtly projecting pilasters and pediments, as in the Atheneum in Troy and the United Methodist Church of Lansingburgh. Brick residences with simple, broad cornices and recessed entrances with fluted columns or pilasters are a third form; remaining examples include 554 First Avenue in Lansingburgh, 110 Third Street

Above: This was the front parlor of the Hart home in the 1880s. The classical details of the woodwork are from the original construction although the Victorian furnishings reflect the family's desire to keep up with changing styles. Courtesy, Rensselaer County Historical Society

Left: The Van Schaick house in Cohoes is one of the few remaining buildings representing the Dutch settlement of the Gateway region in the seventeenth and eighteenth centuries. Courtesy, Rensselaer County Historical Society

Above: This is the First Presbyterian Church on Seminary Park in Troy as it appeared in the late nineteenth century. Courtesy, Rensselaer County Historical Society

Left: The White Homestead, a Greek Revival house with a temple front, is now the Waterford Historical Museum. Photo by Robert Chase

Right: This is Quarters One at the Watervliet Arsenal as it appeared in the 1870s. Courtesy, Watervliet Arsenal Museum, U.S. Army photograph

in Troy, and the Commandant's House at the Watervliet Arsenal.

These buildings incorporate generous quantities of Greek Revival motifs—Doric, Ionic, and Corinthian columns or pilasters, anthemions, dentil moldings, and cabriole brackets, but even in industrial and commercial buildings where detailing is minimal, the studied proportions and simplicity that characterize the Greek Revival are apparent. Examples include the River Street warehouses north of Congress Street and the Cannon Building (1835) designed by Alexander Jackson Davis in Troy

and the Benet Laboratories at the Watervliet Arsenal.

In Troy the wide appeal and versatility of the Greek Revival is well-illustrated by three outstanding structures. Designed in 1834 by architect James H. Dakin, the former First Presbyterian Church, now the Julia Howard Bush Memorial Center, ranks nationally as one of the earliest and most accurate examples of a hexastyle, or six-columned, Doric temple. Its unobstructed auditorium retains the original shallow, coffered dome. To the south Washington Park was laid out in 1840 in the manner of London's private residential squares; the ten rowhouses along

encrusted with crockets, and rib vaults were common features. Consecrated in 1828, Saint Paul's Episcopal Church in Troy recalls the boxy form of a New England meeting-house, but the lancet windows, tracery, and pinnacles of the tower signaled a rising interest in Gothic forms. Smaller Episcopal congregations embraced Gothic forms reminiscent of rural English parish churches; their buildings typically had stone walls braced with buttresses, steeply pitched roofs, and a corner tower. Notable examples include Saint John's in Troy and Saint Mark's in Green Island.

The Warren family of Troy, prosperous from their businesses and rich in intellectual curiosity, traveled to England where they studied church architecture and choral services. The Warrens brought to Troy three prominent architects from New York—Alexander Jackson Davis, Richard Upjohn, and Henry Dudley—and became important architectural patrons, commissioning the Church of the Holy Cross, its parsonage, the Mary Warren Free Institute, a crenellated villa on Mount Ida (whose steep-roofed, picturesque Gothic gatehouse survives at 95 Cottage Avenue), and a private family chapel atop a knoll in Oakwood Cemetery. The Warrens also supported Saint Paul's, which is embellished with plaques in their memory.

Many other congregations also built with the finest materials and craftsmanship. The Jermain Memorial Church (1874) in Watervliet remains resplendently intact with a wood-paneled sanctuary, limestone and sandstone facades, a Victorian Gothic fence, and a pinnacle encircled with an iron railing. Equally distinctive in the skyline is Christ Church United Methodist in Troy, whose soaring limestone spire recalls the steeples of English towns. Many other mid-nineteenth century churches have facades of red brick with corbelled cornices, round-headed windows, and brownstone trim. Remaining examples include the First United Presbyterian Church and Saint John's Lutheran Church in Troy, Saint Agnes Church in Cohoes, and Saint Patrick's Church in Watervliet. Saint Joseph's Catholic Church in South Troy is remarkable for its massive tower and stained glass windows by the studio of Louis Comfort Tiffany.

Mid-nineteenth century American landscapes were influenced by an interest in the picturesque—seemingly casual but carefully arranged grounds dotted with fanciful structures connected by undulating paths. Consecrated in 1850, Oakwood Cemetery in Troy grew from this tradition. Troy industrialists and merchants erected extraordi-

the south side, called Washington Place, have a common pediment, massive brownstone stoops, and elaborate iron-work with female figures and miniature columns. On Second Street, midway between these two monumental structures, are three wooden temples, originally known as Cottage Row, which though more modest in scale, received national recognition in 1843.

For religious buildings, congregations and their architects often looked to a different past for inspiration and created from medieval forms new buildings in a style known as the Gothic Revival. Pointed arches, pinnacles

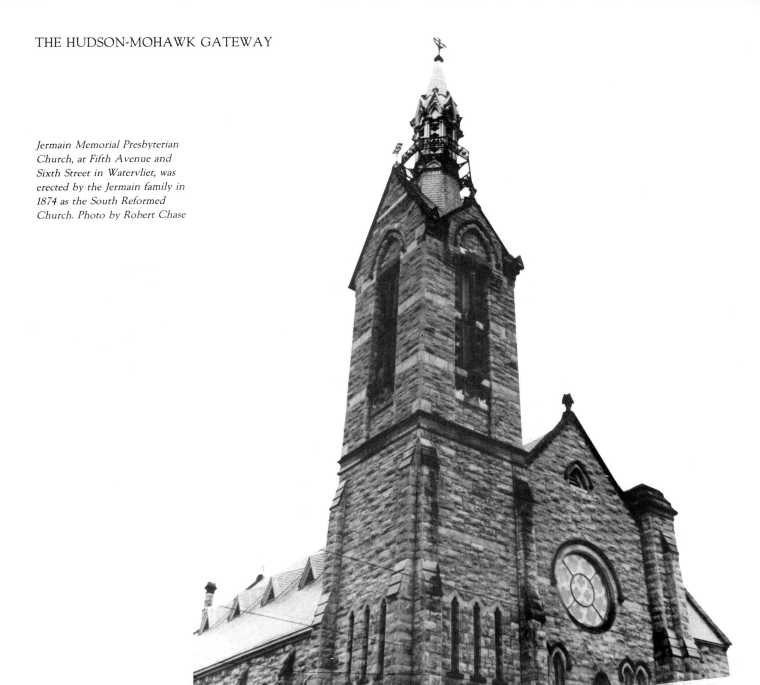

Jermain Memorial Presbyterian Church, at Fifth Avenue and Sixth Street in Watervliet, was erected by the Jermain family in 1874 as the South Reformed Church. Photo by Robert Chase

nary monuments and mausoleums with Greek, Gothic, and even Egyptian motifs amid "its shady dells and breezy heights, its crystal water and noble shade trees."

By mid-century, the Gateway's industrial products— bells, stoves, valves, cotton cloth, and shirts and collars— had won international acclaim. Blocks of modest, flat-roofed brick row houses and detached frame dwellings were erected to meet new demands for workers' housing. Their two-story facades were typically ornamented with bracketed cornices, flat-arched windows, and slightly recessed, paneled doorways. Hundreds of examples remain in South Troy and on Cataract Street and Harmony Hill in Cohoes.

A fire that swept through central Troy in 1862 enabled

the newly prosperous industrial and merchant class to build imposing residences of brick and brownstone, rivaling those found in New York and Brooklyn. Still standing along Fifth Avenue and on First, Second, and Grand streets, their three-story facades have high brownstone stoops, elaborately bracketed cornices, and bay windows, a hallmark of the Troy row house. Only twenty to twenty-eight feet in width, these dwellings were spatially efficient and often lavish; interiors feature deep plaster moldings, marble mantels, paneled woodwork painted in imitation of exotic hardwoods, and parlors of impressive proportions.

Illumination was provided by the Troy Gas Light Company, which constructed a circular, brick gasholder house

*Above: The Vail family mauso-
leum in Oakwood Cemetery is a
Gothic masterpiece constructed in
sandstone. Photo by Robert Chase*

*Left: Washington Place in Troy is
shown here in the late nineteenth
century. The common pediment
was still intact although the central cupola had been removed and
Victorian bay windows had been
added to the second floors. Courtesy, Rensselaer County Historical
Society*

Right: This is an early view of the Hall Building (now Rice Building) at River and First streets in Troy. Courtesy, Rensselaer County Historical Society

Facing page, top: Mid-nineteenth-century housing for the Harmony Mill complex is still standing on North Mohawk Street in Cohoes. Photo by Robert Chase

Bottom: This is the architectural rendering of the building designed by M.F. Cummings & Son for the George P. Ide & Co. in 1907. It was one of the many steel-framed, "fire-proof" collar factories built along River Street in Troy in the early twentieth century. Courtesy, Rensselaer County Historical Society

(1873) embellished with corbels and piers and pierced with slender windows—a commodious structure appropriately scaled to its neighborhood. The four-story W. & L.E. Gurley Company Building, which sits comfortably beside narrow, three-story row houses, is another example of architectural good manners.

The ornamentation for these new structures was seldom made by hand by skilled carvers of stone or wood; usually it was produced by machine for sale at prices the burgeoning middle class could afford. Brackets, doors, windows, balusters, shutters, marbelized slate mantels, and cast-iron window trim could be ordered ready-made from catalogs or purchased from manufacturers in Troy or Cohoes. Other prefabricated building components, such

as cast-iron storefronts and sheet metal cornices, can be found on mid-century commercial structures along Remsen Street in Cohoes, 19th Street in Watervliet, Broad Street in Waterford, George Street in Green Island, and throughout Troy. A prefabricated cast-iron storehouse at the Watervliet Arsenal was supplied ready to assemble by the Architectural Iron Works in New York. The practice of standardized building assumed another form under Troy architect Marcus F. Cummings, who wrote three architectural pattern books between 1865 and 1873 which spread deliberately replicable forms nationwide.

Beginning in the eighteenth century, buildings of the Gateway area were usually built upon the alluvial planes along the rivers, but the close of the Civil War brought suburbanization. Along the thoroughfares ascending the hills—Pawling and Pinewood avenues in Troy and Saratoga Avenue in Waterford—architects and builders took advantage of this spaciousness by building asymmetrical villas, decorated with projecting towers and porches that created fanciful silhouettes against sky and foliage. Later in the century, their verticality and planar boldness gave way to the more horizontal emphasis of Queen Anne houses, which had decorative wooden siding and shingles, capacious porches, and round towers with conical roofs.

Examples stand in Lansingburgh at 842 Second Avenue and in Troy at 162 Pawling Avenue and 7 Collins Avenue.

Another distinctive profile is created by the enormous, curvilinear red slate roof and monitor of the Troy Music Hall, designed by New York architect George B. Post and built in 1871-75. Sheltered within is one of America's most acoustically perfect auditoriums; on the first floor is the banking room of the proprietors, the Troy Savings Bank. The more modest Cohoes Music Hall (1874) is notable for the painted interior.

Industrial growth demanded expanded factories. Between 1857 and 1872 the Harmony Company erected three spectacular mills along North Mohawk Street in Cohoes, including Mill No. 3, an expanse of red brick 1,100 feet long with four tiers of large windows topped by a Mansard roof lighted by tall dormer windows. In Troy and Lansingburgh the demand for collars and cuffs created a new scale of brick construction. The block-long Lion Factory at 120th Street followed a traditional building form, but the steel-framed factories at 547, 599, and 621 River Street have grouped windows that admit large amounts of daylight.

Community growth and civic pride spurred the con-

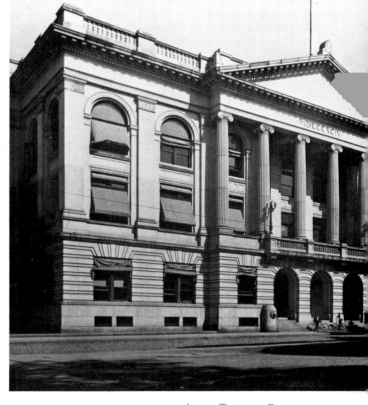

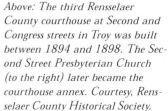

Above: The third Rensselaer County courthouse at Second and Congress streets in Troy was built between 1894 and 1898. The Second Street Presbyterian Church (to the right) later became the courthouse annex. Courtesy, Rensselaer County Historical Society.

Left: Built as the Manufacturers National Bank in 1922, this building became a branch office of Marine Midland Bank in 1965. It stands at the corner of Fourth and Grand streets in Troy, and is now the Franklin Plaza, home of Michael's Catering Service. The room in which the contract was signed to build the U.S.S. Monitor is preserved inside this building. Courtesy, Rensselaer County Historical Society.

Right: The interior of Frear's "Troy Cash Bazaar" was as elaborate as its exterior. Here the employees pose on the main staircase in 1908. Although the first floor of the staircase is now gone, the upper part remains and is now incorporated into the Uncle Sam Atrium office complex. Courtesy, Rensselaer County Historical Society

struction of public buildings. By 1884 Troy boasted four-teen brick schoolhouses and firehouses. Similar civic needs and architectural values prompted construction of the Whipple, Powers, and Haskell schools in Lansing-burgh, the city hall in Cohoes, and Corporation Hall in Green Island.

As the turn of the century approached, an interest in polychromy—the use of contrasting masonry—overtook the earlier combinations of brick and brownstone. An early example is the Rice Building (1871) at the junction of River and First streets in Troy; its red brick walls are

only a backdrop for the brown and tan voussoirs above the windows. Twenty years later, Marcus Cummings ex-perimented with rusticated light and dark masonry in the Gurley and Plum buildings on what is now the Russell Sage campus and the former Young Women's Association at 33 Second Street.

This delight with building materials was carried over to interiors, notably at Saint Paul's Episcopal Church, where the studio of Louis Comfort Tiffany was commissioned to design splendid chandeliers and pews, and J.A. Holzer cre-ated stained glass windows and a baptistry. At Oakwood

Cemetery the parents of Gardner Earl constructed a memorial chapel and crematorium embellished with quartered oak, exotic marbles, and mosaics. The extravagant Paine House (1894) at 49 Second Street, designed by Washington architect P.F. Schneider, has a richly carved limestone facade and tower. The Troy Public Library (1897) was constructed of elegantly tooled white marble and recalls the Boston Public Library at a smaller scale; the collection is stored in steel-framed stacks divided by floors of translucent glass.

As the twentieth century opened, a progressive spirit prevailed, bringing considerable new construction, especially in Troy. The growing influence of classicism is apparent in the Ionic portico of the Rensselaer County Courthouse (1894-98). A later, elegant example of the use of classical forms is the limestone Marine Midland Bank Building (1922-23) at Fourth and Grand streets.

Blocks of small domestic buildings were replaced by six- or seven-story commercial buildings. Two notable examples are the Ilium Building and the National State Bank Building, both built in 1904. Located just two blocks apart, they echo each other's configuration—rusticated ground floors surmounted by clustered windows and an arcade of smaller openings. Located midway between them is the monumental Frear Building (1897), with Corinthian capitals and richly carved spandrels.

Lighter facades and fanciful ornament were considered tasteful at the turn of the century. In Troy white terra cotta was used at Proctor's Theatre and in the McCarthy Building with its remarkably expansive showcase window.

Left: The Caldwell apartment building on the corner of Second and State streets was Troy's first modern apartment house. Courtesy, Rensselaer County Historical Society

Facing page: The library and music building at Emma Willard School was designed by Edward Larrabee Barnes in 1966-67. Photo by Robert Chase

The Caldwell apartment building (1907) was constructed of buff brick and gray litholite, an artificial stone, and had a dining room for tenants; at the opening it was heralded for its "metropolitan-like touch" that marked "another step toward a greater and better Troy." The Arts and Crafts movement is suggested by the facade of the YMCA on Second Street, which has copper roofs that project over broad windows. Emma Willard School boasts a fine campus with Collegiate Gothic elements, the work of Troy architect Frederick M. Cummings.

At the same time many area structures continued to be built of red brick, oftentimes in buildings that recall varied antecedents. The First Presbyterian Church in Waterford, for instance, is reminiscent of New England meetinghouses. The Troy Record newspaper plant (1908-09) operates behind a facade laid up in Flemish bond and surmounted by a Dutch bell gable. The entrance to the Union National Bank (1936) recalls a Roman basilica. Meanwhile, the popularity of the automobile spawned new neighborhoods that spread further up over the hills;

new houses often had traditional center hall plans but the exteriors showed a richness of historical and aesthetic influences. A notable example of a planned "residential park" is Whitman Court in Troy, where architect Frederick Cummings designed comfortable dwellings for himself and others in "modified English, cottage, mission, and colonial forms."

Significant mid-twentieth century architecture has been commissioned by Troy's educational institutions. Among the best examples are the Chapel and Cultural Center (1967-68) on Burdett Avenue, designed by Levatich and Miller of Ithaca, and, at the Emma Willard School, the library and music building (1966-67) by Edward Larrabee Barnes, and the gymnasium (1976-77) by Bohlin and Powell. Other recent building activities have included the adaptive use of significant historic buildings, such as the Julia Howard Bush Memorial Center at Russell Sage, the commercial facade programs in Troy, Lansingburgh, and Cohoes, and the rehabilitation of dwellings by individual owners.

This was graduation day at the Lansingburgh Academy in the late nineteenth century. In 1900 the private school was discontinued and it became part of the public school system. Courtesy, Lansingburgh Historical Society

CHAPTER NINE

A MAJOR EDUCATIONAL CENTER

From its earliest days, the Hudson-Mohawk area has been home to outstanding educators and outstanding educational institutions. Lansingburgh Academy, Emma Willard School and Rensselaer Polytechnic Institute, especially, have each played important roles in the history of American learning. Innovative educators, like Emma Willard, Amos Eaton, Benjamin Franklin Greene, the Kevenys of Cohoes, Palmer C. Ricketts, Lewis A. Froman, and George M. Low were attracted to the Gateway and did their influential work in the area. Harry Pratt Judson, who was teacher and later principal of Troy High School between 1870 and 1885, went on to become President of the University of Chicago in 1907. Educational efforts at all levels were encouraged by the nineteenth century merchants and industrial elites. The twentieth century has witnessed a continuation of this tradition.

Emma Willard was one of the two most innovative educators to settle in the Hudson-Mohawk area. She insisted that young women be schooled in the same disciplines as young men. While living in Middlebury, Vermont, she first learned these subjects from her husband's nephew, a student at what is now Middlebury College. Contact with Amos Eaton, when she moved to Troy in 1821, further broadened her education.

During her residence in Middlebury, Willard authored a "Plan For Improving Female Education" which so inspired Governor DeWitt Clinton of New York, that he invited her to the state. She opened her school in Waterford in 1819, but when financial backing was not forthcoming from that community or the state, the educational pioneer was given a great deal of support by Trojans and moved to their city. The town's Common Council raised $4,000 and initiated "another fund." Moulton's Coffee House, set back from the southwest corner of Congress and Second streets, was subsequently purchased, renovated, and retrofitted. The Troy Female Seminary, with Emma Willard as principal, opened in 1821 with ninety

pupils from as far away as Georgia and South Carolina. Its student body doubled the following year.

Emma Willard was a "pioneer in securing advanced education for women." She instructed her own teachers and wrote textbooks where none existed. Proceeds from these publishing efforts allowed worthy students to enroll in her school, receiving an education which otherwise would have been unaffordable for them. But Emma Willard's interests were hardly parochial; after a trip to Europe in the 1830s, she compiled her *Journal and Letters from France and Great Britain,* using the earnings to found a girls' school in Greece. She also encouraged her teachers to broaden their perspectives through travel.

Following several expansions, in 1837 the school began receiving monies from the state "Literature Fund," which had up to that time supported boys' schools exclusively. The educational innovator retired from the principalship in 1838. She was succeeded by her son, John, as business

director, and his wife, Sarah, as principal. When the lease on the buildings ran out in 1872, the trustees raised $50,000 to purchase them from the city. In that same year, John and Sarah Willard retired and Emily Treat Wilcox, a grandniece of the founder, was chosen principal. She discontinued the boarding division and conducted the school as a day school exclusively. During the 1890s, the gift of donors brought new facilities: Gurley Memorial Hall, the Anna M. Plum Memorial (a music and arts building), and a residence hall awarded by Mrs. Russell Sage. As a result of this latter gift, the school reopened its boarding division.

During the principalship of Anna M. Leach, Russell Sage's widow, Margaret Olivia Slocum Sage, contributed one million dollars for the construction of a new campus on Pawling Avenue. The generous benefactor took a personal interest in this project, helping to select an architect and oversee the design. Its beautiful collegiate Gothic

Left: This was the Troy Female Seminary as seen from Second Street in 1822. Moulton's Coffee House was purchased by the city in 1821 and remodeled for use as the school. The upper floors contained lodging and study rooms for boarding students. From Emma Willard and Her Pupils, *by Mrs. Russell Sage, 1898*

Right: Emma Willard was a pioneer in securing advanced education for women by insisting that they be schooled in the same disciplines as men. In addition to opening the Troy Female Seminary (Emma Willard School), she instructed teachers, wrote textbooks, and founded a girls school in Greece. From Emma Willard and Her Pupils, *by Mrs. Russell Sage, 1898*

Following page: The Emma Willard School campus on Second Street in Troy is seen here at the turn of the century. From the left are Plum Hall, Gurley Hall, and Russell Sage Hall. These buildings were the nucleus of Russell Sage College upon its founding in 1916. Courtesy, Rensselaer County Historical Society

campus remains in use to the present day. Renamed for its foundress in 1895, the school has experienced a continuing prosperity. William M. Deitel, the first male to head the all-girl school, updated both campus and curriculum in the 1960s, making Emma Willard School one of America's first-ranking schools for young women. Faculty housing, an art and music building, and a library were built during Deitel's principalship. Dennis Arthur Collins succeeded as principal in 1970. A children's division, then begun as a nursery school, now extends up to the third grade. Frances Roland O'Connor was appointed principal in 1974 and the new gymnasium was completed three years later. The school continues to flourish under the headship of Trudy Hall.

The Emma Willard School has graduated many notables from Elizabeth Cady Stanton in the nineteenth century to today's activist-film star Jane Fonda. Mary Lyons, the foundress of Mount Holyoke College, was an early alumna. Both the nineteenth and twentieth century women's movements have been well-served by a school founded on the premise that young women should have educational opportunities comparable to those offered young men.

In the meantime, quality academic training for boys was offered by the Lansingburgh Academy. Chester A. Arthur, twenty-first President of the United States, and Herman Melville, author of *Moby Dick,* were sometime students there, and its most distinguished principal, the Reverend Dr. Samuel Blatchford, became the first president of what was to become the Rensselaer Polytechnic Institute. One of only thirteen academies (the basic equivalent of our high schools), founded in New York State before 1800, the Lansingburgh Academy was also the last survivor of this tradition. It had been chartered by the New York Board of Regents in 1796, and was dissolved by the same body in 1911, after having been absorbed into the public school system at the turn of the century. The academy originally occupied a building on the west side of the village green until 1820, when it moved to a new two-story brick structure on the corner of 114th Street and Fourth Avenue.

While the Lansingburgh Academy and Troy Female Academy were precursors to the college preparatory movement, public education also took an early lead in

the Gateway area. In the seventeenth and eighteenth centuries, the Dutch prized both religion and academic training, so it is not surprising that the Lansingburgh community sponsored a tuition-free school, open to boys and girls, as early as 1774. By 1830 William Powers introduced the Lancasterian method which relied on older students to teach younger ones. This method was inexpensive and, therefore, was used in the education of the poor. In 1847 Lansingburgh School District No. 1 was permitted to tax and operate what is reputed to be the oldest free school in the state. The jurisdiction had no high school until 1899, however, and sent its secondary students to the Lansingburgh Academy or to Troy High. On January 1, 1901, the village of Lansingburgh was consolidated into the City of Troy, with the stipulation that the school systems remain separate. For a city of its size, Troy is rather unique in its possession of two school districts.

What is perhaps most unique about Lansingburgh is that the old Lansingburgh Academy building, a relic of the past constructed in 1820, has been completely renovated with community development funds. It now houses the Lansingburgh branch of the Troy Public Library and the Rensselaer Taconic Land Conservancy.

Troy's first school had been established in 1791 on the site of the Rensselaer County Courthouse. Two years after its founding, the school moved to the new government building, occupying a single room. In 1796 a brick English grammar school was constructed on First Street north of Ferry, only a block west of the site of the earliest school. The village was divided into four districts in the first sixteen years of the nineteenth century. A Lancasterian school was built on State Street at Seventh Avenue, and, although the original building was soon destroyed by fire, it was rebuilt in 1819 and eventually became the home of

Troy Academy. Troy Academy evolved into a private preparatory school for Rensselaer Polytechnic Institute, with which it shared teachers. The second school building was razed in the great fire of 1862, but replaced with yet a third structure which served until 1917 when the academy closed its doors. Troy had separate schools for blacks (1821 and 1829) and this minority group was not integrated into the school system until 1873. During the first half of the nineteenth century, the schools were maintained by payment of tuition as follows:

$2.00 per quarter in the upper departments. (above seven yrs of age).
.75 per quarter in the infant schools (4-7 yrs of age)
.0625 per quarter in "African" schools.

Teachers received ten percent of what they collected; books and supplies were furnished.

An early form of high school was established in the top floor of the Lancasterian school in 1828. It employed the same system as its downstairs neighbor: the more advanced instructed the less advanced. There were two grades, junior and senior, and separate classrooms were provided for boys and girls. Troy High School was opened in 1854 and continues to offer secondary education to this day. With the establishment of public schools in 1849, each of Troy's twelve wards developed separate districts and their own schools. Education became free for children five through sixteen years of age, and teachers' salaries at this time were $275 a year. A Board of Commissioners and clerk were authorized in the legislation establishing the free schools. School opened with a rhythmic rendition of the Lord's Prayer and closed with the recitation of the Ten Commandments. Writing and arithmetic were taught in the morning; spelling, reading, and geography filled the afternoon schedule.

The primary and secondary educational systems of Troy have evolved from these early beginnings. In recent years, the number of public schools has been reduced from fifteen to nine. However, in the 1970s, Brunswick School Districts 10 and 11 joined with the Troy School District to form the Enlarged City School District of Troy. Today's Troy High School building opened its doors over three decades ago, offering opportunities for vocational training, as well as traditional academic education.

Waterford's record of education dates back to 1788, when one James Dugan taught there. We also know of the appointment of the Waterford-Halfmoon School Commission roughly eight years later. A district school located in the Waterford-Halfmoon area is first mentioned in 1812. Within a quarter of a century, this institution

Right: Spearheaded by Sage Colleges President Jeanne Neff, the entire central campus of Russell Sage College is undergoing a facelift with a focus on restoration. Photo by Sid Brown

Previous page: This was the Troy Female Seminary in the 1880s, looking southwest from Congress and Second streets. The main building was replaced in the 1890s by those currently used by Russell Sage College. To the right is the First Presbyterian Church, also now part of the college campus. Courtesy, Rensselaer County Historical Society

boasted 232 pupils, but only two instructors. What came to be known as the public schools, and in their early days the "free schools," came into existence with the legislation passed by New York State in 1849. In Waterford a new, three-story structure was erected to accommodate three teachers per floor. Students were not graded at first, and graduating classes were rare, since many children left for private schools. As the century progressed, three schools enlarged the system and its name changed to Union Free School District No. 1. Finally, in 1959 Waterford's District No. 1 and District No. 2, encompassing all of Halfmoon and part of Waterford, were merged. Three years later the new system opened a school which serves kindergarten through senior high. The Waterford-Halfmoon District celebrated its 100th graduating class in 1984.

Aside from its public schools, early Waterford enjoyed considerable private education. The Waterford Classical Institution, housed in the "Classic Hall," was a young men's school with a tuition of three dollars per term for reading, writing, and arithmetic; and an additional four dollars per term for English, grammar, and geography. What was called "higher education," something like secondary education, cost five dollars per term. At the Waterford Ladies' School (1822) a Miss Haight charged her pupils twenty dollars a year for instruction in eight sub-

jects. An additional ten subjects, including chemistry, astronomy, and philosophy cost twenty-four dollars per year, while drawing and painting on velvet hiked tuition by thirty-two dollars. French and music were taught when enough pupils were interested.

Up to approximately 1813, the only school in the Cohoes vicinity was located at the Boght. About this time, however, two institutions opened their doors: the first, "in a building on the main road," and the second, "a short distance above the Heamstreet farmhouse." The latter was apparently the "Red School House." A second school district was formed in 1828. Located near the site of the old freight house of the Rensselaer and Saratoga Railroad's freight station on Oneida Street, its offices were formerly boarding house lodgings. School trustees, chosen in 1850, soon identified a need for more classroom space. The basement of the Reformed Church was rented while the Messrs Fuller built the two-story schoolhouse on Remsen Street, which was subsequently leased by the trustees. Just five years later, in 1855, the *Albany Knickerbocker* noted that:

The advantage of having new public schools entirely free is shown by the experience of Cohoes. Under the past pay system, the number of pupils who attended was less than four hundred. At present, it is over eight hundred.

There were seven schools in Cohoes at the time. By 1876 the Board of Education operated 25 primary, four intermediate, one grammar, and one high school in eight buildings, seven of which belonged to the city. Thirty-eight teachers served the needs of approximately two thousand students. Today's school district is directed by a seven-member Board of Education which oversees three elementary schools, one middle school, and one high school. Two hundred and eight teachers are charged with the instruction of approximately 2,200 pupils. The only documented private school in Cohoes was opened in the mid-nineteenth century under the direction of Rev. Stephen Bush.

Green Island had two schools prior to the passing of the Union Free School Law of the State. A Mr. Doolittle taught in one schoolhouse, while Mrs. Dodge, "a very refined and well-educated woman" who was "held in the greatest respect," headed the other. This sophisticated educator inspired a love of learning in nineteenth-century Green Island residents. On November 17, 1854, Green Island voted for a reorganization of the town district and compliance with the state's public school mandate. Two schools were subsequently built, in 1865 and 1879. James Heatly served as superintendent of schools from 1880 through 1924. Heatly School, built in 1930, commemorates his long service to the education of citizens of the village. Green Island's two earlier schools, in the meantime, were merged and a ninth grade was added, inaugurating a junior high. When a 1934 decision urged further education, the ninth grade expanded into a four-year secondary school program. Completely renovated in 1956, the Heatly School, housing all primary and secondary grades, continues to serve the educational needs of Green Island.

Called "West Troy" until 1897, the city of Watervliet inluded what had earlier been Gibbonsville, Washington, and Port Schuyler. An infant school existed there in 1818, and schoolhouses are mentioned in 1828, 1832, and 1833. The West Troy Female Seminary, with S. Harris and Elizabeth 0. Stowe as teachers, was founded at this time; according to Watervliet's historian it just "bloomed and faded away." Other records describe first and fourth ward "select schools" in the late 1830s. A high school is mentioned in 1881, though it can be assumed that sometime after the mid-nineteenth century when public education came

into existence, a whole system of primary and secondary programs was established.

Watervliet's next benchmark in the field of education came much later, in 1952. City schools then became independent of the government. As the sixties drew to a close, an Enlarged City School District commenced operation, starting out with five elementary school buildings. These buildings were eventually closed, and a Norton Company building was converted to a single primary school, serving the entire district. Along with the Watervliet Junior-Senior High School, this institution meets the educational needs of the jurisdiction.

Parochial and other church-related schools, too, have played an enormous role in educating Gateway youth. In fact, at times these schools have enrolled as many pupils as the public schools. As early as 1825, the Quakers built a schoolhouse adjacent to their meeting house on the corner of Fourth and State streets in Troy. This institution served Trojan children for 43 years. And in Cohoes, St. John's Episcopal Church was operating a parochial school in the mid-nineteenth century. Nevertheless, the Roman Catholic Church, religious beacon for the immigrant masses, has been responsible for most of the Gateway's parochial and church-related academies.

The first parochial elementary school was connected with St. Mary's Church in Troy. The Sisters of Charity began to educate girls in 1847 and the Christian Brothers took boys under their tutelage three years later. St. Peter's, also of Troy, initially employed lay teachers in its school (1854) but the Sisters of St. Joseph took over within a decade. Boasting an enrollment of 500 elementary students from its start in 1861, St. Bernard's of Cohoes operated an evening program for children who worked in the mills. The school became coeducational 31 years later. These nineteenth-century institutions had opened with lay faculty, but soon turned to teaching sisters.

The twentieth century witnessed the continuation of this trend toward parochial education. Some of the schools opened in that century are the strongest primary parochial schools still open today. They include: Sacred Heart, Troy (1927); Our Lady of Victory, Troy (1952); and St. Mary's, Waterford (1953).

In addition, no less than thirteen of the Roman Catholic elementary schools had high schools attached to them at one time. By 1923 the five remaining Troy and Watervliet academies were phased out in favor of Catholic

The first home of Rensselaer Polytechnic Institute, the former Farmer's Bank was at the corner of River and Middleburgh streets in Troy. Courtesy, Rensselaer County Historical Society

Central High School, which was to serve a much larger part of the Gateway. The former Troy Hospital building on Eighth Street in Troy was renovated to house a secondary program, with Rev. Edward J. Burns as its founding principal. He left his stamp of quality education on the school. In 1952 the school purchased the Cluett Peabody Research Laboratory at 116th Street between Sixth and Seventh avenues. Moving there, it annexed the old Country Day School property which had more recently been owned by LaSalle Institute. A gymnasium was erected and, later, a wing was added to the original structure. The school topped off at approximately 1,500 students, and has been taught over the years by Sisters of

Mercy, Sisters of St. Joseph, priests of the Diocese of Albany, Augustinian Fathers, and lay teachers.

The old St. Bernard's Academy, founded in 1878, entered its new building in 1930. To honor three priests, all related, who had been prominent in parish education, the school's name was changed to Keveny Memorial Academy. The Academy closed its doors in 1986. St. Joseph's Academy of Troy (1851) later became La Salle Institute in commemoration of the Christian Brothers' contribution to the learning arts. The school moved from South Troy to a new campus adjacent to Hudson Valley Community College in 1966. A middle school was opened within five years. Today, La Salle is a private middle and secondary school with a Junior Reserve Officers Training program. By 2000 it enrolled over 600 students.

If the Hudson-Mohawk area has done an excellent job of teaching its children and youth, it has also offered outstanding opportunities for advanced education. Earliest and most famous among its institutions of higher learning is Rensselaer Polytechnic Institute, originally the Rensselaer School, founded in 1824. It was named for its founder and patron, Stephen Van Rensselaer, eighth patron of the Upper Hudson who, in a letter addressed to the school's first president, the Rev. Samuel Blatchford, stated:

I have established a school at the north end of Troy ... for the purpose of instructing persons who may choose to apply themselves, in the application of science to the common purposes of life.

Van Rensselaer went on to say:

My principal object is, to qualify teachers for instructing the sons and daughters of farmers and merchants ... I am inclined to believe that competent instructors may be produced ... who will be highly useful to the community in the diffusion of a very useful kind of knowledge, with its application to the business of living. ...

Insofar as this primary document was concerned, the Rensselaer School sought to train teachers of applied science for service in New York schools; it was an innovative educational venture. The patroon may have also had a personal objective in mind, namely, the development of his estate's roughly 900 farms and other holdings which were spread over a three-county area. In the same letter to President Blatchford, Van Rensselaer named as senior professor, or head of the faculty, Amos Eaton, who was to carry the title "Professor of Chemistry and Experimental Philosophy, and Lecturer on Geology, Land Surveying and laws regulating town officers and jurors." Lewis C. Beck, "Professor of Mineralogy, Botany and Zoology, and lecturer on the social duties peculiar to farmers and mechanics," was chosen junior professor.

From its inception the Rensselaer School came under the dominating influence of Amos Eaton. Courses and professorships in science already existed in America's colleges, some dating back to the preceding century, but these were academic in character. Quite apart from the classical tradition, Eaton was interested in popular and practical technical education. His intent was by no means unique, but his methods certainly were. He threw his imaginative and innovative mind into the development of what we now know as the oldest technological university in continuous existence in the English-speaking world. Interestingly, the Rensselaer School from the beginning aspired to grant women an opportunity to prepare them-

Stephen Van Rensselaer III, founder and benefactor of RPI, was the eighth patroon of the Manor of Rensselaerwyck, a vast semi-feudal estate including most of Albany and Rensselaer counties and part of Columbia County. Farmers were bound to him by a leasehold system in which they paid annual rent for the use of his land. Courtesy, Rensselaer Polytechnic Institute Archives

selves for teaching careers. In 1828 Eaton even proposed a "Ladies Department." Finally, a class of eight women was actually presented for public examination seven years later. But the experimental method, involving the student in lecture and demonstrations, was Eaton's most original and significant contribution. Perhaps he was applying Lancasterian techniques to higher education. Whatever the case, in 1826, this noteworthy educator established a "Preparation Branch," intended for students thirteen years of age

Amos Eaton, the progressive senior professor at the Rensselaer School, instituted the experimental method of instruction which involved students in lectures and demonstrations. Courtesy, Rensselaer Polytechnic Institute Archives

and upward who had already completed basic schooling. Within a decade the state legislature enacted a bill authorizing the Rensselaer Institute, as it then became known, to develop a department of mathematical arts for instruction in "Engineering and Technology." The trustees, acting on this mandate, established two branches with corresponding degrees, both new to American education. One was the degree of Bachelor of Natural Science for the course already in existence, and the other, the degree of Civil Engineer, accommodated new technical programs. This second branch and credential were to set the course for the future development of the Rensselaer Institute. By the time Eaton died in 1842, it had awarded ninety-seven degrees in Civil Engineering and forty-two in Natural Science.

Eaton had always had to struggle mightily to keep his fledgling institution fiscally solvent. He turned regularly to his benefactor, the patroon, for approximately $3,000

per year. But Van Rensselaer died in 1839, and Eaton spent his last years struggling to keep the Institute open. He made a claim for $10,000 on Stephen Van Rensselaer's estate, expecting a similar sum to be raised among the Trojans. However, Stephen's son, Alexander, a graduate of the school, replied, "My father no doubt felt vexed to think that they (the Trojans) so little appreciated the vast sum of money he had expended in founding a school in their very midst." Rensselaer's scion therefore declined Eaton's request, calling it "absurd." On his death, Eaton's property and that of the Rensselaer Institute were sold for $382.26 to Dr. Thomas Brinsmade. Brinsmade then consigned all of the holdings to George B. Cook, Eaton's successor as senior professor. Finally, in 1844, Troy turned over the Infant School, appraised at $6,500, to the Institute. William Paterson Van Rensselaer, one of Stephen's sons, matched this with $6,500 to create an endowment which provided an annual income of $455.

Another one of the Institute's exceptional senior professors was Benjamin Franklin Greene. Only twenty-nine years old when he was named senior professor, Greene, like Eaton, his teacher, possessed a brilliant and creative mind. The young educator called Rensselaer "a Polytechnic" and wrote the "True Idea of a Polytechnic." He persisted and after resigning from his post in 1859, this name was legalized by an act of the legislature in 1861. Greene called himself "Director and Professor" and established three departments. The one-year curriculum was extended to three years. He elevated the new Rensselaer Polytechnic Institute to collegiate rank, suggesting a breadth of education which was realized only a full century later. Greene also made Rensselaer a national and even international institution. As early as 1850, for example, a Brazilian student was graduated. The director, too, introduced courses in German, French, and English. Like Eaton, Greene had grand visions and was constrained by limited means, though he did convince the state legislature to appropriate $3,000 for the Rensselaer Institute in 1851. Added funds allowed him to accomplish some of his goals.

Nevertheless, Greene's "True Idea of a Polytechnic" was premature. The board of trustees—which included Greene after 1855—consisted of local persons. State government, in spite of some funding in 1851, was not ready to get involved in private educational enterprises, even the most imaginative of sorts. Local support, too, was not adequate. Finally, in 1859, in a crisis of personality and business behavior with the board of trustees, Greene's directorship and professorship ended in resignation. Rensselaer's most

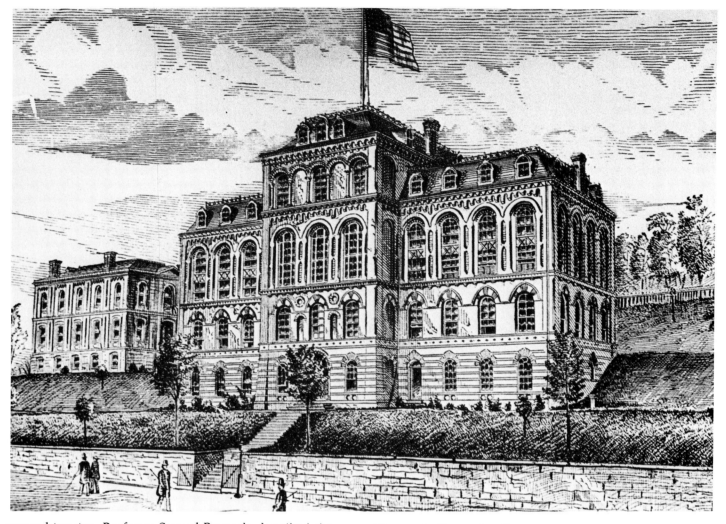

The main building and smaller chemical laboratory of the Rensselaer Polytechnic Institute were constructed on Eighth Street at the head of Broadway after the fire of 1862. After the main building burned in 1904, the campus moved to its present location. From History of the City of Troy, *by A.J. Weise, 1876*

recent historian, Professor Samuel Rezneck, described the post-Greene period as one in which the school "contracted into just another technological institution, claiming age and antiquity rather than novelty of origin and purpose." Nevertheless, after the great fire of 1862 destroyed the Infant School Building near the railroad station which RPI had occupied since 1844, RPI moved into "Old Main," newly built on the site of the "Approach," restored to its original beauty (under the leadership of former President Byron Pipes). A chemistry laboratory (1866) and the Proudfit Observatory (1878) enhanced the campus, and a creditable celebration marked the school's fiftieth anniversary in 1874. Famous graduates of the period included Henry A. Rowland, first professor of physics at Johns Hopkins; George Washington Ferris, inventor of the Ferris wheel; and Mordecai T. Endicott, founder of the Navy's Civil Engineering Corps.

An era of relative inactivity ended with the accession

Several students from RPI's class of 1888 use the nearby Poestenkill Gorge as a classroom for surveying studies. Courtesy, Rensselaer Polytechnic Institute Archives

of Palmer Chamberlaine Ricketts to the directorship in 1892, and subsequently, to the presidency. Ricketts had come to RPI as a freshman in 1871 and remained at the school until his death sixty-three years later. He was a builder. The Carnegie Building was opened in 1904, and the following two years saw the ground-breaking of the Walker and Sage Laboratories, the latter named for former trustee Russell Sage, whose widow had given a handsome sum of one million dollars for the facility's construction. The host of successful Western Pennsylvania alumni made their contribution in the Pittsburgh Building (1907). Five years later the classes of 1886 and 1887 presented the school with an athletic field and gym, named for their respective years. A clubhouse was opened in 1914, as were the quadrangle dormitories. Between 1920-

24, the Troy Building was built, while 1928 saw the completion of Amos Eaton and the former Rensselaer Union, now the Lally Management Building. Greene and Ricketts began their service to the RPI community in the following year.

President Ricketts also fulfilled most of B.F. Greene's vision of the "True Polytechnic." Speaking to the first meeting of the American Society for the Promotion of Engineering Education, he said, "In general the engineer is not liberally educated. Beyond his profession his knowledge is not great. This is a mistake. . . ." Ricketts used some of the first Sage gift to initiate electrical and mechanical engineering and housed them in the Russell Sage Laboratory. Chemical engineering and graduate study in engineering were both introduced in 1913, as Mrs. Sage

Ricketts' first move to broaden the curriculum came in 1915 with the hiring of a young, Harvard-trained, English Ph.D., Ray Palmer Baker. Baker soon headed a Department of Arts, Science, and Business Administration, offering degrees in chemistry, physics, biology, and business administration. History, political science, economics, sociology, psychology, foreign languages, and English were introduced or strengthened, and architecture found its way into the course list as the 1920s drew to a close. Already seventy-seven years of age, Ricketts added three new curricula: metallurgical, aeronautical, and industrial engineering in 1933. When he died one year later, the faculty boasted 145 members. RPI's student body numbered approximately 1,350.

After a short *interregnum,* William Otis Hotchkiss moved from the Houghton School of Mines in Michigan to become Rensselaer's president, the first non-alumnus to head the Institute. His principal contributions were in the area of curriculum development. He also strived for improved faculty salaries, manageable teaching loads, more modern equipment, increased research activity, and better student-faculty relations. As the United States entered World War II, the president had the unenviable job of scaling back most normal activities and gearing up to wartime needs. Undergraduate enrollment slid to a low of 932 in 1945, two-thirds of which were Navy ROTC and V-12 students. The faculty, 160 strong in pre-war years, diminished to less than a hundred.

Taking over the reins from Hotchkiss in 1945, Livingston Waddell Houston, local industrialist and longtime RPI officer, reorganized the administration. He named Dr. Matthew A. Hunter dean of faculty and Dr. Ray Palmer Baker dean of students. An excellent manager, Houston prepared for the post-war boom, utilizing the Committee on Post-War Planning originally established by his predecessor. But no one could have predicted the number of students who descended on universities following the war. They were older, married, very career-oriented—and in a great hurry to get started. Curricular reforms, other than the introduction of an eight-course core of humanities and social sciences, had to be postponed. But an evening school, refresher courses, cooperative education, and ROTC programs by all three major services were introduced. New housing and classrooms came into being. Rensselaerwyck for married students and a large field house were built out of wartime surplus materials; an abandoned orphanage provided lodgings for new faculty. Classrooms and offices were added later. West

provided funds for the establishment of two masters-level fellowships. The publication of a Rensselaer Science and Engineering course also furthered research, but Ricketts was cautious. Restating his primary interest in undergraduate education in 1933, he wrote:

It is believed that teachers should do outside work in the line of their profession, in order that they may be better fitted to teach, but it must be explicitly understood that such work is wholly secondary to their duties as teachers. It's not intended to provide any teacher with a place from which he may pursue professional outside work of any character while neglecting his duty as a teacher. Abuse of this nature has caused endless trouble in another well-known school, and it cannot be permitted to arise here.

The Rensselaer Newman Foundation's Chapel and Cultural Center is on Burdett Avenue in Troy. Photo by Jim Shaughnessy. Courtesy, Rensselaer Polytechnic Institute

Hall, with all its teaching facilities sprung from the former Catholic Central High; freshman dormitories also arose. Enrollment reached 4,000 while assets climbed to fifty-one million dollars.

After the post-war boom, long-range goals were pursued and planning for their achievement followed. Houston raised $27,750,000 before his retirement in 1958. With it, he enlarged the RPI campus, increased student activities, and expanded the endowment. At about the same time, Houston divided the departments into schools, each headed by an academic dean. The School of Management came along a few years later. Dr. Paul Hemke, dean of faculty since 1949, was named vice president and provost. The graduate division was also made a school. On top of these developments, RPI established the Hartford Graduate Center in Connecticut. Houston, in fact, had been so successful as administrator and fundraiser that upon his retirement, he was named chairman of the board.

Richard Gilmore Folsom, director of the University of Michigan's Engineering Research Institute, replaced this managerial expert. Changing times demanded that an essentially undergraduate institution take advantage of growing graduate education and research opportunities. A numerically and qualitatively expanding staff formed a Faculty Council. And, under the new president, development took the form of a Science Center, the Materials Research Center, a Communications Center, the Rensselaer Union, and a new library, named, after his retirement, for Folsom. A linear accelerator was built as were many dormitories, and the old Troy Armory was converted into RPI's Alumni Sports and Recreation Center.

The former dean of engineering at Purdue University, Richard J. Grosh, succeeded Folsom in 1971. His tenure and a bold move towards top quality education, Engineering Initiatives, propelled the construction of the Jonsson Engineering Center. Presiding over RPI in 1976, George M. Low had directed the Apollo space program and served as deputy administrator of the National Aeronautics and Space Administration. Low's leadership brought Engineering Initiatives to a more than successful conclusion. His blueprint for the future, "Rensselaer 2000," states that by the end of the present century, "RPI will be one of a small number of first-rank, internationally renowned technological universities." Low, who died in 1984, spent his eight years at Rensselaer working towards the realization of this overarching goal.

The former chapel of St. Joseph's Seminary, now part of RPI, was converted into a computer center, an effective adaptation which nevertheless allows the previous use to remain obvious. Thelma and Kenneth Lally's name was placed on the management building, reincarnated from the Rensselaer Union Clubhouse, and Sage Laboratory was completely renovated as the home for the School of Humanities and Social Sciences as was the Playhouse. A former Norton Abrasives research laboratory in Watervliet became the Center for Integrated Electronics. Low also convinced the state to join RPI in the building and equipping of a Center for Industrial Innovation—a bold move which, along with the school's Incubator (industrial development) program and Technology Park, forms the basis for a "Second Industrial Revolution" in the Capital District of New York State. Even more importantly, the quality of the faculty and the quantity of research grew greatly during Low's presidency, bringing new national recognition to both the country's oldest engineering school and the Gateway area. At this writing, Dr. Daniel Berg, formerly Provost and Chief Academic Officer, has been named 15th President of RPI to succeed Low.

Although RPI's accomplishments could fill their own book, these educational ventures hardly exhaust the higher education offered in the Hudson-Mohawk Gateway. A mid-nineteenth century advertisement in the *Troy Whig* announced that if the local people could raise $100,000, the Methodist College at Charlottesville (Schoharie County) would move its campus to Troy. Given the city's heady atmosphere at that time, the proposition presented no great problems and the money was quickly subscribed. Jacob D. Vanderheyden's property, some thirty-six acres on the brow of the hill overlooking central Troy, was purchased. Surmounted by four tall spires, the cornerstone for a great neo-Romanesque structure was subsequently laid. Troy University opened in 1858, offering four-year B.S. and B.A. degrees, a three-year program in agriculture or civil engineering, and a bachelor of divinity degree in two years. However, the college's president never left New York City. Perhaps as a result, only four professors and fifty-five students appeared and Troy University soon closed down. The Provincial Theological Seminary of the Roman Catholic Archdiocese of New York came to occupy the site in 1864, but moved to Yonkers twenty-eight years later. After serving as a refuge for victims of disaster, the building eventually was purchased by the Sisters of St. Joseph of Corondolet. When they moved to new and larger quarters in Latham, the property and building were purchased by RPI.

After the Emma Willard School moved to its new cam-

George M. Low was president of Rensselaer Polytechnic Institute from 1976 to 1984. Courtesy, Rensselaer Polytechnic Institute

pus, Russell Sage College—housed on the old campus of the school—was created to provide young women with a practical, as well as a more classical education. Opening with 117 students, it blended secretarial, home economics, and nursing courses with the traditional liberal arts. By 1923 a full-fledged school of nursing developed, and one year later the college boasted a 310-member student body. It shared the Emma Willard School principal as its president, but by 1927, it became obvious that such a successful endeavor required its own full-time administrative head. James Laurence Meader, who greatly strengthened the liberal arts program, became its second president. Within three years, the Central School of Hygiene and Physical Education moved from New York City and joined Russell Sage College.

After Meader resigned to enter the military service, several short-term presidents assumed the leadership role. But Lewis A. Froman's twenty-one-year tenure, from 1948 to 1969, saw truly massive development of the school's facilities, constituent components, and curriculum. Enrollments grew to 1,250. A fine arts center, auditorium, and Ackerson Hall were constructed, and the James Wheelock Clark Library opened in 1955, to be expanded in 1966. Vail House, the federal period seat of a Poestenkill Gorge industrialist, became the president's residence. In addition, Russell Sage College added new campuses and broadened its schedule to include evening classes for both men and women (1941), an Albany division (1949), and the coed Junior College of Albany (1957). Froman then saw the need to unify the growing home campus and built a tunnel to carry traffic beneath Ferry Street.

In 1970 Charles U. Walker became president of Russell Sage and remained in that post for five years. During that period, the Greek temple-like First Presbyterian Church in the midst of the campus was given to the college as the Julia Howard Bush Center. The school's current president, William F. Kahl, arrived at Sage in 1976. His term has brought about the building of the Ellis and Doris Robison Athletic and Recreation Center. Enrollments at the three constituent elements of the college are approximately: 1,400 at Russell Sage, 1,000 at the Junior College of Albany, and 2,500 at the evening divisions in Troy and Albany. Master's degrees are offered in business administration, elementary education, reading, special education, health education, nursing, public service administration, health services administration, and community psychology. The Junior College also offers course work at three New York State correctional institutions and the Job Corps Center in Glenmont.

Yet another Gateway area institution of higher education appeared at mid-century and has grown by leaps and bounds over the past thirty years. Hudson Valley Community College, located in Troy and sponsored by Rensselaer County, had its origins in the Veteran's Vocational School (1946). The two-year program was initially housed in the vacant Earl and Wilson Shirt Company building on Seventh Avenue, a structure earlier occupied by an Army Signal Corps School. At first the school helped returning World War II veterans acquire the technical training necessary for the new industrial era. Having taken care of returning G.I.'s by the early 1950s, many people assumed that this technical institute would close its doors. However, Dwight Marvin, editor of the *Troy Record* newspapers, believed it to be the potential nucleus for a community college. Other new two-year schools were just beginning to gain recognition in New York State, so the Hudson Valley Technical Institute was opened in 1953, with Otto V. Guenther as its first president. Guenther had been chair of the Mechanical Technology Department at Buffalo's Erie County Technical Institute. He also had been recommended by the New York State Department of Education. There was little money during these early days, and instructors did the maintenance and routine construction work in the building.

Guenther's assiduous efforts and those of the first facul-

ty members paid off, however. The name of the institution was changed to Hudson Valley Community College in 1959, reflecting a broader mission. Plans for a new campus were announced as well. Taxpayers then challenged the county's right to assess its citizens for the support of a college, but the New York State Court of Appeals handed down a decision in favor of the taxing. The newly-named Hudson Valley Community College surged ahead. The former Williams farm on the southern border of the city and northern border of North Greenbush was purchased, and five structures costing five million dollars were built by the time of the move. The student body had grown from eighty-eight to 1,200 in just six years. Technical courses were still the bread and butter items of the curriculum, but banking, insurance, and real estate, as well as dental hygiene, were added in 1960. The first two years of the liberal arts program first appeared in 1961. Curricular expansion continued as the post-war baby boomers reached college age. In 1965 Guenther announced his retirement. He inspired a pioneer faculty and staff to create a new higher educational institution in the traditional northeast.

James J. Fitzgibbons, who had moved from department chair to dean at HVCC and later joined the state's education department, returned as second president. The latter half of the 1960s saw enrollment swell to 4,000 students. HVCC subsequently became administrator of new urban centers for the economically disadvantaged which sprang up in the inner cities of the Capital District. Educational offerings extended to some forty curricula. The Middle States Association granted these programs full accreditation in 1968, and a student union and library graced the campus within six years. By this time the HVCC student body had grown to 6,240. Fitzgibbons retired in 1979, to be succeeded by Joseph J. Bulmer, formerly of the General Electric Knolls Atomic Power Laboratory. The college's rapid development has continued apace under Bulmer's leadership. A health technologies building named for Fitzgibbons opened in 1982, and the college acquired the old Henry Burden property, later a Franciscan Seminary complex, two years later. Nearly 300 full- and part-time faculty now teach some 7,500 students at one of the largest community colleges in upstate New York.

Troy also claimed a small business college, founded in the early 1860s, which ultimately merged with the Albany Business College in the middle of the twentieth century. And, as might be expected, Samaritan Hospital still continues to sponsor a nursing school.

The Ford Motor Company plant on Green Island continued to be an important business in the area until its closing in 1989. This was the dedication ceremony for the manufacturing plant in 1923. Courtesy, Rensselaer County Historical Society

CHAPTER TEN

DECLINE AND REVIVAL IN THE TWENTIETH CENTURY

The northeast's "gritty cities," areas that were industrialized earliest in this country, have generally experienced special adjustment problems in the twentieth century. Water was a key to the settlement of these early industrialized areas—falling water for power and waterways for transportation. Steam engines, and later electricity, made industries more independent of water, though water continues to be important for many industrial processes. The freedom provided by steam and electricity allowed industries like textiles to move closer to the center of raw materials. Labor unionization and labor-management conflicts forced industries towards cheaper and more pliable labor markets. There was also the matter of scale: early industry built on such a small scale that the visible remains are barely noticeable in our old cities. As the size of the industrial process and their buildings increased, the larger, open spaces much more easily found in the relatively flat midwest were in increased demand. In addition, there was the inexorable movement west in the second half of the nineteenth century. Those industries which stayed behind tended to become obsolete; this was evidenced in their unwillingness to pursue the research and development that would keep the companies up-to-date with the latest technological advances.

The Gateway area was a victim of all of these forces. By the late nineteenth century, creeping industrial decline was visible to the perceptive, and in the first half of the twentieth century, that decline was obvious and visible to all. Fortunately, however, there were other institutions still in their growth stages that gave the area its needed base for continued existence, and, in fact, relative prosperity even in difficult times like the great Depression. At the same time, Gateway communities in the late twentieth century have been undergoing extensive renewal programs.

Troy's business district was most affected by the ill-fated

121

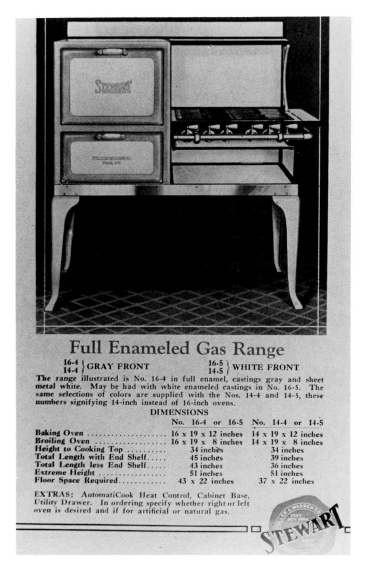

Full Enameled Gas Range

| 16-4 | GRAY FRONT | 16-5 | WHITE FRONT |
| 14-4 | | 14-5 | |

The range illustrated is No. 16-4 in full enamel, castings gray and sheet metal white. May be had with white enameled castings in No. 16-5. The same selections of colors are supplied with the Nos. 14-4 and 14-5, these numbers signifying 14-inch instead of 16-inch ovens.

DIMENSIONS

	No. 16-4 or 16-5	No. 14-4 or 14-5
Baking Oven	16 x 19 x 12 inches	14 x 19 x 12 inches
Broiling Oven	16 x 19 x 8 inches	14 x 19 x 8 inches
Height to Cooking Top	34 inches	34 inches
Total Length with End Shelf	45 inches	39 inches
Total Length less End Shelf	43 inches	36 inches
Extreme Height	51 inches	51 inches
Floor Space Required	43 x 22 inches	37 x 22 inches

EXTRAS: AutomatiCook Heat Control, Cabinet Base, Utility Drawer. In ordering specify whether right or left oven is desired and if for artificial or natural gas.

From Fuller & Warren Company's 1927 catalogue, this is the twentieth-century version of P.P. Stewart's famous cooking range. Courtesy, Rensselaer County Historical Society

federal government Urban Renewal Program. In 1966 the New York State Legislature created the Troy Urban Renewal Agency which, over a period of ten years, demolished central business district stores, the Troy Theater, and Troy Union Railroad Station. A plan had been devised to build a huge downtown Uncle Sam Mall covering twenty-four acres and costing ninety-six million dollars. A preferred developer was named, but that company backed out in 1975. Meanwhile much of the northern section of the central business district of Troy was demolished, leaving what came to be called "the great hole." An offer to build a much diminished one-story mall was made in 1976 and rejected because of the problem of scale. Finally, Carl Grimm of Troy erected the smaller Uncle Sam Atrium with the assistance of a $1,500,000 U.S. Urban Development Action Grant which covered the building of a public central courtyard or atrium.

The central business district of Troy, aided by a facade program and new developers who are taking advantage of a variety of government programs, currently shows clear signs of revival. Major companies like New York Telephone and the John Hancock Insurance Company, as well as a Holiday Inn, new banks, shops, restaurants, and offices, are appearing almost daily.

Meanwhile Cohoes' central business district, which did not undergo the trauma of urban renewal as its industrial area did, has also received a facelifting. A sense of historic preservation, aided by tax incentives, appears to have succeeded in bringing out the quality of the built environment in the business district of Cohoes and the remaining old business district of Troy, and this latter-day renewal appears to be meeting with a much more favorable response from consumers.

During the Depression that began in 1929 and lasted for a decade, not one Gateway area bank failed. Banks were also sufficiently strong to allow mortgagees to postpone payments, thus preventing many foreclosures. In fact, although there were wage cuts and the work week was shortened to spread work to more persons, unemployment was held at less than 5 percent during this economically difficult period. At present a change in the banking laws has resulted in both the absorption of old local banking institutions into large regional banks and an explosion in the number of banking institutions in the area.

The twentieth century has not been the heyday of industry in the Gateway area, nor is the area likely to regain the position of industrial prominence it occupied in the mid-nineteenth century. Nevertheless, there has been significant industrial activity during this period and it appears that the area may well be beginning what is sometimes referred to as the "Second Industrial Revolution" in high technology industries.

One of the most remarkable remains of Troy's early iron industry is both the factory and machinery of Portec

Inc., located immediately west of the Troy approach to the Menands bridge. In 1903 the old Albany Rolling and Slitting mill was taken over by the Continuous Rail Joint Company, which in 1905 merged with the Weber Rail Joint Company and the Independent Supply Company of Chicago to form the Rail Joint Company of New York. From the beginning of the twentieth century, the mill turned out insulated joints used in railroad signal and safety systems, as well as for joining together track. In more recent years the Rail Joint Company became part of Portec Inc., which continued to manufacture insulated joints in the old factory and even with some of the original machinery until it closed down in October 1989. In their latter years, the two rolling mills themselves were no longer powered by steam but by 1,000-horsepower motors.

In the mid-nineteenth century, James Horner acquired the Pompton Furnace in northern New Jersey. James Ludlum joined the company salesman and in 1864 was taken into a partnership with Horner. Eleven years later the Pompton Steel and Iron Company was formed with Ludlum as president. In 1892 James Ludlum died and was succeeded in the presidency by William H. Ludlum. Six years later the firm became the Ludlum Steel and

Built on the site of the Troy Iron & Steel Company, the coke plant in south Troy manufactured gas for power and light and coke for fuel. This photograph was taken in 1937. Courtesy, Rensselaer County Historical Society

Right: Two out of five of the giant water turbines in the Masto-don Mill (Harmony Mill #3) remain to help tell the story of the great cotton mills of Cohoes. Photo by Jim Shaughnessy

Below: The big gun shop at the Watervliet Arsenal in the late 1960s manufactured 175mm cannons among other weapons. Courtesy, Watervliet Arsenal Museum, U.S. Army photograph

Far right: Although the Harmony Mills Company was liquidated in the early 1930s, smaller textile manufacturers continued to occupy the nineteenth-century buildings. Beaunit Manufacturing Company utilized these knitting machines in 1951. Today a variety of manufacturers and outlet stores are part of the Harmony Mills complex.

Spring Company. The company moved to a new plant just outside Watervliet in the town of Colonie in 1907.

By 1938 the Ludlum Steel Company had its main office and a manufacturing plant in Watervliet. It had another large plant at Dunkirk, New York, and interests in three other companies. That year a merger was consummated between Ludlum and Allegheny Steel Company, creating a new name, Allegheny Ludlum Steel Corporation. Following the merger and substantial growth, the new company became the world's largest producer of high alloy specialty steels, with principal emphasis on stainless, tool, and electrical steels. However in 1976 Allegheny Ludlum sold its Bar Products Division to yet another new corporation called Al Tech Specialty Steel Corporation. Al Tech operates the plants at Watervliet and Dunkirk with its headquarters at the Dunkirk plant. More recently, in 1981, Al Tech became a division of GATX Corporation, a major U.S. corporation headquartered in Chicago.

Besides the steel and iron industry, a major automobile company is present today in the area. The Ford Motor Company owes its presence in the Gateway to a camping trip of Henry Ford, Thomas A. Edison, Harvey Firestone, and John Burroughs. In 1919 they pitched a tent on Green Island overlooking the dam at the headwater of navigation on the Hudson. Ford saw in the dam a valu-

able source of hydraulic power and immediately purchased 150 acres from the Tibbetts estate. Work on the power station to take advantage of the falling water at the dam began in 1921 and was completed the following year. Its turbines were capable of developing 8,000 horsepower of electrical energy. The Ford plant construction also began in 1921 and was completed three years later. Since that time a wide variety of automobile parts have been manufactured at the Green Island plant. Before World War II a river-front shipping dock provided for the unloading of steel and assembled automobiles from Detroit which were distributed from the plant. For a time a small landing field allowed Henry Ford to swoop down in his tri-motor "Tin Goose" for occasional plant visits. Although the plant continues to produce replacement radiators, its future at this writing is uncertain.

Troy was still an important collar, cuff, and shirt manufacturing city well into the twentieth century. A 1923 survey by the Troy Chamber of Commerce indicated that approximately 10,000 women and men produced detachable collars and cuffs valued at approximately forty-three million dollars that year. Some of the companies that were manufacturing these products and shirts at that time included: Corliss, Coon and Company; Earl and Wilson; George P. Ide and Company; the James K. P. Pine Lion Factory; Van Zandt's; and Joseph Bowman and Sons. Cluett Peabody and Company, which had its origins in 1850, and has for many years marketed its products under the Arrow name, is the only major shirt company still located in the Gateway area. Though shirts are no longer manufactured here, the company maintains its Technical Service Headquarters subsidiary of the Sanforized Company in Troy. Regretfully, however, the firm recently moved the museum of collars, cuffs, and shirts from Troy to New York City. The old industry which made Troy the "collar city" is thus still alive, if barely. A firm that entered the detachable collar and cuff business as late as 1924, the Standard Manufacturing Co., Inc., is now located in the 100-year old James K.P. Lion of Troy factory in Lansingburgh where it now produces mens' and boys' outerwear jackets.

The old Harmony Mills are now called the Cohoes Industrial Terminal, Inc. and are occupied by companies including Barclay Home Products, Inc.; Swanknit, Inc.; and Troy Town Shirts. And so the textile industry lives on in special ways in the old company town.

One of the oldest industries in the Gateway, paper manufacturing, is still operating. The Mount Ida Paper

The Troy that never was. An artist's optimistic conception of Troy in the year 2016, drawn for the souvenir booklet of the Troy Centennial Celebration in 1916. Courtesy, Rensselaer County Historical Society

Mill operated up to 1962, but its closure signaled only a pause in the 300-year history of water power on the Poestenkill at Troy's Gorge. Having consolidated their operations in Green Island, the Manning Paper Company became a division of Hammermill Paper Company with a world-wide distributing system for their long-fibered manila stock. Another Gateway area paper manufacturer of equal note is the Mohawk Paper Mills, Inc. of Cohoes and Waterford, manufacturers of the highest quality stock.

Only one manufacturing operation, the Mohawk Paper Mills, survives on what in the nineteenth century was the King Power Canal in Waterford. Gilbert, Murdock and Creighton founded the Enterprise Paper Company on the

Matton shipyard on Van Schaick Island in Cohoes originally built canal boats and later, as in this 1966 launching, police boats, tugboats, and barges. This shipyard, the last in the Gateway, closed in the fall of 1982. Photo by Gene Baxter

canal in the early nineteenth century. In 1931 George O'Connor of Waterford took over the failing Frank Gilbert Company mills in both Cohoes and Waterford. The company is still owned and led by a member of the O'Connor family, Thomas D. O'Connor.

Even in its most depressed twentieth-century days, the Gateway's economy has actually proven more solid than it appeared. Besides industry, New York State government and education have contributed largely to the area's viability. But now a new factor has been added that promises an even brighter future. It is the visionary contribution of the late George M. Low, the fourteenth president of Rensselaer Polytechnic Institute. Low had introduced both

incubator companies and the Rensselaer Technology Park as new components in the area's growth pattern.

Rensselaer Polytechnic Institute in the last decade has grown to become one of the leading technological universities in this country, in fact, in the world. The quality of the faculty has become an irresistible attraction to new high technology industries. And, of course, other Gateway area institutions of higher education, especially Hudson Valley Community College, have contributed to this attractive ambience. At present many new corporations or new subsidiaries of older companies, with names as old and famous as Bolt, Beranek and Newman, Inc. and as new and exciting as Bioreactor Technology, Inc., have set-

This was Cluett, Peabody & Co. and the collar shop district in Troy in the 1920s. Courtesy, Rensselaer County Historical Society

tled in the incubator space on the Rensselaer campus.

Two companies, National Semiconductor and Pac-AmOr Bearings, have built or are building plants at the Rensselaer Technology Park, south of Troy on the highlands overlooking the Hudson, and RPI has constructed multi-tenant facilities. In all, seven corporations have settled in the newly formed park making everything from cathode ray tubes to multi-player, cross-country board and card games. The park is expected to fill up gradually as the century ends, bringing new industries which are geared to keeping the U.S. at the forefront of progress. Besides these assets, Rensselaer Polytechnic Institute, in partnership with the State of New York, is currently building a huge Center for Industrial Innovation where campus research will aid corporations eager to stay at the cutting edge of world industrial development.

Over a decade ago when the Rensselaer County Historical Society formed a committee on preservation, it was decided to focus on industries and industrial properties. The

committee soon broke off from the parent organization to become the Hudson-Mohawk Industrial Gateway. Among its goals was the encouragement of continued operation of historic industries and preservation of historic industrial buildings and sites through adaptive reuse.

The early successes of the Gateway organization led to the establishment of the area as an urban cultural park, a concept that emphasizes special built areas as important cultural resources to be emphasized and preserved much as parklands are preserved. The Hudson-Mohawk Urban Cultural Park was established by the State Legislature in 1979, the first in New York State. Since that time a total of thirteen urban cultural parks, from lower New York City to the Niagara Frontier, have been established and the Gateway has been designated as the park that focuses on industry and labor. Recently on completion of a mandated management study plan, the area park was renamed Riverspark and a timetable set that will have the park completed in 1996. The continuing efforts of the Gateway area and Riverspark promise to make the region much more attractive to both new high-tech industry and to people who come to see sites associated with America's Industrial Revolution, giving the Gateway area both an additional purpose and an additional prominence. It is estimated that when the park is completed, 250,000 persons will visit the Hudson-Mohawk Gateway each year.

This is the architect's rendering of the Troy Savings Bank on Second Street designed by George B. Post and completed in 1875. The Music Hall, located on the upper level, is nationally renowned for its fine acoustics. It is home of the Troy Savings Bank Music Hall Corporation and Troy Chromatics which provide concerts of popular and classical music. Courtesy, Troy Savings Bank

Right: United Shirt and Collar Company of Lansingburgh produced this tin advertising sign circa 1900. The company's block-long building on Second Avenue is now occupied by Standard Manufacturing Company. Courtesy, Thomas Phelan

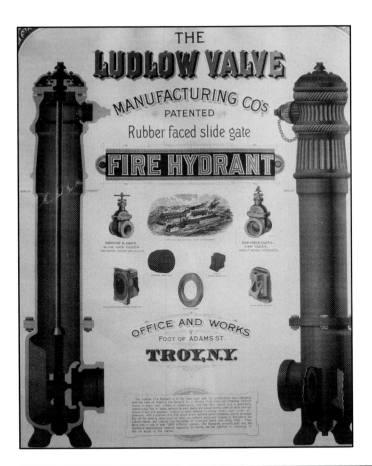

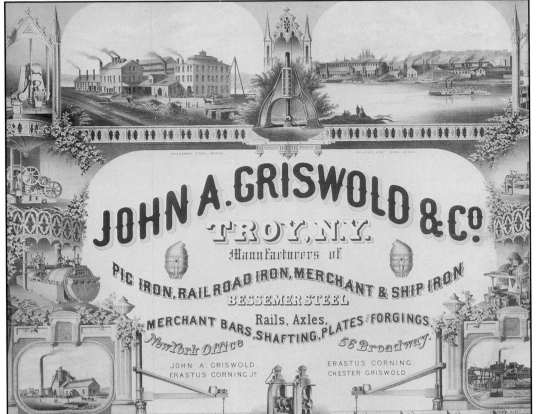

Above left: Ludlow Valve Manufacturing Company began in 1861 in Lansingburgh, moved to Waterford for several years, and then returned to Lansingburgh until 1896 when it took over the rail mill of the old Troy Iron and Steel Company on the banks of the Poestenkill. Courtesy, Thomas Phelan

Above right: The now-famous image of Uncle Sam originated with this 1917 U.S. Army recruiting poster by illustrator James Montgomery Flagg. Courtesy, Rensselaer County Historical Society

Left: This advertising lithograph was produced for John A. Griswold & Co. circa 1870. The Bessemer works in South Troy, established in 1865, were the first of their kind in the U.S. Located on the banks of the Hudson River near the Poestenkill, the Rensselaer Iron Works eventually became the Troy Iron & Steel Company. Courtesy, Rensselaer County Historical Society

Above: Poestenkill Gorge is depicted in this early-nineteenth-century lithograph made from a painting by T. Milbert. Benjamin Marshall developed the gorge in 1840 when he constructed a dam and 600-foot tunnel at the top of the upper falls to power his cotton mill. Courtesy, Rensselaer County Historical Society

Facing page: Troy was still a small port city in 1820, as seen in this engraving based on a watercolor by William Guy Wall. Water from the hills to the left was being used to run mills, but the Erie Canal was not yet completed, and the only bridges across the river were in Lansingburgh to the north. Courtesy, Rensselaer County Historical Society

Right: Major General John Ellis Wool was presented with this gold sword in 1848 for his service in the Mexican War. Photo by Greg Troop

Facing page: The Cohoes Music Hall, restored to its Victorian splendor in the early 1970s, provides a unique setting for a variety of theatrical and musical performances. Courtesy, Mendel, Mesick, Cohen, Waite, Hall Architects

Below: Margaret Olivia Slocum of Syracuse graduated from the Troy Female Seminary in 1847 and married New York financier Russell Sage in 1869. Following her husband's death, Mrs. Sage generously endowed many charities and founded Russell Sage College and the second campus of Emma Willard School.

Above: Troy was already beginning to outgrow the narrow strip of flat land along the Hudson River in 1848 when this lithograph was made. Directly above the people in the foreground are St. Paul's Episcopal Church and the newly completed First Baptist Church. Courtesy, Rensselaer County Historical Society

Right: This was the architect's rendering of William H. Frear & Co. department store. William Frear opened his grand "Troy Cash Bazaar" in 1897 and continued here until 1941. Courtesy, Rensselaer County Historical Society

Left: Proctor's Theater in Troy, now unused, provided entertainment for the Gateway for over 60 years. Opened in 1914 as a vaudeville theater, it switched to movies in the 1930s. It was purchased by a developer from New York City who plans to convert the office portion of the facility into an upscale hotel.

Facing page, top: This is the central tower of Harmony Mill #3 in Cohoes with a statue of Thomas Gardner, one of the mill's founders. Constructed between 1866 and 1872, the building was the largest cotton mill in the country with 1,600 operatives and 2,600 looms. Photo by Robert Chase

Bottom left: The acoustically-splendid Troy Savings Bank Music Hall has attracted not only music lovers but also ancillary recording companies and musical instrument shops. Photo by J. Malouf, www.albany.net/ ~jmalouf

Bottom right: A home along Third Street in Troy's famous Washington Park provides a typical example of the elegance to be found there. Photo by Sloane Bullough

Above, left: Downtown Troy storefronts provide the perfect setting for creative merchants to install Victorian-style window decorations. Photo by Sloane Bullough

Above, right: Noted architects Calvert Vaux and Frederick Withers designed the historic Hall-Rice Building, now used as incubator space for high-tech startup firms from Rensselaer Polytechnic Institute. Photo by Sid Brown

Right: The Anna M. Plum Memorial Hall, on the Russell Sage College campus, was designed by Troy architect Marcus Cummings for the Troy Female Seminary in the early 1890s. Photo by Robert Chase

Left: St. Mark's Church in Green Island is now a community center.

Below, left: The bright entrance to The Arts Center of the Capital Region adds life to the Monument Square region of downtown Troy. Photo by Dave Feiden. Courtesy, The Arts Center of the Capital Region

Below, right: St. Paul's Episcopal Church in Troy was remodeled in the 1890s with windows and furnishings designed by Tiffany and Holzer. Photo by Ned Pratt

Top: This trolley car was built in 1905 by the Jones Trolley Car Company of Watervliet. Jones streetcars were once used all over the world. This one is on display at the trolley museum in Kennebunkport, Maine. Photo by G. Steven Draper

Bottom: Dance is one of the many arts at The Arts Center of the Capital Region. Photo by Dave Feiden. Courtesy, The Arts Center of the Capital Region

Facing page, top: The annual arts festival at the Riverfront Park in Troy is sponsored by The Arts Center of the Capital Region.

Below, right: Nineteenth-century townhouses line the streets of downtown Troy near the commercial district. Photo by G. Steven Draper

Below, left: Troy's youth frolic in the water below the historic Mount Ida Falls in the Poestenkill Gorge. Photo by Sloane Bullough

Left: The first microbrewery in New York's Capital District, the award-winning Troy Pub & Brewery shares a commanding view of the Hudson River with its neighbors The River Street Café and The Troy Town Dock & Marina. Photo by Dave Saehrig

Below: A ladle car, once used for transporting molten iron, is one of the few reminders of the great Burden Iron Works and Republic Steel in South Troy. It now stands alongside the Burden Iron Works Museum at the Foot of Polk Street. Photo by G. Steven Draper

Above: The second most powerful waterfall east of the Mississippi, topped only by Niagara Falls, the Cohoes Falls provided the power that made Cohoes a major textile city. Photo by Denise Scammell

Below: As is obvious from an aerial view, the elevated ramps of the 1980 Collar City Bridge dwarf and decimate the brick mixed-use neighborhood at the foot of Hoosick Street in Troy. Photo by Sid Brown

The reconstructed Approach provides a popular vista upon downtown Troy from the western boundary of Rensselaer Polytechnic Institute. Photo by Sid Brown

CHAPTER ELEVEN

TRANSITION TO A POST-INDUSTRIAL WORLD

As fate would have it, the many heroic attempts to revive the Gateway communities in the 1970s and 1980s faced some unanticipated hurdles, and only after these were overcome would the hurdles eventually lead to some positive outcomes. Perhaps most importantly, at just about that time, the nation and indeed the entire world began to experience a massive cultural transformation similar to that pioneered in nineteenth-century Troy, when the country metamorphosed from a rural-agrarian culture to an urban-industrial, or modern, one. At the time, pundits tried vaguely to understand the oncoming changes in books like Alvin Toffler's *Future Shock* and in terms such as the "second industrial revolution." No one, however, understood at all clearly back then how what is now described as an emerging, post-modern, post-industrial, global economy would affect the fortunes of a struggling region such as the Gateway. But affect it this transformation did indeed, as it did most of the other embattled urban areas of North America.

The indicators of the arrival of this new worldwide political economy were subtle in the Gateway communities—a "made in China" appearing on the bottom of a coffee mug, computerized cash registers in checkout lines, the appearance of instructions in a half-dozen languages in owners' manuals for consumer products—but the implications for what would and would not work for cities like Troy or Cohoes were profound. Aerospace and shipbuilding innovations had teamed with land-based highway and trucking developments to link the entire planet via breathtakingly inexpensive transportation. In a city like Troy, it was once so rare to see a tropical pineapple that wrought-iron images of them on the finials of the ornamental ironwork in front of a home bespoke the wealth of the occupants and their hospitality in sharing such a rarity with guests. In contrast, with the coming of global transportation systems, Troy's everyday consumers could daily find fresh pineapples and much more in vast supermarkets that had reduced the offerings of corner grocers to cigarettes, milk, lottery tickets, and an occasional ethnic specialty. Satellites, undersea fiber-optic cabling, and a breathtaking increase in the speed, capacity, and affordability of electronic computers revolutionized communication, making a global village in which to grow the global economy. It became profitable for major magazines to arrange for all the slips containing the names and addresses of new subscribers to be routed through a central consolidating facility in Ohio, shipped by the ton to Ireland for data entry by low-wage English-speaking clerks, and then conveyed electronically back to the United States for instant use.

Under such circumstances, the strategy of retaining traditional high-paying manufacturing industries in the Gateway region had a very limited chance of success indeed. In October 1989, for example, both Cluett-Peabody in the collar district of north-central Troy, and Portec, Inc., in the iron-working heart of South Troy, closed their doors. The rise of the Sunbelt had already killed much rust belt manufacturing. By 1990, the rise of the "Asian tiger" nations, the World Trade Organization, and the North American Free Trade Agreement (NAFTA) was killing even more. To be sure, a healthy sprinkling of firms remained in the area. Indeed, at the dawn of the new millennium two firms in Troy, the Ross Valve Manufacturing Co., Inc., and the Bruno Machinery Corp., find themselves forced to relocate elsewhere in the region not by a decline in sales but by the need to expand to accommodate their growth into global marketplaces. But the proportion of the region's economy represented by heavy manufacturing is nothing compared to its nineteenth-century heyday, giving the term "reindustrialization" an antique flavor in discussions about the future of the Gateway communities. Compounding that phenomenon

Above: A symbolic pineapple adorns an ornate finial along downtown Troy's architecturally resplendent Second Street. Photo by Sloane Bullough

Left: Once jammed with employees, a fully-modern manufacturing facility stands virtually idle at the Watervliet Arsenal. U.S. Army photo

was the collapse of the Soviet Union and the end of the Cold War, which led to a precipitous decrease in business for such Gateway facilities as the Watervliet Arsenal, which by the year 2000 saw its employment drop from its World War II peak of roughly 10,000 to under 500.

The rise of the global economy also reinforced the threats to traditional cities already posed by the appearance of the automobile suburbs. Wired, computerized "edge cities" began to spring up alongside bedroom communities outside the Gateway proper, in places like Clifton Park and Halfmoon and Malta where one had seen nothing but cornfields, cow pastures, and woodlands a mere two decades earlier. This undermined the hopes of those supporting the "urban renewal" movement of the 1960s and 1970s, which had bulldozed hundreds of urban brownstones and similar structures in downtowns like Troy in the hope that more up-to-date cityscapes would rise from the rubble. Compounding the problem, transportation improvements continued to focus on the automobile and on suburban models, leading to the obliteration of riverfronts to make way for Interstates and, in the case of Troy, the radical redesign of the collar and cuff district by the choice of an elevated rampway for the Collar City Bridge on Hoosick Street that overshadowed the area with a concrete overpass and hastened the deterioration of the surrounding residential neighborhood.

Meanwhile, populated by increasingly computerized, globalized chain retailers, glitzy suburban mega-malls, most notably the Crossgates Mall in nearby Guilderland,

undermined any attempts at keeping department-store-style retail in urban downtowns. Consequently, the noble attempt to undo the damage of wholesale urban renewal demolitions by building the Uncle Sam Atrium indoor shopping mall in downtown Troy failed to lure a critical mass of shoppers from suburbia, and one by one the retailers in the Atrium closed their doors. For a brief while, various Gateway communities attracted some significant shoppers to "factory outlet" destinations, first in former mill complexes such as the Harmony Mills and then in custom-built facilities such as the Cohoes Fashions department store. In the year 2000, however, Cohoes Fashions relocated to Crossgates Mall, and the discounts available in suburban "big box" retailers such as Wal-Mart had undermined the main attraction of the outlet marts, namely, the prospect of bargains.

Compounding all these challenges were a series of financial setbacks at the national, state, and local levels. The early 1980s witnessed a variety of federal budget changes, such as the elimination in 1983 of the Comprehensive Employment and Training Act (CETA) worker program that had helped fund various projects in the Gateway communities. There was also a spike of unemployment that peaked at 10.6 per cent in late 1982, which weakened the tax base in hard-hit states such as New York. When employment rose again in the later 1980s, and when the ample Reagan budgets fueled something of an economic boom in the mid-1980s, however, upstate New York did not partake heartily in that growth. To the

The uninviting "recreational" space below the ramps of the Collar City Bridge attracts only an occasional resident and no visitors. Photo by Sloane Bullough

contrary, the Reagan prosperity reinforced the ability of other regions of the country to compete with Gateway cities for businesses and young citizens.

The arrival of a far more widespread national recession in 1989-1990 hit the Gateway communities—and indeed much of the surrounding area—particularly hard. Long-established businesses, like Cluett and Portec, closed their doors, driving up the need for social services in the inner cities. Municipal revenues, however, declined as the need for them increased. First, the 1980s boom in real estate prices went flat, compromising urban property tax revenues in upstate New York. Second, and simultaneously, New York State revenues tightened, and appropriations to Gateway communities declined accordingly. For example, appropriations to the New York State Council on the Arts were drastically slashed, which stunned the many not-for-profit cultural organizations working to revive places like Troy. Exacerbating the effect of the State budget cutbacks were the layoffs of State workers in the Gateway region. Meanwhile, as "downsizing" became a corporate commonplace throughout the country, General Electric continued to scale down its workforce in nearby Schenectady to a tenth its size at the end of World War II, putting an even greater strain upon the region's attempts at economic and cultural revival.

All the Gateway communities struggled to cope with these setbacks, but nowhere was the effect as devastating as in Troy. Several promising initiatives there were stalled when the municipal government found itself facing staggering budget deficits. Instead of drastically cutting expenses (which would have reduced services to barely-acceptable levels at best) or increasing taxes (which were already high enough to discourage homeownership), city leaders opted for a complicated scheme of financing that included such features as the mortgaging of City Hall to pay operating expenses. After six straight years of deficits, the city's financial rating had dropped below junk bond status, leaving it unable to float any additional debt. Only through a bailout by the New York State Legislature in 1995, which required the management of Troy's budget by a five-member Supervisory Board chaired by the New York State Comptroller, was municipal bankruptcy avoided. Other Gateway cities were more fortunate than Troy at this time, but all faced challenges.

Just when the situation was looking particularly dire, several new departures began to take root, portending some exciting developments as they matured. In one way or another, all of them grew from a cultural movement

Below: Second Street, as it approaches Broadway in downtown Troy, presents a classic example of the kind of downtown streetscape most desired by the New Urbanism. Photo by Sid Brown

that would come to be known as the "New Urbanism," championed by some maverick architects and publicized by enthusiasts such as Roberta Brandes Gratz in *Cities Back from the Edge,* and nearby Saratoga Springs author James Howard Kunstler in *The Geography of Nowhere.* A revolt against suburban values, the New Urbanism condemned the ongoing conversion of open spaces outside the city into housing developments and strip malls, branding it with the name "sprawl." It also rejected suburban zoning codes that required such features as setbacks for retail facilities, huge streetside parking lots, and the elimination of sidewalks. In place of these suburban landscapes, the New Urbanists offered the traditional downtown village streetscape, with welcoming store windows lining curbside sidewalks, human-scale pocket parks, and other pedestrian-friendly amenities. In addi-

"*I want you two to meet some people who just bought a fabulous five-story brownstone with a garden in Troy, New York.*"

tion, this school of reformers advocated mixed use zoning, so that people could live, shop, work, go to school, worship, and play entirely on foot, face-to-face with others. Finally, the formula called for putting people back in touch with natural features such as waterways and green spaces.

Such a movement made a perfect fit with the communities of the Gateway region, possessed as they are with river frontage and quaint downtowns designed around mixed-use, pedestrian living. As disenchantment with the sterility and the commuting congestion of suburban life increased, certain groups such as healthy "empty nesters" began opting to become "urban pioneers" and to reinvest in downtown living. Others already living a cosmopolitan life began relocating to the less-expensive Hudson-Mohawk area from larger cities where costs were skyrocketing. As recent Census figures indicate, the arrival of such newcomers has not yet stopped the downward trend in the Gateway area's urban population, but it has slowed the trend down. In addition, such new arrivals have infused new cultural life into these cities.

In Troy, part of this new vitality has taken on the coloration of an urban arts subculture. Starting over two decades earlier, a dedicated band of arts champions, led by Raona Roy, slowly built up the Rensselaer County Council for the Arts into a powerful regional presence, eventually changing its name to the Arts Center of the Capital Region. With considerable creativity, they took ownership of five contiguous downtown buildings, raised over $5 million for renovations, and converted nearly a half-block

of the city into a state-of-the-art facility for artists and artisans to produce and display their craft. Around that base is beginning to grow a host of ancillary components of an urban arts subculture, including several new art galleries, a row of antiques stores, a crafts cooperative, and loft space occupied by urban arts pioneers from elsewhere. Complementing that are some spin-offs from the acoustically-superb Troy Savings Bank Music Hall, namely, the recording firm Dorian Recordings and some musical instrument shops, and the arrival in 1992 of the New York State Theatre Institute on the campus of Russell Sage College. The consequent arts-based revival is akin to the revitalization of the TriBeCa area of Manhattan in New York City.

In a related development, a cluster of preservation-oriented architects, artisans, designers, and other professionals have begun restoring a section of town they have dubbed "The Pottery District," lending further momentum to an urban resettlement movement that, arguably, got its start in Troy in the revival of the city's famed Washington Park. Like Gramercy Park in New York City, after which the

Above: The annual sidewalk drawing competition at downtown Troy's Riverfront Arts Fest attracts both chalk artists and throngs of admirers. Photo by Dave Feiden. Courtesy, The Arts Center of the Capital Region

Left: The luxurious Paine Mansion near Second and State streets in downtown Troy was the site of several important interior scenes for Martin Scorsese's The Age of Innocence. *Photo by Sloane Bullough*

Top: A Dreamworks crew sprays Troy's Second Street with artificial snow in preparation for a pivotal scene in The Time Machine. *Photo by Sloane Bullough*

Bottom: One of the few cities in the Upper Hudson area to have avoided the construction of a highway bypass along its waterfront, Troy enjoys a number of convenient riverfront overlooks. Photo by Honorah Donovan

Troy variant was modeled, Troy's Washington Park is one of the nation's rare privately-owned city parks.

Reinforcing the appeal of Troy as the place where the New Urbanism could first take root in the Gateway region are certain features of its surviving infrastructure. First and foremost, despite the loss of some 500 buildings during the ill-fated enthusiasm for "urban renewal," the city retains some of the nation's finest surviving downtown houses and storefronts from the Victorian era. Indeed, the streetscapes in Troy have been so appealing that filmmakers have repeatedly used them as a backdrop for period-piece location shooting. A considerable part of Martin Scorsese's *The Age of Innocence* was shot in Troy, as were portions of *The Bostonians, Ironweed, The Scent of a Woman,* and most recently, *The Time Machine.*

Second, while many of the other cities of the Gateway region have endured the construction of Interstate highways along their rivers, cutting off their downtowns from their waterways, Troy enjoys an almost unspoiled waterfront, particularly in the downtown area. As the New Urbanism has caught on, various efforts have been made to capitalize upon the river's appeal. Among the earlier waterfront developments was the opening of several eateries with a river view, including the award-winning River Street Café,

Above: Pleasure boaters form some of the more colorful and exotic of the tourists who are now coming to Troy to sample its attractions. Photo by Sid Brown

Right: A stunning stained-glass window by Tiffany associate Maitland Armstrong joins with equally stunning marble, onyx, and mosaic appointments to inspire visitors to the Gardner Earl Memorial Chapel and Crematorium at Troy's Oakwood Cemetery. Photo by Denise Scammell

the Troy Pub and Brewery (the Capital Region's first brewpub), and the Castaways (currently being returned to its original status as a chain restaurant after its intermediate owner's recent death). Later, a block of former riverfront warehouses were converted into the Quayside Apartments, some with spectacular riverfront views.

In combination, the attractions of the arts, quality restaurants, stunning architecture, and a welcoming riverfront have begun to attract a modest visitor and tourist clientele for Troy. Certain other features of the city lure still further visitors. For example, it is at least arguable that Troy has more Tiffany windows per square mile than any other downtown in the nation. Particularly striking is St. Paul's Episcopal Church, with an entire interior designed by Tiffany Studios, St. John's Episcopal Church, with its renowned five-lancet all-landscape Tiffany depiction of "St. John's Vision of the Holy City," the Hart Memorial Library's Tiffany rendering of printer and typographer Aldus demonstrating the octavo-format book to a gathering of Venetian admirers, and the huge number of Tiffany windows in St. Joseph's Roman Catholic Church in South Troy. Patriotic visitors come to see the city where Samuel Wilson lived and is buried, because Wilson is generally considered to be the inspiration for the national symbol, Uncle Sam. The romantic come to see the storefront of the *Troy Sentinel* newspaper, which on 23 December 1823 became the first place in the world to publish a rendering of "A Visit from St. Nicholas," the holiday poem better known by its first line, "Twas the Night before Christmas." Those curious about nineteenth-century lifestyles have come to Troy to see the marvelously well-preserved and well-documented Hart-Cluett Mansion, headquarters of the Rensselaer County Historical Society. As the nation shows increasing interest in North America's industrial heritage, Troy and the other Gateway communities have also attracted those wishing to see such sites as: the place where the replacement for the Liberty Bell was cast; the remains of the Erie Canal; the birthplace of Arrow collars and shirts; the spectacular Harmony Mills of Cohoes; the Hudson Mohawk Industrial Gateway's Burden Iron Works Museum; and the former home of Kate Mullaney, founder of the first truly all-female labor union in the United States.

Complementing all these facets of New Urbanism is a different kind of post-modern development that brings back to the Gateway communities something that was once a hallmark of the region. In the early to mid-1800s, the Hudson-Mohawk area witnessed a deliberate, coordinated attempt by a self-conscious elite to make cutting-edge technology the focus for the prosperity of the region. The record-breaking Erie Canal, Henry Burden's giant wheel and horseshoe machine, South Troy's Bessemer plant, the innovative design of the *U.S.S. Monitor*, the use of aluminum in surveying instruments at W. & L.E. Gurley, and the introduction of the detachable collar were just a few of the more striking indicators of the willingness of the Gateway's nineteenth-century leaders to depart radically from tradition and to outpace others in making progress toward the modern industrialized world. That phenomenon bears a striking resemblance to the strategy pursued by Frederick Terman at Stanford University, and others in his circle, to transform the apricot orchards of the Santa Clara Valley in California into high-technology computer firms. In certain respects, then, one might think of the Gateway region as a sort of "Silicon Valley" for the nineteenth century. In the past ten years, seeds planted by the visionary George Low, late President of Rensselaer Polytechnic Institute in the 1970s and early 1980s, have grown into a full-blown regional effort to transform the Gateway area into "Tech Valley." Already the enterprise is bearing fruit, with the Institute's Technology Park filling with first-rate firms such as MapInfo Corporation, a

First Lady Hillary Rodham Clinton (shown here with an actor portraying Kate Mullaney, founder of the first truly all-female labor union in the United States) shows a gift from the City of Troy, and prepared by the Hudson Mohawk Industrial Gateway, as she declares the Kate Mullaney House a National Historic Landmark. Photo by Sid Brown

Left: First Lady Hillary Rodham Clinton presented this bronze plaque for installation at the home of Kate Mullany, American labor pioneer. Photo by Sloane Bullough

Former NASA Adminstrator and Rensselaer Polytechnic Institute President George Low breaks ground for the Rensselaer Technology Park. Photo by Thomas V. Griffin. Courtesy, Rensselaer Polytechnic Institute

successful development of an undergraduate student project, and other promising high-tech firms such as Intermagnetics General, Albany Molecular Research, and Molecular Opto-Electronics Corporation (MOEC) taking root elsewhere in the area. Adding significant momentum is Rensselaer's current President, Shirley Ann Jackson. She recently procured for Rensselaer the largest single academic gift in the history of American higher education, an anonymous unrestricted $360 million donation that, among other things, will allow the university to move aggressively into both biotechnology and the electronic arts.

One particularly striking feature of the Tech Valley phenomenon is its occasional tendency to blend the past and the future in creative ways. For example, the headquarters of the Rensselaer Technology Park is not located in a gleaming glass cube, but rather occupies the historic DeFreest House, the home of the Dutch family that originally farmed the land where the Technology Park is now located. Similarly, Rensselaer Polytechnic Institute has teamed up with the Troy Savings Bank and TAP, Inc., a local architectural services firm, to rehabilitate the historic Hall/Rice Building in downtown Troy, designed by famous architects Calvert Vaux and Frederick Withers and filmed by Martin Scorsese in *The Age of Innocence*, as incubator space for high-tech startup firms. It has also teamed up with Gurley Precision Instruments to convert the top two floors of the landmark Gurley Building in downtown Troy into the world-class Lighting Research Center, prompting punsters to quip—justifiably—that the Gateway community's future is looking brighter again.

To some extent, the Gateway communities can credit this astonishing turnaround from the dire situation of a decade or so ago to the nationwide economic boom of the 1990s and to the newfound attraction of cities to at least a sophisticated cosmopolitan sub-population. But many other cities in upstate New York have fared far more poorly than the Gateway communities have done during this time. Consequently, the credit for capitalizing on the trends of the later 1990s also should go very largely to support from some visionary political and other allies.

Without question, the most important figure in this regard is New York State Senator Joseph L. Bruno. Elected to the New York State Senate in 1976, Senator Bruno has been Senate Majority Leader and President Pro Tem since 1995. A strong advocate of economic development and public-private partnerships to foster it, he has worked closely with Rensselaer Polytechnic Institute to cultivate the Rensselaer Technology Park. When the City of Troy

Left: New York State Senate Majority Leader Joseph L. Bruno announces a $1 million state grant to assist in the restoration of the historic Hart-Cluett Mansion, headquarters of the Rensselaer County Historical Society. Courtesy, Office of Senator Joseph L. Bruno

Right: Mark S. Rea, director of the world-famous Lighting Research Center, confers with LRC researcher John Bullough outside the entrance to their newly-renovated facility on the top two floors of the historic Gurley Building in downtown Troy. Photo by Sloane Bullough

began tottering on the brink of bankruptcy, he helped pass statewide Distressed Cities Aid legislation that has funneled several million dollars of state money into Troy's operating budget, allowing it to stave off creditors while it paved streets, replaced worn-out equipment, and otherwise engaged in its recovery. In addition to finding support for dozens of smaller projects, Senator Bruno has also secured several substantial and critical grants for various heritage and high-technology initiatives in the greater Troy area. He has been instrumental in finding subventions in the millions of dollars for the Arts Center project, for the Rice Building renovation,

Above: A lighting system designed by the Lighting Research Center's Watts Up program illuminates the historic Rice Building in downtown Troy. Photo by Jennifer Brons, designer of this lighting system

Right: Shirley Ann Jackson, President of Rensselaer Polytechnic Institute, speaks at her inauguration not long before landing for her institution a $360 million donation, thereby setting a record for the largest single gift ever made to an American college or university. Photo by Fred Ricard. Courtesy, Rensselaer Polytechnic Institute

for the restoration of the Hart-Cluett Mansion, for the Troy headquarters of the New York State Theatre Institute, for the conversion of the old Rensselaer County Jail into a state-of-the-art Family Court facility, and for the conversion of Rensselaer Polytechnic Institute's Winslow Building into a new, state-of-the-art Junior Museum, with a world-class planetarium donated by Kenneth and Thelma Lally. Also critical to the revival of at least Troy in the Gateway region has been Senator Bruno's involvement in transferring the offices of many hundreds of New York State employees to the Collar City. This move has infused new life into vacant downtown office space, allowing the conversion of the failing Uncle Sam Atrium into a bustling workplace, the conversion of the old Cluett, Peabody headquarters into the equally busy Hedley Park Place (named after its visionary owner, John Hedley), and the conversion of another collar factory into the Flanigan Square office complex, named after the locally-revered Father Thomas Flanigan from St. Peter's Roman Catholic Church.

Supplementing all this assistance have been a number of New York State programs that have been particularly helpful to the Gateway communities. In 1992, New York transferred control of the New York State Canal (including the former Erie Canal) to the New York State Thruway Authority, beginning a string of changes in the way the canal is utilized as a resource. In 1996 under current Governor George E. Pataki, $32 million was devoted to a Canal Revitalization Program aimed at bolstering the recreational uses of the Canal system. These changes have resulted in an appreciable increase in the use of the Canal

The Rensselaer County Court, formerly the Rensselaer County Jail, provides a stunning example of adaptive use. Courtesy, John G. Waite Associates, Architects

as a heritage and recreational resource, which has had particularly beneficial effects in Waterford, where a new Visitor Center alongside the Canal has attracted considerable traffic.

Along the Hudson River, the creation in 1991 of the Hudson River Valley Greenway, spearheaded by then-Assemblyman Maurice D. Hinchey, launched a state-level attempt to facilitate the cultivation of the Hudson River Valley as a regional resource. In 1996, then-Congressman Hinchey followed that with sponsorship of federal legislation to create a Hudson River Valley National Heritage Area, managed by the Greenway, that promises in the upcoming decade to provide some $10 million in federal funds to assist in the development of the Hudson River as a resource. Greenway and National Heritage Area support have provided assistance to a number of Gateway-area projects. Meanwhile, Congressman Mike McNulty has been especially devoted to finding private partners to occupy the vacated manufacturing capacity of the Watervliet Arsenal. Also of particular importance has been the creation in 1993 of the state's Environmental Protection Fund, supplemented in 1996 by the state's Clean Water/Clean Air Bond Act, which has been heavily promoted by Governor Pataki. These sources of funds have also helped make possible a number of the initiatives mentioned in this chapter.

In Troy, a critical catalyst for the ongoing revival has been Mark P. Pattison, who in 1995 was elected the first "strong" mayor of the city in over three decades following

The Hart Memorial Library in downtown Troy is one of many facilities in the Gateway region to be helped by a grant from the 1993 New York State Environmental Protection Fund. Photo by Sid Brown

Facing page, top: The new Waterford Visitor Center attracts considerable boat traffic near Lock 2 of the New York State Canal. Photo by Edmund J. Hunea

Facing page, bottom: In the center of this photograph, the New York State Canal heads west from the Hudson River through Waterford. Photo by Sid Brown

the citizenry's vote to restore strong-mayor governance as a response to the fiscal crisis. Descended from a family that has been in Troy for over 200 years, Pattison quickly cut budgets, refinanced the city's debt, and convinced the City Council to approve controversial tax hikes that brought the municipal budget back into the black. Operating on a shoestring ever since, he has nonetheless been creative at finding outside funding to refurbish the downtown area. He has similarly revived Troy's *RiverSpark* Visitor Center with help from Marine Midland Bank (now HSBC Bank USA), the Troy Savings Bank, and the Chase Manhattan Foundation, at the same time that he concentrated its efforts on marketing downtown retail interests. He has also built fruitful public-private partnerships with the various not-for-profits working to promote the city.

At the core of those partnerships has been the Troy Redevelopment Foundation, formed by five of the largest not-for-profit entities in Troy (Emma Willard School, Northeast Health, Rensselaer Polytechnic Institute, the Sage Colleges, and Seton Health). Spearheaded by the heads of all five organizations, in 1995 it made a commitment to provide $400,000 annually for five years to assist Troy in its revival. These funds have helped to reconstruct

Facing page, top: Troy Mayor Mark P. Pattison, right, assists Troy Gateway Initiative Director Jeff Paules to beautify one of the entrances to the City of Troy. Photo by Craig Pettinger. Courtesy, Troy City Hall

Facing page, bottom: Revitalized via a partnership among the City of Troy, the Hudson Mohawk Industrial Gateway, the Troy Redevelopment Foundation, HSBC Bank USA, the Troy Savings Bank, and the Chase Manhattan Foundation, Troy's RiverSpark Visitor Center orients tourists amid a theme of labor and industry. Photo by Sid Brown

Garrett Hamlin, who helps promote Troy home ownership for TAP, Inc., enjoys a moment of reflection in his own historic home on Second Street in downtown Troy. Photo by Donna Abott Vlahos. Courtesy, Capital District Business Review

the famous Approach on the hillside connecting the downtown with the Rensselaer Polytechnic Institute campus. They have helped to rebuild the Broadway Corridor downtown and to wire that corridor for the Internet. Among other things, they have also helped to revitalize Congress Street, to reopen Troy's *RiverSpark* Visitor Center, and to attract artists to live and work in Troy. Complementing that partnership has been the Sage/ TRIP Home Ownership Incentive Program, a campaign assembled of many components by visionary President Jeanne Neff of the Sage Colleges and the not-for-profit Troy Rehabilitation and Improvement Program (TRIP) to encourage single-family homeownership in the area around Russell Sage College. In March 1999, with the strong encouragement of Senator Bruno, the many parties undertaking to revive Troy in one way or another have united together in a long-term planning exercise known as "Historic Troy 2020." Its leaders aim to build a broad consensus in the community for steps that should be taken to ensure the long-term revival of Troy.

Following Troy's lead, a number of the other Gateway communities have shown similar eagerness to get on the "New Urbanism" bandwagon. Just a few examples will make the case. In Waterford, a consortium of boosters has been making good progress at cultivating the town's canal frontage as a tourist destination. In nearby Cohoes, a new young mayor, John McDonald, has taken budget-controlling steps similar to those employed by Mayor Pattison, and he is now pushing eagerly for the development of the historic Harmony Mills complex as a high-tech zone. The identification of the site as ideal for this purpose by a study team from Milan, and the recent purchase of

Top: Purchased by an experienced developer of industrial sites in the New York City area, the historic Harmony Mills complex of Cohoes is beginning a revival as loft space. Photo by Sloane Bullough

Bottom: Father Christmas greets children on the streets of downtown Troy during one of its most charming moments, the annual Victorian Stroll. Photo by Sid Brown

the facility by a sympathetic developer, bode well for ultimate success. Elsewhere in town, the local Peter Gansevoort Chapter of the Daughters of the American Revolution (DAR) is on the brink of purchasing the historic Van Schaick House, the charming site of important planning for the Battle of Saratoga and similar significant events. Helping in that regard is a recent grant from New York State's Clean Water/Clean Air Bond Act program, plus strong interest from Governor Pataki's new Revolutionary War Trail initiative for New York State. The Town of Colonie has also benefited from similar state grants as it has sought to attract tourist attention to the archaeological treasures at their Schuyler Flatts historic site. In Green Island, New York State Assemblyman Ron Canestrari has secured $1 million in infrastructure funding for Molecular Opto-Electronic Corporation (MOEC), a rapidly-expanding incubator firm at Rensselaer Polytechnic Instiute, to retain their corporate headquarters near the banks of the Hudson River in this municipality. Meanwhile, a little further south, the recently-formed Watervliet Business and Technology Partnership has just secured the first of what it hopes will be many private corporate tenants to make use of the reserve capacity of the Watervliet Arsenal. Congressman Mike McNulty and Senator Charles Schumer have teamed to lobby aggressively for federal contracts at the Arsenal.

All these recent developments show every sign of undoing the setbacks of roughly a decade ago. Perhaps most important, they no longer focus nostalgically on "returning" to a bygone regional formula based on the Industrial Age. Instead, taken together, they provide a new formulation for a fast-changing world, an emerging alternative to the increasingly maligned suburban sprawl and an antidote to road rage and other maladies of the mall era in American history. At the same time, this new formulation is maturing in tandem with a growing national appreciation for the nation's industrial heritage, offering hope that heritage tourism can complement the postmodern core of the region's rebirth. Although much further work is necessary on this score, the emerging partnerships among government, business, academe, and the not-for-profits; the broad cooperation among proponents of "Tech Valley;" and the collaborations among communities up and down the Hudson River and all along the New York State Canal system; promise a coordinated approach to building the region's future. Indicative of the success of the recent strategies for the Gateway communities has been an increasing stream of positive media pieces about the Gateway communities. The tourism sections of both *Newsday* and the *Washington Times* have recently included positive reports on the tourism experience in the Upper Hudson region. Not long ago, *Hudson Valley Magazine* chose a Tiffany windows tour in Troy as the top event of the month for the entire Hudson River Valley. The *New York Times* provided very positive coverage of Troy's remarkable economic recovery.

And the various "Tech Valley" developments are getting national mention in the high-technology and venture capital press, especially after the announcement of Rensselaer Polytechnic Institute's $360 million gift. With a little luck, the Gateway region can look forward to becoming the poster child for the post-suburban recovery of America's cities and a major player in the global economy of the twenty-first century. If so, it will exemplify the wisdom of simultaneously acting and thinking at the local, the regional, and the global levels—a decidedly post-industrial and new role for one of the industrial centers of the New World.

A new iron gateway into Russell Sage College, designed by Lepera & Ward, PC, adds character to a revitalized Congress Street in downtown Troy. Photo by Sloane Bullough

Following page: A period replica street lamp frames the view of downtown Troy looking westward from the renovated Approach of Rensselaer Polytechnic Institute. Such appointments help signal Troy's accommodation to the New Urbanism. Photo by Sloane Bullough

CHRONICLES OF LEADERSHIP

If there is a single determining factor in the development of the Hudson-Mohawk Gateway area, it has to be water. Not the water of the prehistoric Lake Albany which covered the area about 20,000 years ago (although that left its contribution in iron-molder's sand), but the water that has flowed and bubbled down out of the glacial remnant hills to the two scenic rivers—the Hudson and the Mohawk—pausing on its way to turn mill wheels.

It is the water of the rivers themselves which has carried the boats of trade into and out of the area.

The land now occupied by Troy and Watervliet, being at the head of navigation on the Hudson, was a natural place for explorers and settlers to break their journeys, Because they found tillable land, they soon needed gristmills, and the streams tumbling down from the hill country provided the power.

The settlers also used the rivers to transport the crops of their fields to the markets down the river and to bring back needed goods.

Second to the abundant water—and contingent upon it—is technology, a factor that today outreaches water in its importance. This started with the development of machinery and the installation of mills along the waterways.

This, in turn, brought more people into the area and, with them, more providers of the services people need. Banking came early to the Gateway area because the wealthy mill owners saw a way to help their employees and themselves in the business of money handling. Prominent among the industries were the cotton and iron mills, and their natural offspring: shirt, collar, and stove making.

Schools and colleges followed—the earliest and most important being Emma Willard School and Rensselaer Polytechnic Institute in Troy. Many of the future engineers who learned their life's skills at RPI remained in the area to work in existing businesses and often to start their own new ones. Today the Gateway area is synonymous with the term "high tech."

With education and industry, culture couldn't be far behind.

Troy had a wide variety of theaters in its early days-businesses that no longer exist—and both Troy and Cohoes built elaborate music halls in the later nineteenth century. Those halls are in use today; Troy's has never closed and the Cohoes hall reopened after renovation several years ago.

The Gateway cities were known too for the contributions made by their ethnic "pockets" of Frenchmen, Italians, Armenians, Ukranians, Germans, Danes, and others, most of whom came to the area to work in one or another of the industries.

Much of the manufacturing has moved elsewhere or has changed in character. Most of the theaters have closed and been torn down or remodeled. Banks still flourish and education has assumed increased importance in the area. In the Hudson-Mohawk Gateway the computer has replaced the mill wheel.

The organizations whose stories are detailed on the following pages have chosen to support this important literary and civic project. They illustrate the variety of ways in which individuals and their businesses have contributed to the growth and development of the Hudson-Mohawk Gateway. The civic involvement of the region's businesses, learning institutions, and local governments, in partnership with its citizens, has made the Gateway an exceptional place to live and work.

ALBANY INTERNATIONAL AIRPORT

The Legacy of A Century of Heroes and Progress: America's oldest municipal airport was born in Albany almost a century ago. What was once a tiny, crude landing strip has evolved into Albany International Airport, today serving as a major transportation center for the Capital Region, upstate New York and western New England. A parade of national figures, events and site changes have marked the airport's evolution through the decades.

The first "airport" was located on a former polo field three miles north of the city and quickly proved inadequate. A year later, in 1909, the airport was transferred to Westerlo Island, south of Albany, where it was originally maintained through a special fund provided by the Albany Chamber of Commerce.

The airport became part of aviation history on May 10, 1910 when Glenn Curtiss, an adventurer and manufacturer, shattered a long-distance flight record of 24 miles by piloting his *Albany Flier* biplane from the Westerlo field to New York City, a journey of 143 miles. Curtiss stopped only once to refuel south of Poughkeepsie. His feat christened Albany as home to the nation's first municipal airport. As for Curtiss, the flight marked his successful passage as bicycle maker to motorcycle manufacturer to airplane assembler, all of which took place at Hammondsport in the Finger Lakes Region of New York.

Albany's Westerlo Island municipal airport was eventually named Quentin Roosevelt Field to honor the youngest son of former New York Governor Theodore Roosevelt. Quentin was killed in July 1918 while flying on a mission behind enemy lines, only four months before World War I ended.

On July 27, 1927, soon after his historic trans-Atlantic flight from New York to Paris, Charles Lindbergh landed his *Spirit of Saint Louis* at Quentin Roosevelt Field, part of his

Albany Airport terminal and air traffic control tower circa 1950s.

triumphant 22,000-mile tour of the United States. Amelia Earhart, Jimmy Doolittle and Clarence Chamberland were other great pilots who touched down in Albany during aviation's early years.

As air travel increased, Albany's progressive mayor, John Boyd Thatcher, urged creation of a new, modern airport and spearheaded preparations for a site to be located on farmland owned by the Watervliet Shaker Community. Thatcher said a city "without foresight" could soon fall victim to changing times. The Shakers sold the land to Albany in 1928, when construction began. The Shakers continued to play an important part by loaning machinery and tools to work crews and by often sharing lunch with them.

The new airport, located on Albany-Shaker Road, originally occupied 249 acres with two brick hangars and three runways. Albany Municipal Airport was opened for westbound mail on June 1, 1928. In October, flights out of Montreal carried passengers and mail to Albany and Newark, New Jersey.

In 1932, Governor Franklin D. Roosevelt flew from Albany Airport to Chicago to capture the presidential nomination at the National Democratic Convention. Will Rogers noted that FDR's Albany flight gave commercial aviation an immeasurable boost. Presidential candidates who have flown into Albany include John F. Kennedy and Richard M. Nixon.

Aviator Douglas "Wrong Way" Corrigan flew to Albany to promote his movie, *The Flying Irishman* in 1939. The Texas native had gained notoriety the previous year when he flew out of New York for Los Angeles, and landed in Ireland instead. Corrigan claimed he had made a mistake, disregarding the fact that federal authorities had denied him clearance to try to cross the Atlantic in his tiny single-engine aircraft.

New times brought new challenges and problems. Mayor Erastus Corning determined in 1960 that Albany no longer could afford the airport. The facility was sold to Albany County for $4.4 million. The county completed construction of a new terminal in 1962. Other additions during this period included freight and air cargo buildings, and a rescue and fire-fighting facility.

Perhaps the most significant turning point in airport history took place in 1993 when the county legislature established the Albany County Airport Authority, a seven-member body that has functioned as a model of non-partisanship while fostering cooperation among government, business and community leaders of the Capital Region.

On January 10, 1996, the authority announced plans for a huge multi-million-dollar project to include a new terminal, parking garage, air traffic control tower and cargo facility. The county granted the authority a 40-year lease to operate the airport on May 16, 1996. The new 230,000-square-foot terminal opened in June 1998, under budget and four months ahead of schedule. The terminal can accommodate 3 million passengers annually, and is designed to reflect the Capital Region's colonial Dutch and Shaker heritage. Different types of brick, coupled with large round windows and sky lights provide a bright, comfortable environment that can be summed up in one word: *Welcome*.

In February 1999, the airport opened a 1,600-car parking garage linked to the terminal via a heated pedestrian bridge. A new 800-car addition to the garage was completed in November 2000. Additional ground parking has raised overall parking capacity to over 5,000 spaces.

The authority's aggressive pursuit of lower fares, new airlines, a wider range of top-flight services and dramatically expanded parking capacity has attracted increasing numbers of passengers. They consist of business and government travelers, educators, students, military, families and tourists.

The authority has achieved such results by combining innovative thinking with purposeful action and state-of-the-art technology. But the accomplishments also mean much more. Albany International Airport is helping to shape the future by stimulating economic, social and cultural growth across the region and in neighboring communities.

Today the terminal is a center for many kinds of activities and services:
• A curved observation deck on the

Albany International Airport terminal and parking gargage opened in June of 1998.

third level offers travelers and visitors an outstanding view of runways, aircraft taxi ways and the Federal Aviation Administration control tower. Conversation between flight crews and air traffic controllers is piped onto the deck via loudspeakers. A *Kids' Flight Deck* airport tour for children includes visits to the observation deck. In addition, the observation level can seat up to 150 people for dinners and receptions.

• The terminal's design is enhanced by the imaginative use of vertical space, making the facility ideal for the display of large-scale contemporary sculpture, including a work on the first level by Alexander Calder. In addition, rotating historical and artistic exhibits are featured on the third level. Topics have included important 20th century events captured by Associated Press photojournalists, children's art, women's history, African-American art, the Lake Placid Winter Olympics of 1932 and 1980, and horse racing at Saratoga Springs.

• A business center, including three conference rooms, is on the second level. The center has no membership fee. Video conferencing, computer use and faxing are among the services offered. A community room on the second level is made available to not-for-profit, public benefit and private business organizations.

• Shops include Departure, a regional museum shop that offers art, handicrafts and books furnished by dozens of regional museums. Also in the terminal are a food court and combination gift shops and news stands that offer merchandise of interest to travelers.

• A striking interfaith prayer room featuring etched art glass panels and water sculptures is ideal for reflection and meditation when travelers seek a bit of quiet and solitude.

Albany International Airport has been transformed into a symbol of regional civic pride because of the cooperative "can-do" effort that individuals and organizations of all kinds constantly bring to the challenge of welcoming the 21st century as an ally rather than a foe.

ALBANY LAW SCHOOL

"The onward spirit of the age must …have its way. The law is made for the times, and it will be made or modified by them," said Ira Harris, state legislator and one of Albany Law School's three founders. The year was 1851, and Harris was quoting from a case more than a decade old, but it was this vision which prompted Harris, along with Amasa J. Parker and Amos Dean, to form Albany Law School that same year. Albany Law School is the nation's oldest independent law school and the oldest law school in New York State. It was organized under an act of the legislature enacted April 17, 1851, giving the powers to grant degrees and confer honors. Under this grant of power the Law School was established and the school opened to receive its first class of 23 students on December 16, 1851.

At that time, the founding of law schools marked a great change in the bar's approach to legal education. In 1851 almost all lawyers came to the bar after a prescribed period of study in a lawyer's office, and there was no formal instruction. After the prescribed time had expired the clerk was "called to the bar." The course of study at the Law School was designed to complement the practical experience a student received in clerkship, with only one term of study per year so students did not have to give up their affiliation in a law office. Albany Law School first charged a tuition of $40 per term.

The education provided by Albany Law School was considered valuable by many notable and distinguished alumni. These alumni include: William McKinley, 25th president of the United States; Kate Stoneman, first female member of the New York State Bar; James C. Mathews, first African American judge in New York; the Honorable Robert H. Jackson, Supreme Court Justice; the Honorable Lawrence H. Cooke, former chief judge of New York; Mary O. Donohue, lieutenant governor of New

Albany Law School's home at 80 New Scotland Avenue in the capital of New York State offers a rich educational environment for students interested in the workings of government and the judicial system.

York; Andrew Cuomo, former secretary of the U.S. Department of Housing and Urban Development; Richard Parsons, co-chief operating officer of AOL Time Warner, Inc.; and Thomas Vilsack, governor of Iowa.

From its original site in the Exchange Building at the northeast corner of State Street and Broadway (the old post office building), to its permanent location at 80 New Scotland Avenue, Albany Law School has continued to expand, offering an exceptional education to students through a rigorous curriculum. Currently, 43 faculty and 32 adjunct faculty teach approximately 700 students at the Law School, which offers three- and four-year programs leading to a juris doctor degree, joint degree programs in business, public administration and social work, and a new master of science in legal studies degree for professionals in other fields. Its graduates have consistently per-

formed well on the New York Bar examination and have distinguished themselves in the legal profession.

Although the days of clerkship as a substitute for a law education are over, Albany Law School provides practical experience to students through its award-winning Clinical Legal Studies Program, where student attorneys take on pro bono projects addressing the legal aspects of many vital issues, such as AIDS, civil rights, disabilities, and domestic violence. Albany Law School employs the doctrine of "learning through doing," helping students build professional skills through hands-on experience in the real world, serving clients with real issues.

As the capital of New York and the home of one of the largest government structures in the world, Albany provides a rich environment for students interested in the workings of government and the judicial system. The close proximity of the New York State Legislature, Court of Appeals (New York's highest court), federal courts and numerous state agencies provides students with excellent opportunities to study and actively participate in the development, implementation and judicial review of legislation, public policy and regulation oversight. The Law School established the Government Law Center (GLC) in 1978, which has become a national model for other law schools. The Center conducts interdisciplinary study and research on government and the problems facing governments, and introduces law students to policy analysis and public service through research programs, externships, public conferences and legislative seminars.

In the interest of the rapidly expanding high technology industry, Albany Law School established the Science and Technology Law Center in 1998. Conveniently located in the Rensselaer Technology Park, the Center provides affordable legal assistance

Amasa J. Parker, Ira Harris and Amos Dean (pictured left to right) founded Albany Law School in 1851; it is the nation's oldest independent law school, and the oldest law school in New York State.

for start-up and early stage companies critical to forming, attracting and retaining high technology industries. Called the Entrepreneurial Legal Assistance Program, it allows students, under the supervision of staff and volunteer attorneys, the opportunity to get hands-on experience dealing with technology and entrepreneurial legal issues. A unique asset to the Law School and the Capital Region, the Center is undertaking a whole new agenda of projects for a law school-related entity. By providing educational programs in entrepreneurship and intellectual property law and facilitating technology transfer relationships in the local economy, the Center is building the infrastructure for high-technology start-up companies in the region.

The year 2001 marks the sesquicentennial anniversary of Albany Law School as well as the conclusion of a major construction and renovation project, with the Law School building a new 45,000-square-foot facility and making significant improvements

Albany Law School employs the hands-on approach of "learning through doing," giving students a greater educational experience through direct involvement in actual or simulated lawyering situations.

to the existing site. The result will be a state-of-the-art complex that will put the institution at the forefront of changing legal education in the United States. Additionally, the University Heights Association has brought together the Law School and its partners, Albany Medical Center, Albany College of Pharmacy and the Sage Colleges, as a consortium to create a world-class learning center. The member institutions will enjoy the benefits of a larger campus environment and the local community will benefit from a revitalization of the neighborhood with an attractive medical/academic complex as well as a revamped landscape with new walkways and lighting. This exciting and historic venture will provide faculty and students with the vital resources to go beyond the traditional realm of studies to another level of professional excellence.

ALBANY STEEL INC.

In the early 1920s, F. Arthur Hunsdorfer worked as regional sales manager for Carnegie Steel Corporation. Hunsdorfer was responsible for covering all of upstate New York, from Newburgh to the Canadian border, on both sides of the Hudson River. Due to the lack of bridges across the Hudson in the 1920s, Hunsdorfer usually only made sales calls on the eastern side of the river in the winter when he could drive across the ice. He would put the car in neutral and place a weight on the accelerator to hold it down. Then, exiting the vehicle, he would stand on the running board outside the car, reach in and jam the shifting lever into gear. The car would start its slow progress across the river with Hunsdorfer ready to jump off at the first sign that the ice was cracking. He had a few close calls but never got wet.

It may have been this early experience that made him decide to start his own business; building a warehouse in one place and letting most of his customers come to him.

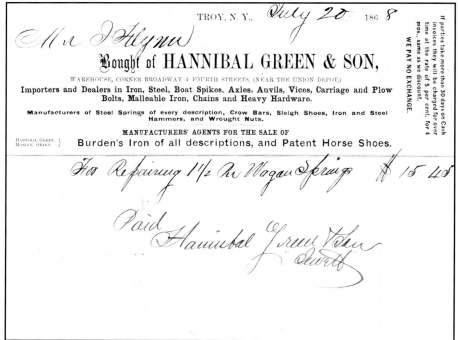

A July 20, 1868 invoice from Hannibal Green.

In 1922, Hunsdorfer joined forces with two of his business associates, Ben Gifford, president of Gifford-Wood Company of Hudson and Walter Strope, purchasing agent for McKinney Steel of Albany. Gifford provided funding; Hunsdorfer and Strope were to run the business. The first business, named General Mill and Contractors Supply Company, was located in a vacant greenhouse at 899 Broadway, just north of steam fire engine no. 3 (currently near the Miss Albany Diner).

After one year, Strope split off and started a competing business, Strope Steel, on Terminal Street in Albany. Hunsdorfer, with Gifford's financial support, moved across the street to much larger quarters at 892 Broadway (now called 900 Broadway, housing Universal Auto Parts) and incorporated the new company as Albany Steel and Iron Supply Company.

The main product of Albany Steel and Iron Supply Company in 1922 was reinforcing bar. The City of Albany was slowly converting from cobblestone to concrete streets. Large blankets of steel reinforcing bars were fabricated to strengthen the concrete. Other products fabricated and warehoused by Albany Steel included hot and cold rolled steel bars, rolled bands and hoops (for making barrels), beams, angles, plate, sheet, tin plate and rail track.

Albany Steel's first location in 1922, near site of Miss Albany diner.

Since Strope stored most of his inventory outside in an open yard, Hunsdorfer would drive up to Terminal Street whenever a large rebar bid was requested to see if Strope had enough inventory to bid the job. Hunsdorfer adjusted his bid accordingly.

Albany Steel moved in 1929 to new, much larger quarters at 45 Broadway, Menands. This location, currently Cranesville Block, was located across the street from Albany's Hawkins Stadium, home of the Eastern Baseball League's Albany Senators. Each season could count on about a dozen broken windows from baseballs fouled straight back over the roof. Albany Steel always paid to repair the broken window, but at least they got to keep the ball.

When this plant was first opened, Hunsdorfer worried that he had built it too far out of the city. Broadway was unpaved at that time and early photographs show a trolley track running along a dirt road flanked by weeds.

In the '20s and '30s, Albany Steel started to build one of the area's first trucking fleets to deliver steel. The stake trucks and flatbed trucks of the day were about the size of a pickup truck today. These trucks were used to deliver reinforcing bar and steel beams up to 40 feet long. This was accomplished by running the beam up along the side of the truck and securing it to the side and front bumper. It was not unusual to have beams running along both sides of the truck, making it impossible to open either door, requiring the driver to climb in through the window.

The 1920s were a time of great prosperity in the Albany area. The country as a whole, and Albany Steel, prospered and grew rapidly. The stock market crash and depression in 1929 and the 1930s slowed growth, but Albany Steel was always prosperous. In the early 1940s, the preparations for war and the later outbreak of war

brought a large increase in government contracts, many originating through the Watervliet Arsenal. At the same time, steel shortages reached epidemic proportions. Albany Steel had many more orders than they could fill. Steel mills went into production 24 hours a day, seven days a week trying to meet demand for raw material. Albany Steel's military contracts, including one to fabricate escape hatches to be mounted to the bottom of tanks, got priority over other work.

Albany Steel's expansion included the purchase of Hannibal Green's Sons of Troy. Hannibal Green had been originally formed in 1809, by Henry Nazro and Jacob Hart on Six Lane's Row, east of River Street. It was completely gutted by the great fire in downtown Troy in 1820, but rebuilt at Three Lane's Row shortly thereafter. In the earliest days, Hannibal Green sold hardware, nails, iron bars, anvils, vices, Smith's bellows, mill saws, cutlery, horseshoe iron, and manufactured "steel springs of every description." They were also listed as

distributors of Fairbanks Celebrated Scales.

Nazro and Hart (1809) became Nazro and Green (1834), Green and Cramer (1838), Hannibal Green (1852) and later, Hannibal Green's Sons (1875). In 1855, they moved from 231 - 233 River Street to the corner of Albany (later Broadway) and Fourth Street, that at the time, was called "the old Corning lot."

Ads from the 1870s listed Hannibal Green as "importers and dealers in iron, steel, and heavy hardware, Agents for Burden's Iron, horseshoes and boiler rivets." An early 1800s Troy newspaper said that Hannibal Green was "...the direct representative of the Burden Iron Company for its iron, a product which has a world wide reputation." On their 100th anniversary in 1909, Hannibal Green received congratulatory letters from steel companies from Maine and Boston to Buffalo and Chicago, from Watertown to New York City, Penn-

Second location of Albany Steel, 1923. Currently Universal Auto Parts.

sylvania and Louisville, Kentucky (probably a purchaser of Burden's patented horseshoes). Some of the letters came from the New York Central and Hudson River Railroad, Delaware and Hudson Railroad, Boston and Maine Railroad, Carnegie Steel of Illinois, Townsend Furnace of Albany, and Robert Cluett of Troy.

Remarkably, one of the congratulatory letters came from the Lake George Steamboat Company and sent along a copy of an order sent to Hannibal Green in 1826.

When Hannibal Green was purchased by Albany Steel, they were housed in one of the Burden Iron Buildings at the foot of Monroe Street. The purchase of Hannibal Green expanded Albany Steel's products into hardware and fasteners, as well as specialty steels.

Albany Steel expanded into the fabrication of structural steel for buildings and bridges through the purchase of the Claussen Iron Company of Tivoli Street in Albany. Claussen was

Albany Steel after 1929. Currently Cranesville Block.

comprised of three buildings and a large warehouse and structural yard on the south side of Tivoli Street, just west of Pearl Street. One of Albany's most historic and beautiful buildings, the D&H Building, now State University Plaza, was fabricated here. The building was designed by Marcus T. Reynolds and construction started in 1916. Also, part of this project was

the fabrication of the adjacent Albany Evening Journal Building, thought by most people to be part of the D&H, but actually a separate building.

Albany Steel purchased a building in Glenmont in 1946 and developed a machining division at that location.

Richard Hunsdorfer succeeded his father as president of Albany Steel in January 1965. Charles Straney, Marvin Hinkelman and Walter Fredenburgh continued as department managers. The top priority of Albany Steel continued to be expansion.

On July 10, 1976, Albany Steel officially moved into a newly constructed modern facility at 566 Broadway in Menands. This facility, approximately 200,000 square feet, comprises 3 divisions in eight contiguous buildings:

• Service Center—warehousing and cutting plate, sheet, bar, structural, and specialty steel with the area's largest stacker crane system housing 10,000 tons of bar stock;

• Fabrication—since the Claussen Iron days, Albany Steel fabricates and erects buildings, bridges, towers, stairs,

Clausen Iron circa 1917. Purchased by Albany Steel.

Steel Fabrication on the D&H Building and the Albany Evening Journal.

railings, and almost any steel structure. A computer controlled drill line drills structural steel and plate. The Fabrication Department also does shotblasting and painting, as well as bending and rolling of shapes;

• Reinforcing Bar Fabrication–rebar was Albany Steel's largest product at their formation 75 years ago, and continues to be a large factor today. They bend, roll and cut rebar for use in concrete structures;

• Machining is still done in Glenmont.

Peter Hess, former vice president and general manager of Albany Steel bought the company in June 1985 from Richard Hunsdorfer, who retired. Current managers include: Mark Heroux, Benjamin J. Van Duzer, Brian Keefe, William Bedard, Deanna Mantica, Michael LaFlamme

and Kimberly O'Rourke.

Today, Albany Steel is Albany's largest and oldest steel center. Their history goes back almost 200 years to 1809. They have survived major fires, the War of 1812, the Civil War, two world wars, major depressions, 5 major strikes, and many periods of iron and

steel shortages and rationing. As the elder Mr. Hunsdorfer demonstrated by crossing the river on the ice, the ability to survive lies in the ability to adapt to constant challenges.

Albany Steel's current 200,000 square foot plant at 566 Broadway.

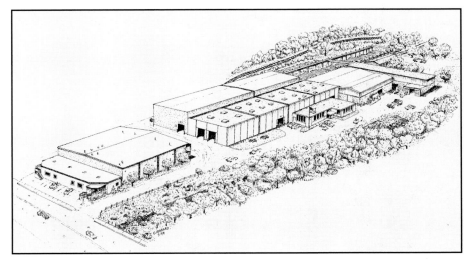

MATTHEW BENDER & COMPANY

A two room walk-up office at the corner of State Street and Broadway was the location of Matthew Bender, "law bookseller," in 1887. At that time, Bender sold other firms' publications, but quickly emerged as a publisher of quality New York State lawbooks. Matthew Jr. ("Max") was already working for his father when younger brother John joined the business. The family concern soon moved around the corner, to 36 State Street, and then to a Broadway storefront in 1892, when the city directory first listed Bender as "law bookseller and publisher." That year, Matthew Bender began issuing an annual "Lawyers' Diary," a desk book successful for the next 56 years. Issuance of William M. Collier's treatise on bankruptcy in 1898 marked the advent of Bender's most long-lived series. Abreast of the times, Bender published early books on streetcar and automobile laws.

Matthew Bender became partners with his sons, Max and John T. Bender, in 1905, and within a year they had three salesmen on the road. In 1910, the firm consumed 108 tons of paper and employed seven salesmen, with gross sales exceeding $188,000. By 1915 Bender had nationwide clientele, with additional customers in Paris, London, Havana, and Berlin; the company established a New York City office at that time.

Matthew Bender, Sr. died in 1920; his son Max succeeded him as president of the company, a position he held for 21 years. During his tenure, Matthew Bender & Company prospered in the 1920s and successfully weathered the Great Depression. His son, Matthew Bender III, and his nephew, John T. Bender, Jr., entered the firm during the '30s. Nephew John took charge of the New York City operation, displaying considerable ability in recruiting writers. It was John Jr. who pioneered loose-leaf binders for ease in updating Bender publications, a system employed thereafter.

Although World War II inhibited the growth of Matthew Bender & Company, the postwar years were ones of continual growth. As late as 1960 the State Street offices were "straight out of Dickens." The company was seeking improved facilities and relocated in 1952 to modern offices at 255 Orange Street. In 1963, Matthew Bender & Company became a subsidiary of The Times Mirror Company and shortly thereafter occupied its 1275 Broadway headquarters. By 1980, Bender employed 1,000 persons, 300 of them at its Albany operation, and also had offices in San Francisco, New York and Washington, D.C. Printing its first international catalogue in 1980 to service customers throughout the world, Matthew Bender & Company has continually increased its international market. In 1998, Matthew Bender & Co., Inc. was acquired by Reed-Elsevier, a British-Dutch leader in the U.S. legal information industry. This move provided even greater opportunities to expand the reach of Matthew Bender's unique content around the globe and in all media (i.e., print, CD-ROM, on-line and over the Internet). The company has offices in New York City, San Francisco (CA), Binghamton (NY), Minneapolis (MN), and Provo (UT), in addition to Albany, where operations now employ 380 people. The overall picture of this old Albany firm is one of dynamic growth in a highly competitive and specialized field.

In 1892, the Benders—Matthew, Matthew Jr., John, and Melvin—were photographed standing in front of their store at 511-513 Broadway. Fred Bender, far right, was no relation.

BOYD PRINTING COMPANY, INC.

For more than 100 years—spread over three centuries—Boyd Printing Company has been building customer loyalty with its reliability, excellence, capabilities and flexibility. From its plant in Albany, it provides clients in Washington D.C, New York City and Europe with a full range of printing services.

Boyd Printing came into being in 1889. Founder William Boyd and six employees ran a treadle-operated press in a world before horseless carriages and electricity were taken for granted. They printed their first full text in 1890, a 500-page loose-leaf legal publication for Matthew Bender Company.

Setting a pattern that is the core of Boyd's success, Bender is still a client. More than 60 percent of Boyd's customers have been working with them for in excess of 40 years. These are relationships passed on through generations.

Thomas Lynch purchased Boyd Printing in 1919 and it has been in the Lynch family ever since. When Thomas died in 1954, his daughter, Marion Lynch Quellmalz and her husband, Henry, took over. Their daughter, Jane Quellmalz Carey now runs the company, working with brother-in-law Carl Johnson and niece and nephew Marcus Lynch Johnson and Kathryn Johnson Koonce. They employ 80 people, operating an 81,000 square-foot complex filled with state-of-the-art technology and equipment.

Left to right: A new generation of Boyd—Kathryn Johnson Koonce, Jane Quellmalz Carey, and Marcus Lynch Johnson. Photo by Colleen Brescia.

Looking for increased space, Boyd occupied its current building in 1961. The plant is the only manufacturing facility in its downtown area of Albany; its neighbors are government offices and retailers. The location is close to 15 major paper mills, allowing overnight delivery and a fast response to its customers' needs.

In 1973, when Jane Carey started with the company, sales were about $2 million a year. In 2000, they were more than $9 million.

That same year, Boyd went to offset printing, and at the end of the decade it commissioned a web press suitable for journals and perfect-bound books. It continues to stay current with the latest technologies, and can convert disk to film in both Mac and PC.

Today, Boyd operates three sheet-fed presses (one for two-color), a heat-set web press, and equipment for making plates, perfect binding, saddle stitching, shrink wrapping and shipping. Through sister companies, it offers clients four-color process work. It specializes in loose-leaf publications, bound books and journals of every kind, catalogs, brochures and direct mail campaigns. Boyd's wholly owned subsidiary, Johnson Press, provides subscription and order fulfillment, warehousing and mailing list maintenance and management.

Boyd relies for business largely on word-of-mouth. This makes its dedication to great quality, price and service essential, since happy customers are the keys to its success. And customers, such as the American Sociological Association (ASA), RIA Group, and Mercy College, are indeed happy.

"Boyd first published an ASA journal in 1951," says its director of publications, Karen Gray Edwards. "I began working with Henry years ago, and he probably saved my job at times. When his daughter, Jane, became president, the same level of service continued. Boyd and ASA have truly been partners through the generations."

"The number one thing I turn to Boyd for is their extraordinary reliability," adds Rick Beardsley, purchasing director of RIA, a New-York-City-based provider of educational materials for tax and accounting professionals. "They do what they say they are going to do. They will actually turn down work if they don't believe they can deliver it on time."

For Mercy College, Boyd prints college catalogs. Said Donna Gordon Mitchell, director of publications at Mercy, "Even the catalog specialty companies don't have Boyd's ability and flexibility. Boyd works to our schedule, our budget and our quality standards."

One of Boyd Printing's presses. Photo by Timothy Raab.

BRUNO MACHINERY CORPORATION

Bruno Machinery designs, manufactures and services its own line of die cutting, embossing, heat-sealing, molding and trimming presses. It also manufactures a full line of accessories (i.e., unwind and rewind stands, scrap conveyors, storage racks, die cart movers, etc.). These press systems are sold worldwide with approximately 60 percent going to the automotive industry for cutting interior car parts (i.e., door panels, trunk liners, headliners, sun visors, carpet, seats, acoustical liners, HVAC seals, gaskets, air bags, steering wheels, consoles, arm rests, etc.) The next time you sit in your car, look at the interior. There is a very good possibility that some of these parts were cut on a Bruno press.

In fact, there are many other examples of products cut on Bruno presses that one may see everyday and take for granted. Bruno Machinery Corporation has considerable and growing sales in the toy industry, household products, packaging, graphic printing, carpet and tile, medical, paper, rubber, plastic, furniture, aircraft, and many other industries that cut, trim, emboss, heat-seal or mold products.

BMC sells presses to Fortune 500 companies (or their suppliers) around

Patrick Bruno, founder.

Left to right: Robert F. Bruno, Jr., Robert F. Bruno, Sr., and Sean P. Bruno.

the world. All of the major car manufacturers, including Daimler-Chrysler, Ford, General Motors, etc., either directly use Bruno presses or contract with tier I or tier II suppliers that produce interior parts on Bruno presses. Johnson Controls, Inc. and Lear Corporation are two of the top automotive interior part suppliers in the world. Both companies are using high tonnage Bruno presses to maintain their competitive advantage. Hasbro (Milton Bradley) uses Bruno presses to cut their puzzles. And, Owens Corning has Bruno presses to cut and mold insulation products.

Bruno Machinery Corporation is one of only a few press manufacturers left in the United States that designs, manufactures and services its own product line. BMC currently produces approximately 40 press systems per year. Plans are in place, however, to double production within the next five years.

Bruno's competition is mainly foreign. Many of these companies produce high-volume, smaller, low tonnage presses and have distribution

centers throughout the world, including the United States. BMC's market strength is in the higher tonnage, customized press systems. Bruno manufactures presses ranging from 10 tons of pressure to 4,000 tons.

The company got its start in the press business in 1972, when it entered into an agreement with the Harris Corporation to service and provide parts to Sheridan presses. Harris Corporation (known then as Harris Intertype) had purchased the rights and assets to the Sheridan press business in 1964. T. W. & C.B. Sheridan was one of the largest manufacturers of mechanical die cutting presses in the United States. The Sheridan press company was founded in 1835 and produced presses until the 1970s. The main factory was located approximately 170 miles north of the Hudson-Mohawk area in Champlain, New York.

Two thousand five hundred ton shuttle press.

This experience with Sheridan presses and parts eventually led BMC to hire more engineers and to develop its own line of die cutting presses. The engineers took the principals of the Sheridan mechanical design and combined it with modern-day hydraulics. The result was a hydraulic-mechanical toggle press that started Bruno Machinery Corporation on its way to becoming a world-class press manufacturer.

Bruno Machinery Corporation was formed in Albany, New York in 1965. Increased business and the emergence of its own product line resulted in a

Computer illustration of Bruno Machinery Corporation's factory and offices located on River Road in Glenmont.

move to Troy, New York in 1979. In 2001, BMC will again move its offices and factory to a new location, in Glenmont, New York. As with the previous moves, increased business and the need for additional space, capacity and higher tonnage overhead cranes will force Bruno Machinery Corporation to relocate. This time the company will construct a new, 80,000 square foot factory and office complex that will assist BMC with its goal of doubling press production within five years.

BMC president Robert Bruno, Sr. made the decision to stay in the Hudson-Mohawk area because of its current workforce. There were opportunities to move to other locations in the country, but BMC's skilled and highly-trained workforce would be difficult to replace. "We have invested a great deal of time and money training our employees," said Robert Bruno, Sr. "The press business is becoming very high-tech. Presses used to operate with simple electrical relays. Now, they have sophisticated electronic programs that integrate mechanical, electrical and hydraulic functions. All of our employees, including salesmen, purchasing agents,

machinists, assembly and service mechanics, mechanical and electrical engineers, etc., have to be continually trained and apprised of fast-changing technology."

No technology has had a more dramatic effect on business than the Internet, increasing sales inquiries each month. As a result, BMC is looking for ways to expand its international sales force. BMC currently has sales offices in Canada, Mexico, England and Europe. It is only a matter of time before there are BMC offices in South America and Asia.

The next decade should be very interesting for Bruno Machinery Corporation and its employees. There are very strong possibilities for expansion, acquisition and partnerships at home and abroad. BMC has established itself as a major player in the press business. In the late 1990s, BMC had been approached by several competitors with the purpose of merging or purchasing the business. It is obvious that the quality and reliability of the rugged Bruno presses and the service provided by BMC employees have the competition nervous.

Companies cannot be successful without great leadership. Continuing the dream of a family-owned business started by his father Patrick Bruno in 1965, Robert Bruno, Sr. has been able to build upon the past, keep his eye on the future, and stay firmly planted in the present. As a result of his vision, BMC has been able to continually expand its horizons. Under the guidance of the Bruno family, Bruno Machinery Corporation should be a major manufacturing force in the Hudson-Mohawk area and the world for generations to come.

Electrical control panel for press and program functions.

CALLANAN INDUSTRIES, INC.

In 1883, an enterprising South Bethlehem, New York hay farmer, Peter Callanan, foresaw a need for quarried stone for road building. He founded the Callanan Road Improvement Company (later to be renamed Callanan Industries), in the northern part of the town of Coeymans in Albany County, at a location on his property where there were exposed limestone rock ledges.

During the following 117 years Peter's vision proved prophetic and the company grew beyond the Capital District to become one of the oldest companies of its kind in the country and one of the largest of its type in New York State.

Peter Callanan felt that better roads would be a benefit to the economy of his time because they would improve the ability to move agricultural and manufactured products to market. He was so strong in his opinion that he traveled New York State speaking to various town and governmental bodies as an advocate for better roads and promoting a system to finance them.

In 1889 he published a 40 page "practical treatise" titled *Roads and Road Making*, in which he described the state of American roads in the late 1800s as "inferior to those of any other civilized country." He reminded the reader that good roads reduce the cost of hauling and provided evidence that defective highways cost the State "annually an extra $15,346,230." And this was in 1889!

About the same time, the Buffalo and Weehawken Railroad (later called the New York Central) was building its West Shore line along the Hudson River valley and the need for crushed stone became substantial. A quote from the *Albany Angus*, a newspaper of 1909 stated, "When the West Shore Railroad was built, passing through South Bethlehem in the '80s, it needed rock ballast for its roadbed. Peter Callanan's farm had all the rock that

The Callanan South Bethlehem quarry of the 1890s. By hand and shovel the "loaders and pickers" piled the stone onto wooden cars for the horses to pull to a steam driven crusher. Kerosene lanterns (hanging from the poles) provided enough light to allow for the 4 a.m. start and the loaders were paid by the number of cars they filled in a day.

the West Shore could use, and Peter Callanan's quarries became an established institution. In time, South Bethlehem came to depend upon the quarries as its principal industry."

In the first years of the business the stone was quarried from the ledges at South Bethlehem literally by hand. A speech written for the company's 65th anniversary celebration in 1948 describes the quarry methods prior to the turn of the century: "Drillers used sledges and steel points to put down the holes for blasting. It took iron men to swing a sledge from dawn to dusk. Screening as well as loading was done by hand. In fact, no power except manpower was used. The loaders, or pickers as they were called, usually came out at 4 a.m. and tried to load at

least three cars before the quarry started. These men worked on piece work and were paid a fixed sum for each car loaded."

The company thrived. A steam driven crusher and mill were built and in 1895 the business incorporated as the Callanan Road Improvement Company.

During its first 30 years, the company endured severe trials which could have put it out of business. In 1896, one short year after incorporation, Peter Callanan died of a heart attack. Devastated by this loss and with six children to care for, Peter's wife, Hannah Whitbeck Callanan was determined in her belief in Peter's vision. In testimony to her resolve, Hannah Callanan managed to keep the stone business going.

With the landmark Highway Act of 1898 a newly formed New York State Highway Commission awarded Contract #1 to the Callanan Road Improvement Company for two miles of road leading out of Albany in the Northern Blvd. area. Peter Callanan's wisdom and advocacy for better roads was being realized.

Three days after Christmas in 1902, another test of Hannah's fortitude occurred when the entire crushing plant burned to the ground. Then facing a business crippled by a second major loss in eight years, Hannah was urged to sell out, but clinging to Peter's beliefs and the business promise of her eldest son, John, she rebuilt the plant.

In 1909, calamity struck with great force. A premature explosion in the quarry took the lives of Hannah's sons, John and Charles, along with 21 others. With a husband gone, a company having been ravaged by fire, and now the lives of two sons as well as others lost, Hannah was, in the words of her youngest son Reid, "prostrate with grief."

Again, Hannah was advised to give up and offers were made to buy the 26-year-old company. But as Reid (later the company's president) put it, "...finally she made her decision. She would not sell. Again she was determined to keep the family business going. I don't know how she had the strength and courage to do it."

In 1923, a competitive stone company, Albany Crushed Stone, was formed not far away near Feura Bush. Without sufficient business in the area to support two stone companies, a price war ensued.

The competition finally sold out to Callanan in defeat in 1929. As Reid Callanan described it, "We ourselves didn't come out of this struggle unscathed and it was some little time before our company was really healthy once again."

Taken as a whole, the trials of Hannah and the early Callanan Road Improvement Company were awesome, yet the recovery process from each disaster strengthened and moved the company a little farther ahead than it had been before. The mill was

rebuilt in better fashion following the fire and more productive equipment replaced the old. Steam, and eventually compressed air drills, caused the steel points and sledges to become outmoded. The first quarry-loading shovel was purchased in 1916. It was steam powered, moved on rails and took nine men and a track gang to keep it in operation.

Around 1937 a new quarry was started at Kingston with equipment

from the Albany Crushed Stone buyout. This operation established a market in New York City via barges on the Hudson River and supplied the heavy fill in Flushing Meadows for the 1939 World's Fair (now the site of the U.S. Tennis Center).

Modern day paving of I-787 in downtown Albany, with the former Delaware and Hudson Railroad building (now New York State University offices) in the background.

In the 1940s and 1950s the company was coming into its own and was operating three crushed stone operations and five blacktop plants, performing construction on many projects and supplying materials on many more.

During the 1950s the company was a major contributor to the construction of the New York State Thruway supplying over 1.5 million tons of materials for the building of 67 miles of mainline, 31 miles of access roads, 6 interchanges and numerous bridges.

In the 1960s the Callanan South Bethlehem quarry supplied in excess of 2.5 million tons of stone for the construction of the Empire State Plaza, which, at the time, was the largest construction project in the world.

Also during the 1960s Penn Dixie Cement, a public corporation of N.Y.C, acquired the company from family ownership. Following a 15 year relationship with Penn Dixie during which the company name was changed to Callanan Industries, Inc. to reflect its diversification beyond road building, the company was acquired by a partnership led by A.J. "Doc" Marcelle, a lifetime Callanan employee and chief executive during the Penn Dixie ownership. During the Marcelle tenure and ownership, success continued, allowing the expansion of operations and the acquisition of several other construction material based companies including Fitzgerald Brothers of Troy, Crushed Rock and Asphalt Stone Products of Schenectady and Pattersonville, and Oxbow Stone and Asphalt, near Canastota, N.Y.

In 1985, Callanan Industries was acquired by CRH of Dublin, Ireland, an international building materials group that, through its subsidiary Oldcastle Inc. has operations throughout America.

As part of Oldcastle, successes and growth have continued with King Road Materials, Clemente Latham Concrete, Sullivan Materials, Fane Concrete and Asphalt, Ritangela Construction, Maybrook Materials and, most recently in 2000, the Dolomite Group of the Rochester area, joining the Callanan Industries "New York Group" of companies.

All of these organizations give testimony to Peter Callanan's sustained vision for road building. The survival and growth of Callanan Industries remains an example for business and industry as we enter the 21st Century.

Currently, Callanan Industries and its New York Group consists of over 40 locations, with more than 1500 employees producing and supplying over 8 million tons of sand and stone, more than 3 million tons of hot mix asphalt and over 0.6 million yards of concrete annually for infrastructure, building and home projects. Their operational area extends from the Orange/Sullivan County region in the south, northward to the Glens Falls, Warren County area and westward from the Capital District to the Rochester region of the Empire State.

Above: A 1920s drill gang. This early drill sat on a tripod and was driven by compressed air coming through pipes and hoses from a steam driven compressor.

Below: In the mid 1930s the first electric shovel was put into operation at South Bethlehem to load the blasted rock onto the wooden rail cars that were then towed by a steam dinky (engine) for the trip to the crushing mill. A blast hole drill is visible on top of the quarry ledge.

CARTER, CONBOY, CASE, BLACKMORE, MALONEY & LAIRD, P.C.

In 1920, with a handshake, J. Stanley Carter and M. James Conboy became partners in the practice of law. Their first office was located over Calkins Drug Store at the north end of Remsen Street, Cohoes, New York. The Carter, Conboy firm opened a second office in 1927 in the old Chamber of Commerce building at 74 Chapel Street, Albany, New York. The firm moved to its present location in 1992 at 20 Corporate Woods Boulevard, Albany, New York.

Carter, Conboy, Case, Blackmore, Maloney & Laird, P.C. combine expertise and experience with a deep commitment to upholding the highest standards and tenets of the legal profession. Their attorneys are active in the Albany County, New York State and American Bar Associations, as well as the Defense Research Institute and Trial Lawyers Associations and the National Panel of Administrators of

James M. Conboy (left) and James S. Carter.

Founders: J. Stanley Carter (left) 1915-1954 and M. James Conboy, 1919-1969.

the American Arbitration Association. The firm is the only Capital District law firm that is a member of ALFA International, an international association of independent law firms. Four members of the firm, M. James Conboy (deceased), James S. Carter (retired), James M. Conboy, Clayton T. Bardwell (deceased) and Forrest N. Case became Fellows of the prestigious American College of Trial Lawyers, which limits its membership invitations to one percent of the attorneys in each state in the nation.

More than 80 years later the name and outstanding reputation of Carter, Conboy endures. The founding partners' sons, James S. Carter and James M. Conboy, went on to become senior partners in the firm.

The firm's attorneys are frequent lecturers on health-related matters at the area's medical colleges, hospitals and medical societies, and on civil practice

in the continuing education programs of the State and County Bar Associations.

Insurance company representation has been a mainstay of the firm practice throughout its 80 year history. Their lawyers have extensive experience in all forms of tort liability defense, including negligence, product liability, toxic torts, labor law, medical malpractice and appellate advocacy.

Carter, Conboy, Case, Blackmore, Maloney & Laird, P.C. is one of Albany's largest firms, with nearly 30 attorneys and a staff of 34. Their lawyers are admitted to practice before the Courts of New York State, various U.S. District Courts, the U.S. Court of Appeals for the Second Circuit and the U.S. Supreme Court.

Located just outside of downtown Albany, Carter, Conboy has access to all local and state courts. The firm handles cases from Poughkeepsie in the southern part of the state to Plattsburgh in the northern part of the state and Syracuse in the western part of New York State. The firm prides itself on the quality of client communications and personal service. Prompt and regular updates and cost-conscious handling of legal matters are an important part of its practice. The firm is ready to serve its clients in meeting the legal challenges that lie ahead in the 21st century.

COMFORTEX WINDOW FASHIONS

Comfortex Window Fashions owes its existence to two complementary entrepreneurs—Thomas J. Marusak, an aerospace engineer turned business-man, and John Schnebly, a window treatment product researcher. The two combined their creative talents, and in 1986, founded Comfortex Window Fashions to fill the growing need for shades in the residential solarium market.

Together Marusak and Schnebly devised a motorized shading system that combined insulating cellular fabric and solar battery technology. They established a fabrication facility with 12 employees in the Harmony Mill Textile Complex located at the confluence of the Hudson and

This spacious Watervliet complex currently houses the Comfortex corporate offices and New York manufacturing and fabrication facility.

All Comfortex products are custom made by trained shade builders. Each window treatment is assembled by hand to meet individual specifications.

Mohawk Rivers in Cohoes. Originally constructed in 1837 and officially closing its doors in 1984, it was the largest textile mill of its kind in all of New York State. The two entrepreneurs hoped to capitalize on the Harmony Mills legacy by employing a local workforce, many of whom had experience in textile manufacturing.

From 1986 through 1991, Comfortex evolved from a small

regional fabricator of solarium shades to a national manufacturer of innovative window treatment products. The Harmony Mill site lent marketing inspiration to the new products Comfortex developed. *Symphony Cellular Shades, Serenade Roman Shades* and *Woodwinds Blinds* are just some of the product names that were created from a decidedly musical theme.

The early 1990s presented a changing business landscape in the United States. The growing number of "big box" stores were squeezing independent window treatment retailers into bankruptcy. Looking for a way to keep its core customer base in business, Comfortex conceived a retail fabrica-

The historic Harmony Mills complex in Cohoes served as Comfortex corporate headquarters from 1986 through 1995.

Today, Comfortex continues to manufacture high quality window treatments as a wholly-owned, independent subsidiary of the Netherlands-based Hunter Douglas company. It employs over 600 people nationally, two-thirds of whom work at the Watervliet facility. Comfortex remains at the forefront of both technology and style, and is nationally recognized as an innovative leader in the window treatment industry.

Left: Introduced in 1998, Shangri-La™ Sheer Window Shadings gently diffuse light while offering the many viewing options of a Venetian blind

Below: The first products fabricated by Comfortex were insulating honeycomb shades that operated with solar recharging batteries and accommodated the curves of the greenhouse glass.

tion program that helped transform these small retailers into mini factories, allowing them to easily compete with the national chain stores. Comfortex's innovative *Composer* Program created a new distribution channel that eliminated the middleman for hundreds of small retail businesses worldwide.

Growth and change highlighted the following years. Comfortex established plants in Florida and Nevada to service the southeastern and western markets, respectively. In 1995, the Harmony Mills operation moved to its current 125,000 square-foot modern office and manufacturing complex in Watervliet. A year later, Comfortex opened another facility in Arizona to manufacture its patented wood alloy material for the company's innovative line of *Woodwinds* blinds.

Further growth, this time in the international sector, followed the 1998 launch of its *Shangri-La* line of sheer window shadings. Currently, Comfortex distributes products globally in 28 countries on five continents.

COOKSON PLASTIC MOLDING CORPORATION

Innovation in the design and manufacture of plastic goods for a variety of applications is a hallmark of Cookson Plastic Molding Corporation (CPM). The Latham-based company pioneered the use of structural foam molding in the 1970s and is today a primary supplier of polymer swimming pools and pallets.

With manufacturing facilities in Latham and Scotia, New York; Atlanta, Georgia; Toronto, Ontario; and Essex, United Kingdom, CPM employs approximately 500 people in its two divisions: Recreational Products and Material Handling.

As the world's largest producer of plastic pallets, the Material Handling Division helps to transport everything from vitamins and potato chips to auto parts and telephone books. Cookson's technologically advanced products serve a broad range of international markets, including automotive, pharmaceutical, food and beverage, retail, printing and chemical processing.

The Recreational Products Division leads the industry in innovative swimming pool design and manufacture

Seven hundred fifty-ton structural foam machine used to mold plastic pallets, swimming pool wall panels and braces.

Bruce Quay, president and chief executive officer.

under the brand names of Pacific Pools, Performance Pool Products and Graphex pool panels.

CPM had its origins in the family business of Alfred and Merrill Laven, who ran a small Latham-based construction business. In 1956, the father-and-son team decided to expand their business and purchased several in-ground woodwall vinyl liner swimming pools, which they installed in homes in the Albany area.

The business transitioned to the manufacture of galvanized steel walls in 1963, and in 1968 Pacific Pools opened its corporate headquarters in Latham, New York. "The evolution of our pallet business is an interesting study in business innovation," said president and chief executive officer Bruce Quay, who joined Cookson Plastics in 1990. "Pacific Pools was already recognized as a leading manufacturer of steel swimming pool panels. In 1975, the company bought several structural foam molding machines and introduced the first plastic molded pool panels. But at the same time, we could not ignore a growing need for contract molding services, particularly in material handling."

Accordingly, in 1981 company executives formed the Loudon Plastics Division of Pacific Industries. The new unit manufactured custom parts for material handling and other applications, including large industrial containers, storage tubs for Pratt & Whitney, cheese boxes for the dairy industry, film trays for Eastman Kodak and game tables for Fisher-Price.

Loudon Plastics also began making custom plastic pallets for General Motors and other members of the automotive industry. In 1981, Loudon began designing and manufacturing its own line of proprietary plastic pallets. "What began as a good business move to keep the molding machines busy grew into a very successful business in its own right," added Mr. Quay.

The innovation did not end there. To complement its pools—and to serve the broader market of quality inground swimming pool owners—Pacific expanded its existing production of vinyl pool liners from Latham to a larger facility in Scotia, New York, and in 1994 opened its South Pacific Vinyl plant in Atlanta. In 1995 Pacific launched its "Dimensional" liner patterns which revolutionized the look of vinyl liners and spawned numerous

imitators. Another accessory product, the pool step, is patented for its Totally Encapsulated System (TES) design using advanced engineering to support a one-piece, watertight unit. Thermoformed from a solid sheet of ABS plastic, the Performance Step line is today sold in several sizes and styles.

Pacific Industries and its subsidiary, Loudon Plastics, were sold to Cookson Group PLC—a multi-billion dollar, diversified manufacturer of industrial materials based in London—in 1989. Pacific Industries began a new phase of growth with the acquisition of several distribution organizations in the Northeast. Pacific has since divested its distribution operations to SCP Pool Corporation in exchange for a long-term supply agreement. "The distribution network we built in the 1990s has been key to our success, and SCP remains our largest customer," said Mr. Quay.

As a leading designer and manufacturer of pools and pool products, Pacific developed many products as "world firsts," including: tile-printed vinyl liners (1974); eight-inch top polymer walls (1975) and 48-inch polymer walls with an eight-inch top (1976); Permalife pool with polymer pool steps (1980); honeycomb design Graphex pool (1987); 42-inch flat-top garden panel (1990); Dimensional vinyl liners (1994); and safety covers with Invisi-Drain (1999).

"No other manufacturer has had such a large impact on the swimming pool industry," said Mr. Quay. "We have integrated processes, materials, design, and aesthetics to produce the broadest selection of pool components of any one company."

Mr. Quay predicts continued growth in both

The conveyor cutting machine is so sophisticated it can be programmed to cut out almost any shaped liner. In this case, they cut out the shape of New York State.

the pool and the plastic pallet businesses and is directing CPM to meet expected demands, adding financial and human resources to Recreational Products and the Material Handling divisions. Mr. Quay anticipates dramatic growth as the "Baby Boom" generation ages: "Only 15 percent of American homes that could support a swimming pool have one. With the

Cookson's Racko Cell™ plastic pallet in use at McCormick Spice, Maryland.

growth in disposable income, there's a great opportunity for our recreational products."

In the material handling industry, a gradual global shift from wooden to plastic pallets in many applications—for a variety of reasons including safety and hygiene—creates a bright future for CPM. Because they are manufactured to precise standards and are dimensionally consistent, Cookson plastic pallets are better suited to automated warehouse and production systems, which are growing in applications worldwide.

Pallets manufactured by CPM's facilities in the United States and Europe are available with a wide range of options including custom colors, friction discs to reduce slippage, and various identification features including bar coding, molding and hot stamping. Each pallet carries its own manufacturing details and the internationally recognized recycling logos. Many customers have pallets molded in custom colors with their company

Pacific Pools' "mountain lake" graphex pool systems.

logos molded in or hot stamped on their pallets. In 1993, CPM was the first company to design and manufacture pallets for in-store display use; the resulting POP Display Base is now used throughout many Wal-Mart stores. "By serving as a ready-made display unit, it eliminates several labor-intensive steps in unloading, moving and arranging products for display," explained Mr. Quay.

When it comes to moving things from one place to another, there's a good chance that a plastic pallet manufactured by Cookson is on a forklift. Since 1970, with the development of the flagship one-piece StructoCell pallet, the company that is now Cookson Plastic Molding has introduced many product innovations including:
• The structural foam Freezer Spacer (1973)
• The first automotive 45" by 48"' pallet for power train assembly plants (1985)
• The nestable 40" by 48" downstream

pallet for grocery distribution (1989)
• The 44" by 56" beverage can pallet (1991)
• The DuroCell pallet technology using a proprietary EMABond welding process from Ashland
• The Point of Purchase (POP) Display Base for retail applications (1993)
• Anti-slip grip coating, and welded Friction Disks, for load stability (1997, 2000)
• The TD (Tapered Drum) Pallet

developed for citrus industry (1997)
• The world's first UL-listed pallet, the AdvantEDGE, developed of fire-retardant resin with GE (1998)
• The high-performance Rack'R rackable pallet, using EMABond welding and CPM's patented pultrusion technology (1998)
• The RackoCell Pallet for the food manufacturing industry and the 40" by 40" Dairy Pallet for fluid milk processors (1999)
• The innovative small-footprint 32" by 38" automotive pallet (2000).

The demand for plastic pallets, particularly for use in Automated Storage and Retrieval Systems (ASRS), has steadily increased around the world since the StructoCell was first manufactured in 1970. Although the initial cost of plastic is higher than the cost of a wooden pallet, the advantages make plastic safer and more economical in the long run, explained Mr. Quay.

"Plastic is more hygienic; it's easier to clean. Unlike wood, plastic is dimensionally consistent, and there's no shrinkage or warping, or problem with moisture. With wooden pallets, a nail sticking out can cause a customer's

Pacific is the world's largest manufacturer of in-ground pool vinyl liners.

entire $20 million automatic system to shut down. That doesn't happen with plastic."

Another advantage that CPM promotes, along with improved safety conditions for workers, is that plastic pallets are 100 percent recyclable, thus eliminating disposal costs and reducing timber demand. As for the cost factor, Mr. Quay noted that the dozens of pallet styles and sizes that CPM makes for various applications are "highly competitive with wood pallets on a cost/performance measure due to their significantly longer useful life."

To help customers with the initial cost, Cookson launched its Pallet Leasing Program through Citicorp in 1998.

"We began the program after managers asked for a way to introduce plastic pallets into their systems without the associated investment up front," said Tom Gibbs, senior vice president of finance and administration. Nabisco was among the first customers to take advantage of the leasing pro-

State-of-the-art Emabond™ weld machines for plastic pallets.

gram, with good results, according to Bob Holland, shipping and receiving manager at the Planter's Life Savers Company facility in Suffolk, Virginia. Converting from wood to plastic "has made a real difference," he says. "'The plastic is cleaner and the new pallets have eliminated difficulties and costs encountered with wood, including safety and infestation problems associated with grain-type products."

This kind of product innovation and market awareness is what has made CPM, and the companies that preceded it, so successful in the highly competitive global industry of plastic goods manufacture. The staff of engineers at CPM simultaneously develops new products for both the pallet and pool lines. In 1999, CPM unveiled its new state-of-the-art testing laboratory in Albany. The new facility creates a working warehouse environment to test the performance of each pallet to meet ASTM D1185 and International Standard ISO 8611 criteria. "Our test

lab is an extension of our commitment to technological leadership," said Mr. Quay.

Along with developing its technologies and retaining good employees, CPM is also focused on developing its role in community affairs in all its locations, including Latham, Atlanta, Canada and the United Kingdom. Mr. Quay is a member of the Board of Managers for the Colonie Community Foundation, which has plans to expand facilities for a community center for the Albany community. CPM also supports local and regional food banks and other community organizations. "We continue to feel that it is essential to look at other ways to support community development in all our locations," said Mr. Quay.

"Worldwide," he added, "Cookson is successful because of a strong commitment to being number one. My challenge as president is to continue to provide vision and support for our businesses, and to focus on our core strategies of leading-edge technology and low-cost production, while continuing to attract and develop talented, motivated people."

Resin used in the manufacture of structural foam molded products. Courtesy, Thoen & Associates.

W. J. COWEE, INC.

The year was 1898. William McKinley was President. Nickelodeons were all the rage. And Willis Judson Cowee was planting the seeds of a new company.

Around this time, American florists were asking for an easy, affordable tool to help strengthen and secure fragile flower stems in arrangements. Judson, as he was called, was working at General Electric in Pittsfield, Massachusetts, but in his spare time he experimented in an unheated room above a local sawmill. He finally came up with a slim stick, pointed at both ends, with a length of fine wire attached to one tip. He also found a way to mass-produce these sticks, designing a special machine that fixed the wires to their ends. The "winding machine" was ready for production in late 1898 and a new business was born.

W. J. Cowee, Inc. is a family owned wood products and land management company in Berlin, New York. It is a small town in the semi-rural Taconic Valley in Eastern Rensselaer County. The company has been in Berlin for over 100 years and employs, for the most part, people from Berlin and the surrounding communities. It is the largest company in the area and has about 100 employees. Four generations of the Cowee, Gutermuth and

Willis Judson Cowee.

Davis families—all closely related—have been involved, one always in the president's chair.

The first employee was a Berlin boy, hired to run the winding machines. He worked in a large, unheated room with no partitions. The machines were driven by a belt, which came up from the sawmill down below. In the winter, he would work a while and then go over to a greenhouse next door to get warm.

In spite of all this, the wire pick business was an immediate success and the operation was moved to the nearby John Hewitt and Sons Wagon and Bicycle shop, where they worked by the light of kerosene lamps and grew to 10 employees.

In about 1915, the company was moved to its present location in Berlin. The picks were packed in wooden boxes and wheeled in a wheel-

barrow to the nearby train station for shipment. Now UPS trucks and common carriers load up at their shipping docks. Buildings were added during the next few years and W. J. Cowee, Inc. was incorporated in 1923. The workforce continued to grow and was paid in cash. Someone had to "ride shotgun" to the bank and back to pick up the payroll. The pistol stayed in the vault for many years and was disposed of only recently.

From these modest beginnings, the company has grown into a thriving 50-acre factory complex, employing 100 people and managing 26,000 acres of timberland. Today, Cowee is the largest manufacturer of wooden floral picks in the world, with distribution all over the United States, Canada and Mexico. It is interesting to note that the product is almost unchanged from the original and has been a part of floral design over a span of several generations. It has been used throughout the ebb and flow of changing approaches to design and styles of teaching for over 100 years.

The product line has been broadened to include many sizes of wood picks, plant stakes and design accessories for florists.

The 1920s saw the development of a woodturning line. Variety lathes were added to make small turnings, mostly for toy companies such as Fisher-Price and Milton Bradley. One of the Cowee specialties for Fisher-Price was a little train of wooden ducks. The duck train was so successful that a large reproduction was made out of papier-mâché

One of the original manufacturing buildings.

and proudly entered in the Fourth of July parade in Berlin.

With the introduction of plastics for toy parts in the 1970s, Cowee's toy business dwindled and there was more concentration on turnings for the craft, hobby, furniture and industrial markets. They still make yo-yos and several types of spin tops.

Much of the wood used in manufacturing comes from their own selectively cut forests in New York, Vermont and Massachusetts. The company works with foresters and loggers who are specially trained to mark and harvest trees in a responsible way. They practice sustained yield management where larger more mature trees are harvested and smaller ones are left to flourish, much like weeding a garden. Thus their forests remain intact and naturally regenerate, ensuring a steady supply of wood for generations to come.

Special steps are taken to enhance wildlife habitat for such things as food, cover and nesting sites. Watershed protection, positive clean air, climate influence and general enjoyment of the outdoors are all made possible by careful and thoughtful forestland management. This renewable resource is, therefore made available for houses, furniture and paper products—many

Wired wood floral picks.

things people use everyday. Contrary to what many people think, economic development and environmental protection and enhancement are not mutually exclusive—they can go hand in hand.

W. J. Cowee works closely with the state of New York in preserving open space by selling hundreds of acres in conservation easements to protect the Taconic Crest Trail. Much of Cowee Woodlands is open to the public for hiking, hunting and wildlife observation.

Cowee belongs to the American Tree Farm system, a nationwide group of 60,000 landowners all linked by a desire to manage their woodlands according to sustainable principles.

Cowee's commitment to protecting the environment doesn't stop in the forest. For example, their dyes are water based and are not harmful, the wood products decompose quickly when exposed to the elements so they won't clog the landfills, and all timber brought into the plant is fully utilized. That which cannot be used in manufacturing is burned in their cogeneration plant and creates about 65% of the energy used in their operations.

The company also does its share in community service. They partner with the local volunteer Fire Department and Rescue Squad, allowing those members who are Cowee employees to attend to emergencies on the clock. They work with the local schools in a school-to-work program, JOBBS (Joint Opportunities between Businesses and Berlin Schools), and have been awarded the Rensselaer County Regional Chamber of Commerce's Van Rensselaer Award for good corporate citizenship.

Efforts have been made over the last hundred years, needless to say, to keep as up-to-date as possible with technology. Even though the company has grown dramatically, they are still very much a small family business. They haven't gotten so big that they forget their biggest asset—friends and neighbors from Berlin and surrounding communities who work hard and give much to the enterprise. There is personal service and fast delivery of a quality product to their customers.

Making a useful product, caring for the environment and involvement in the community are things W. J. Cowee hopes to continue well into its second century.

Some of current woodturnings.

THE COLLEGE OF SAINT ROSE

The College of Saint Rose was founded in 1920 by the Sisters of Saint Joseph of Carondelet who dreamed of establishing the only catholic college for women between New York City and Buffalo. Under the leadership of Sister Blanche Rooney and with the encouragement of the Roman Catholic Diocese of Albany, the Sisters built an institution of higher education dedicated to intellectual progress and an awareness of the spiritual dimension of learning.

On June 28, 1920, the New York State Board of Regents granted a provisional charter that allowed the College to award bachelor's degrees in the arts, sciences and music. The Class of '24 consisted of 19 young women and 8 professors.

In 1927, the Middle States Association of Colleges and Universities accredited the College without the customary period of probation. By the College's Silver Anniversary in 1945, the College had grown from 19 to 360 students and from one house and a garage to 14 houses and two major buildings. By the mid '40s, over 1,000 graduates had been awarded degrees and the College was fast becoming a leading educator of teachers for the Capital Region.

The curricula also grew and intensified and in 1949, the College became the first Catholic women's college in

The College of Saint Rose began with a vision, $1,000 and the house pictured below, Saint Rose Hall. The first 19 students attended class, ate their meals and made their home in this building. It is known today as Moran Hall.

New York state to be given the right to award masters' degrees in the arts, sciences and education.

The College's largest change since its founding came about in 1969, when it became fully co-educational. Thomas Hart, a four-year Marine Corps veteran, who served in Vietnam, became the College's first full-time, male day student.

As the College reached its 50-year milestone in 1970, new seeds of tradition were being sown. The College legally became an independent institution while maintaining its Catholic traditions. Dr. Alphonse R. Miele became the College's first lay president in 1970, followed by Dr. Thomas A. Manion, Dr. Louis C. Vaccaro, and the current president, Dr. R. Mark Sullivan.

In 1971, The College was again at the educational forefront, establishing the Experienced Adult Program (EAP), enabling adult students to receive undergraduate credit for documented life learning experiences. The EAP was one

Today, the 27,000 square foot Science Center is the entryway to the 25-acre Saint Rose campus. The College serves nearly 4,000 students with 36 undergraduate and 21 graduate programs.

of the first programs of its kind in the country and still stands as a national model. The College's athletic programs also blossomed throughout the '80s, and by 1991 the Colleges Golden Knights were invited into the National Collegiate Athletic (NCAA) Division II.

There is no doubt that the dreams of a few can impact the lives of thousands. The College has awarded degrees to more than 23,000 students and the early vision of the Sisters of Saint Joseph of Carondelet continues to form the underpinnings of the institution. The College's mission remains the same: to provide quality educational opportunities to students of all backgrounds and create an atmosphere in which students are empowered to improve themselves and the world around them.

GE SILICONES

Just north of the Saratoga County village of Waterford is the manufacturing site of GE Silicones. A business unit of GE Plastics, GE Silicones has been part of the community since 1947 and today is a global leader in a wide range of silicone rubber, fluids, adhesives and related products. Total sales in 2000 amounted to $1.4 billion.

Silicones are a synthetic material initially developed as an alternative to natural rubber. They are used widely in many industries such as electronics, where they help protect circuit boards and keep computer disk drives spinning, and in consumer applications, such as personal care, where they help make lotions creamier and cosmetics smoother. The most widely-recognized product is caulk sealant, used to create a waterproof seam around windows, doors, tubs and sinks.

Silicone rubber became widely known as "bouncing putty" in the 1950s, and in 1969, man's first walk on the moon was made possible by boots made from GE Silicone rubber.

The 800-acre site on Hudson River Road serves as both the primary manufacturing site for the Americas and also as its global headquarters. With more than 1,300 employees at Waterford, GE Silicones is one of the largest private employers in the Capital District of New York State. (The business employs an additional 2,000 employees

Silicones formulated for use at home provide seals that won't shrink or yellow.

GE Silicones Manufacturing Site in Waterford, NY

at plants throughout the U.S., Europe and the Pacific.) The Waterford site's payroll alone generates in excess of $90 million into the local economy each year.

The direct process for manufacturing silicones was invented in the late 1930s by a GE scientist, Dr. Eugene G. Rochow. Construction of the Waterford plant began in 1945. It opened for business on the initial 65-acre site with 100 employees. One portion of the property included a small cemetery—still protected and maintained by GE—in which several founding members of the village of Waterford are buried. A narrow stone lock from the original Champlain Canal is also located just south of the GE property; an effort is underway to make it a point of interest on the regional bike trail.

A strong culture of emergency preparedness and concern for safety and the environment is evident at GE Silicones. This is strengthened by training and equipment, but is ultimately drawn from the experience of production workers, most of whom are natives of nearby river towns where dealing with the deadly fury of flooding has been a way of life. The Waterford plant proudly received a federal safety award in 2000 for its practices, one of only a handful given to facilities of its type.

GE Silicones maintains two fully-equipped firehouses, and is a member of the mutual aid system in the region. The employee Fire Brigade has helped douse house fires in Waterford, assist car accident victims in Halfmoon and used its special expertise to help characterize and safely handle chemical spills throughout the Capital region. Additionally, each year employees donate hundreds of volunteer hours in area schools and community groups. Employees have also been honored by the United Way for leadership in charitable giving, which helps thousands of the less fortunate in the region.

The uses for silicones continue to present new opportunities for growth. GE Silicones enters the new millennium with market leadership, a strong community presence, an e-commerce site at www.GESilicones.com, and most importantly, employees committed to delighting customers with quality products and service.

Silicone is used to provide protection and enhance the reliability of computer circuit boards.

GRASSLAND EQUIPMENT

Horst Pogge regularly walks the eight acres at 892 Troy-Schenectady Road, Latham, New York, the Grassland Equipment's headquarters. While walking, he will stop to talk with one of the company's managers, warehouse men, drivers, or the parts or service technicians. Often, he will run into a customer and stop to chat. His interest in his business has not diminished even though he became chairman of the board when he recently turned over the presidency and the position of chief executive officer of his company to his son, Kirk Pogge. To his son, Hans Pogge, he gave the position of chief operating officer. He presently remains as treasurer of Grassland.

Horst Pogge, along with his sons, has built Grassland into an impressive and unique multimillion dollar conglomeration of commercial, consumer, and irrigation sales, parts, and service which does business in certain areas of three northeastern states.

Grassland's commercial division deals with golf courses, schools, cemeteries, nurseries, parks, large estates, and state and city agencies. The

Left to right: Kirk H. Pogge, president, Hans J. Pogge, executive vice president, James Young, banker and Horst Pogge, chairman of the board.

company markets specialty mowing equipment for large areas, fertilizer, seed, and various tools and parts needed to maintain large turf areas. Turf irrigation systems are also designed and marketed.

The Latham operation houses a large service department, as well as a retail store. Toro industrial equipment is featured. The company employs 67 people in their various locations. Grassland has been recognized by its

vendors for excellence in sales and customer service on many occasions.

In 1994, Grassland purchased Eaton Equipment, a Toro distributor in western New York State. This enabled Grassland to be appointed distributor for Toro products in the entire upstate New York area, in addition to the state of Vermont. Grassland now has three locations which are located in Latham, Liverpool and Blasdell.

The oldest of four sons, Pogge was born in Klingendorf, Germany. He grew up and went to school in Rostock on the Baltic Sea in northern Germany.

When the war was over, Horst lived in Holzminden and returned to Agricultural College. After he completed his education, he became a farm manager. While working there, he married his first wife Irena Kant, who passed away from leukemia in 1993. His first child, Karin, was born in Germany in 1950.

Liverpool, New York branch.

Horst gained the respect of his employer and other farmers for being an efficient and clever business person. With much of his family property lost in the war and inaccessible to him in East Germany, and wanting more opportunity, he decided to bring his family to America.

In 1952, the family was sponsored by Catholic Relief Services to come to America. They arrived in New York just before Christmas on a snowy evening. After completing processing through immigration and buying something to eat, they had $6.00 with which to begin their new life in America, hoping it would be a land of opportunity where hard work and effort could bring success.

They lived for a short time with relatives in Delmar. Pogge, armed with a willingness to learn English and to work long hours, rose through the ranks of several local businesses to finally take a position with a Toro distributor called Hudson Toro, located in Latham. The owner of the company, Glen Larson, appreciated Pogge's interest in his business, and soon they opened a new company together. After a few years Horst was able to find financing to purchase the controlling shares of what was by then Grassland Equipment.

The spark and enthusiasm that Horst Pogge generates continues to keep the level of excitement high and productivity flowing at Grassland. This demonstrates Pogge's ability to see opportunity in every situation. He continues to contribute greatly to the community and has been an active driving force in every community group or civic organization in which he has been involved.

For many years he has been associated with the Friends of Pruyn House, a Colonie Town Cultural Center. He raises funds and actively participates in the renovation of the historical house, barns, tool museum, patting shed, and

Latham showroom.

presently the carriage house, while directing improvements to the grounds.

Horst serves on the local Industrial Development Agency and is a trustee on the Board of the Albany Rural Cemetery Association. He is a member and has held offices in the Albany Regional Chamber of Commerce and the Latham Chamber of Commerce. He also is a member of the Board of the Greater Loudonville Association and oversees the planting and care of the flower beds which are the focal point of Loudonville.

At his residence in Loudonville, with his wife Pat, he continues to be an avid gardener, creating outstanding and creative plantings.

Horst Pogge, throughout his life, has tapped a tireless spirit and resourcefulness to achieve where others would have failed, to gain respect and admiration from others, to inspire others to action, and most importantly to make the world around him a better place. Truly, Horst Pogge is a credit to his German heritage and a shining example of an American success story.

Latham facility.

HAMILTON PRINTING COMPANY

Named after Hamilton Street in Albany, New York, Hamilton Printing Company opened it's doors to the public in 1912. Founding fathers Fred Corey, Ira Payne and H. Hull were former employees of the Weed Parson Company. Once their doors closed, Hamilton Printing's opened.

As business began to grow, the owners decided in 1923 to move the company from downtown Albany to East Greenbush, NY. At the time, this was a risky business move. Employees worried about finding transportation to the suburban location. The owners knew that due to the reasonable cost of land at the time, this would provide an opportunity for the future growth they wanted. Hamilton Printing Company had a small, letterpress shop and was focused on pamphlet binding. The trend was turning to

book manufacturing, so Ira Payne traveled to New York City to acquire business from the publishing and typesetting industries. Publishers soon began to solicit Hamilton Printing for their printing, typesetting and shipping jobs.

In 1933, Judson Payne, son of Ira, made his way into the business. He began to learn all facets of the company, focusing on the development of the sales and administrative areas. After Ira Payne's death in 1953, Fred Corey became the sole owner. He ran the production side at Hamilton and agreed to a deal. Fred would give Judson a chance to run the business for six months. If Judson was successful, Fred would, in time, sell his shares to Judson. Twelve years later, Judson became owner of Hamilton Printing Company.

Throughout the 1950s to the early 1970s, the company continued to expand. Due to their success, they were able to purchase new printing presses and add a paperback bindery in 1966. This benefited their business, allowing them to make a complete sale on paperback books. These books would be created from start to finish at Hamilton. But, they still continued to send out printed sheets to hardcover binderies in order to keep all their customers happy.

By 1971, it was time for Hamilton Printing to merge in to the world of technology. The purchase of it's first offset perfecting press not only increased business by thirty percent, but

Original plant built in 1923 with three additions (65,000 square feet).

it allowed a streamlined and efficient way to reduce the time and cost of producing books. Over the next three years, Hamilton expanded by purchasing three additional offset presses.

A third generation Payne joined Hamilton in 1966. Brian Payne, Judson's son, began his Hamilton career in the bindery and quickly moved his way up the ladder, learning the intricacies of how to run a successful business. As Judson began to slow down, Brian took over the daily operation responsibilities. By 1974, Hamilton had expanded its manufacturing space to 65,000 square feet and tallied six offset printing presses. A significant turning point occurred in 1976 when Hamilton Printing bought a hardcover trade bindery in Chester, NY. Now Hamilton would not have to rely on outside vendors to fulfill their hardcover book requests.

Hamilton was now an established, full service soft and hardcover book manufacturing company.

Following in his father's footsteps, Brian was made president upon Judson's retirement in 1979. After several years of conducting business from two locations, Chester and East Greenbush, the company decided to close the Chester location and move the manufacturing facilities to a 40,000 square foot building in Castleton, NY. With only 10 miles separating them, East Greenbush was now responsible for printing and the Castleton location performed the bookbinding. Inevitably, the company's goal was to complete all business in one location. 1984 brought the expansion of an additional 60,000 square feet to the Castleton building and by 1989, all of Hamilton Printing was settled in one location.

Innovations in printing press technologies were prevalent in the 1990s. Hamilton acquired two web presses to increase productivity and efficiency. Today the company employs over 150 dedicated staff members and generates over six million books a year. A third web press is in the plans for 2001. Today, after 88 years in business and three generations of leadership, Hamilton Printing continues to expand and serve the needs of the demanding book industry. In a world today that is focused on the Internet and e-mail, Hamilton Printing Company's longevity proves that people still find importance in the printed word.

Current plant of 100,000 square feet in Castleton on 26 acres.

GURLEY PRECISION INSTRUMENTS

The history of Gurley Precision Instruments is the history of the technology of measuring.

The Troy enterprise, which until 1968 was known as W. & L.E. Gurley, had its beginnings in Ephraim Gurley's foundry in Gibbonsville, now Watervliet. William and Lewis E. Gurley, from whom the firm took its original name, were Ephraim's sons.

In 1845, William Gurley formed a partnership with Jonas Phelps to make mathematical and measuring instruments. Lewis became a partner in 1851, and the following year the Gurleys bought out Phelps and the company became W. & L.E. Gurley. The Gurley Building, at the corner of Fulton Street and Fifth Avenue in Troy, was completed in 1862 after the great fire that destroyed much of the city.

Lewis, who succeeded his brother as president, was followed first by his son, William Frank Gurley, and then by William's son-in-law, Paul Cook, as head of the firm. One of Lewis's daughters married Edgar Hayes Betts, a manufacturer of collars and shirts, who later became president of both the shirt firm and the Gurley enterprise.

After Betts's death in 1951, leadership of the company left the family for some years before it passed back to the

The Gurley Building, constructed in 1862, is a national historic landmark. It still houses a firm, now known as Gurley Precision Instruments.

hands of Robert Gurley Betts, grandson of Lewis Gurley. Aside from these leaders, the firm's best-known employee was probably Edward W. Arms, who worked at Gurley from 1862 to 1932. He designed the first, fully-automated dividing engine in America, the first mountain transit, and made the first aluminum transit.

Local entrepreneur Kenneth T. Lally bought the company in 1963. In 1968, the enterprise became part of Teledyne, a major high technology, multi-product corporation, and its name was changed to Teledyne Gurley. Teledyne sold the company to O. Patrick Brady, current president and CEO, and Ronald H. Laberge in 1993. Now known as Gurley Precision Instruments, the company is once again locally owned and managed.

In the firm's early years, it developed and manufactured surveying instruments, hydrological instruments, standard weights and measures, paper-testing instruments, and meteorological instruments.

During the World War II era, W. & L.E. Gurley perfected methods for producing complex patterns on glass and other materials. This technology, known as optographics, is employed in producing high-resolution targets, reticles, scales, step wedges and code discs. During the Korean War the company produced as many as 20,000 reticles each month for tank range finders.

The combination of optographics with mechanical and electronic techniques led to the development of electro-optical encoders, which translate rotary or linear motion into electronic signals. These have become the most significant part of the firm's business.

Gurley's encoders, which achieve accuracy of a few parts per million, are used in factory automation, robotics, semiconductor manufacturing machinery, radar pedestals, telescope gimbals, spacecraft, medical equipment and many other areas that require the

Gurley Precision Instruments' electro-optical encoders are used in a wide variety of precision applications.

precise measurement or control of speed or position. The firm was recently awarded a U.S. patent for a technology that has enabled it to introduce a new type of optical encoder to the world.

As a natural extension of its encoder business, the firm produces packaged digital-readout (DRO) systems to improve the productivity of machine tools. The DRO combines an encoder with a visual display to provide an easily-read digital indication of a machine's worktable position.

In addition, Gurley continues to produce hydrological instruments for measuring the velocity of water flow, and paper-testing instruments for determining porosity, stiffness, smoothness and other properties of paper and similar materials.

Gurley looks forward to maintaining its leadership role in the precision instruments field.

HUDSON MOHAWK INDUSTRIAL GATEWAY

Although most of the iron works, the bell and stove foundries, the textile mills, and the collar and cuff factories located near the confluence of the Hudson and Mohawk rivers are now closed, and many are demolished, much of the Victorian splendor of the region remains, and an appreciation of its significance lives on among area residents and visitors. Moreover, the region's industrial past is being put to good use through adaptive uses, heritage tourism, and school programs.

For much of that, residents of the area can thank the Hudson Mohawk Industrial Gateway. For almost 30 years this organization has helped inform our understanding of the nation's industrial heritage. Whether one argues that the area was the birthplace of America's industrial revolution, or the Silicon Valley of the nineteenth century, or the prototype of the modern American city during the urban-industrial era, there is no question that the entire nation took inspiration from the region in the mid-nineteenth century.

Nowhere else in North America was there a more felicitous marriage of horizontal water for shipping and the cascading waters of the Mohawk, the Poestenkill, and the Wynantskill for powering machinery. Once the nation achieved its independence, that mix attracted entrepreneurs like Henry Burden and Samuel Wilson (the progenitor of today's Uncle Sam symbol), who enhanced those assets with such improvements as the Erie Canal and the famous Burden Water Wheel at the same time as they exploited them to build a thriving regional economy based on the cutting-edge technology of the day, much of it of their own invention.

Organized to spearhead the revitalization of the area using the old industries and industrial buildings as assets, the Gateway grew out of the work of the Preservation Committee of the Rensselaer County Historical Society. It was chartered in 1972 by the Regents of the University of the State of New York as a not-for-profit educational corporation with the responsibilities of public education and the development of tourism.

Since 1974, the Gateway has been developing the Burden Iron Works Museum, a rehabilitation of the historic office building of the Burden Iron Company, which the Gateway rescued from certain demolition, and which it also uses as its headquarters. At the moment, it has over $400,000 in grants and donations for the next phase of that work. It has proposed adaptive uses for certain Troy firehouses, was instrumental in the preservation and reuse of the Cluett Peabody Bleachery complex on historic Peebles Island, has provided advice and technical assistance to the owners of several local historic properties, and continually encourages new investors in the area.

Gateway advocacy was instrumental in the façade-rehabilitation programs in downtown Troy and Cohoes, and the group was a force in the formation of the Hudson-Mohawk ("*RiverSpark*") Urban Cultural Park (now Heritage Area) in 1977. The first in the state, *RiverSpark* has served as a model for a statewide system of 17 such entities that is still growing. Since 1997, the Gateway has served as the management entity for Troy's *RiverSpark* Visitor Center, one of two such facilities in the *RiverSpark* Heritage Area.

Over the years, the Hudson Mohawk Industrial Gateway has been most evident to residents of the surrounding community via its tours, attractive to local residents and tourists alike. The Gateway introduced river cruises to the area, which are now a thriving for-profit industry. Its annual tour of Troy's Tiffany Treasures attracts busloads of tourists from considerable distances. The Gateway has also played a pivotal role in the production of several films about the history of the area, and it has generated a variety of popular and scholarly publications about the region's industrial heritage, of which this book is an example.

From the outset, no doubt because of the richly significant heritage of the area, demand for the Gateway's services has far outstripped its ability to provide them, despite the great financial generosity of its members, the surrounding community, corporate and foundation sponsors near and far, and government agencies at all levels, as well as the many hours invested by its trustees, its staff, and its many selfless volunteers. The Gateway appreciates any and all support as it aims to become the best regional industrial heritage program in the nation.

The Burden Iron Works Museum is framed by a ladle car, used to transport molten steel from the blast furnace to the foundry buildings at the Burden Iron Company. Photo by Sid Brown.

KAPLAN INTERNATIONAL PROGRAMS AT RENSSELAER

The natural beauty of upstate New York makes Rensselaer an idyllic setting for Kaplan's international students. Students travel from all over the world to take advantage of Kaplan's test preparation and English language programs. This flow of students is increasing as American college and graduate degrees become more desirable and English language skills become crucial for international business professionals.

For many years people around the world have been taking standardized test to apply for entrance into college and graduate school, to practice in their respective fields and to advance in their careers. The increased importance society places on education makes competition more intense in both the admissions process and career advancement. In turn, performing well on standardized tests becomes crucial. That is when students turn to Kaplan.

Kaplan has quite a history. Sixty years ago a young man named

Students enjoy the natural beauty of upstate New York.

Stanley H. Kaplan, who had been tutoring students in the basement of his parents home in Brooklyn, NY, invented test preparation for admissions exams and a business was born. Kaplan, now owned by The Washington Post Company, has helped more than three million people worldwide prepare for over 35 standardized tests, including entrance exams for secondary school, college and graduate school as well as English language and professional licensing exams. Kaplan now operates nearly 200 centers and more than 3000 classroom locations worldwide.

As Kaplan expands into new areas in the educational and career

services arena, its international programs unit grows enormously. Kaplan is proud of its success in preparing international students for university programs, as well as its record of placing students at some of the finest universities in the U.S. Seeing students meet their goals and obtain acceptance into the university or college of their choice is not only exciting to Kaplan's staff, but it also fulfills Kaplan's mission of helping individuals achieve their educational and career goals.

That is where the Kaplan Center in Troy, New York fits into the corporate picture. Located on the 260-acre campus of Rensselaer Polytechnic Institute (RPI), one of the most prominent engineering schools in the United States, Kaplan's RPI center offers English language and test preparation programs to students from all over the world. The center is currently located in West Hall, an historic building with high ceilings, spacious hallways, and attractive views of the city. The building, constructed in 1843, previously housed a hospital and a high school.

Kaplan chose Rensselaer Polytechnic Institute in part because it has been at the forefront of scientific and technological education since 1824. RPI's Lally School of Management is among the top business schools in the country. This enables international students to interact with high-level students and professors in addition to the many people they meet at the Kaplan Center.

The students at the RPI Kaplan Center study English to prepare for admission into American universities or to enhance their language abilities for business and professional purposes. The highly skilled and dedicated teachers help them with all facets of second language acquisition: listening, speaking, reading, writing and grammar. Kaplan's International program uses a lexical approach to learning

Students form lifelong friendships at the Kaplan RPI Center.

International students are proud to study on the campus of a world class Institution.

English, teaching students to build their vocabularies by learning and using "chunks" of words. The students also work in instructor-guided personalized computer labs, concentrating on areas that are the most difficult for them. Kaplan uses its years of experience, focus on research and development and extensive interaction with students to ensure that its students gain the communication skills necessary to succeed in school and beyond.

Kaplan students also meet with a University Placement Advisor who assists with all phases of a student's possible placement into an American university.

In addition to providing English language instruction to the students, the staff at the Kaplan Center assists

Studying in the Computer Assisted Learning Lab (CALL) helps students learn English.

the students in finding housing with American host families in nearby communities, in the campus dormitories or in local apartments. By living with an American family the students experience American life and culture while improving their English language skills. They often form long lasting, joyous relationships with their host families.

For example, one family has hosted all the children in their original "son's" family. In 1998 a boy from Taiwan came to study at the Kaplan Center and later went on to do research at RPI. In 1999 his brother came to study and a year later his sister came to study too. The parents of the three children have also stayed with the host family; now everyone knows each other and the host family hopes one day to travel to Taiwan. Another host mother reported receiving Mother's Day cards from seven different countries. Still another was invited, all expenses paid, to attend her host son's wedding in Germany.

Many international students choose instead to live in the campus dormito-

ries and are able to experience American university life 24-hours-a-day. For many, this is the first time they have lived on their own. They learn to be independent by living alone in a foreign country, always knowing that Kaplan's support system can help them through potential difficulties. It is a rewarding and fascinating experience for Kaplan instructors and staff to help students surpass challenges and learn to live in the "real world."

Of course, students also have fun at the Kaplan Center at RPI. The staff provides opportunities for the international students to visit other parts of New York and the surrounding states. Students can organize activities for themselves, other students and a Kaplan staff member. Some of the activities include bowling on campus, watching an RPI hockey game, outlet shopping, skiing, swimming at Lake George, a day trip to New York City or Boston, or an overnight trip to Montreal. Many times the host families accompany the students and participate in activities with them.

The students at the RPI Kaplan Center also get involved with the community. They have done volunteer work at various local agencies, helped political campaigns, assisted children in camp activities and recruited senior citizens to come to the Center to engage in conversation allowing the students to practice their speaking skills. By giving back to the community, the students experience a rewarding part of American life.

Regardless of their reasons for being here, the students at the Kaplan Center at RPI form life-long friendships, supporting each other and working together. As the world becomes smaller and smaller and more companies expand internationally, the students who study English at the Kaplan Center will have had the advantage of having a true American educational experience.

LEVONIAN BROTHERS, INC.

Levonian Brothers, Inc. was established on April 1, 1947 in the state of New York and is located in Troy. The company manufactures and distributes meat and allied products throughout the eastern seaboard. The company's products are sold by an internal sales staff and a network of manufacturer's representatives.

Levonian Brothers has been owned and operated as a family business since it was founded by an Armenian immigrant family, Elia Y. and Levon Y. Levonian and their nephews Elia M. and Levon M. Levonian, now deceased. This business was located on North Pearl Street in Albany, New York. They later moved across the river to Troy to begin serving customers in the wholesale market located in that densely-populated manufacturing city. Levonian Bros., Inc. was started with a purchase price of $10,000 and a $25,000 loan. To save money, equipment was purchased at auction. At first the enterprise was engaged only in meat distribution to family-owned grocers, butchers, and other small service businesses scattered throughout the neighborhood. By this time, two other nephews, Greg Nazarian and Ralph Darian were growing up in the family business, serving as apprentices in the wholesale plant. During the 1950s and 1960s the independent out-

The first home of Levonian Brothers, Inc., was this frame building on Troy's River Street, at the same location as the present plant. This 1947 photo shows one of the founders, the late Levon Y. Levonian (center), with two unidentified friends.

lets were gradually disappearing and the stores were becoming larger, prompting the organization's entry into the manufacturing end of the meat business in the early 1970s. Uncooked corned beef, still one of the firm's best-known and most prestigious products, was the first item produced. Gradually the line was expanded to include cooked corned beef, roast beef, pastrami, ham, and various sausage items. The business had grown so much that in order to accommodate their rapidly growing customer base and demand for products, they razed the original building, and invested $1 million in a modern plant where they began processing meats on a vastly larger scale. In 1982, a neighboring structure was purchased and converted into the company's distribution center, leaving

the original building for the manufacturing operation.

More recently, Robert Nazarian, the third generation in the family, joined the company and today provides the spirited leadership needed to move the Levonian Brothers, Inc. into a new century. The company points with pride to a continuing family-owned business that represents a long tradition and believes that only with hands-on management will they be assured of a successful company that manufactures quality products.

Levonian Brothers, Inc. has survived over 50 years in meat processing—a very competitive, rigorous and technical manufacturing business in the national arena. Large numbers of meat processors in the United States are no longer in business because they were unable to endure the hardships of the industry and could not keep up with advancing technology.

Levonian Brothers, Inc. has always believed in serving the niche market and taking innovative approaches. With its management team having over 150 years experience in the technical business of meat processing, they are able to produce over 70 different kinds of items within four major categories: roast beef, corned beef/pastrami, hams and sausages, which are shipped mostly in the northeastern region of the U.S. A growing number of customers are outside the original service region, including in Florida, Georgia, Michigan, Missouri, Ohio, Oregon, and Washington. Levonian Brothers also exports to Toronto, Canada. In addition, the company was one of the first in the upstate New York area to become a U.S. Government inspected plant—the highest and most stringent inspection system in the world, allowing Levonian Brothers, Inc. to participate in interstate commerce. They are one of seven processors worldwide licensed to produce Certified Angus Beef™ Value Added

Levonian Brother's delivery truck in front of their facility.

Deli Products, which are distributed to major supermarket chains and food service distributors in the United States and Canada. The latest innovation is a product designed to appeal to an increasing number of consumers demanding easy to prepare meals—Meals-to-Go. These are marinated kabobs, ribs and pork tenderloins, vacuum-sealed and ready to prepare. Available in area supermarkets, they are proving to be popular with the public and a complementary product to Levonian's other product lines.

Maintaining their belief in innovation, the company was the first in the United States to install thermal processing equipment to cook roast beef, using the Delta T system for dry roasting. Other companies followed their example soon after. Levonian Brothers, Inc. was the first in their region to produce an exact fat content, ground beef suitable for supermarkets, and was the first in their area to produce fabricated beef cuts with vacuum packaging for longer shelf life.

Levonian Brothers expects to continue their growth into more areas of the United States and Canada and to develop new products.

On July 12, 1998, Levonian Brothers, Inc. and Yingkou Zhongchen Group Corp. of China entered into a joint venture contract establishing Yingkou Shuangchen-Levonian Meat Processing Co., Ltd. The joint venture company is a limited liability company and is a legal corporation of China governed by the laws of China. The production and business scope of the joint venture is to manufacture meat products such as ham, sausage, canned and packaged meats, and to distribute such products within the People's Republic of China. In this joint venture, the Chinese participants look to Levonian Brothers, Inc. to provide the manufacturing and distribution process expertise that makes the company so successful in the United States market.

From left to right: Gregory Nazarian, Robert Nazarian, and Ralph Darian.

Levonian Brothers, Inc. has long been committed to safety in the workplace and has instituted a number of incentives to assure safety. Regular safety meetings take place and work teams were created, with a bonus system, to promote an accident-free environment. Regular inspection and maintenance schedules assure that equipment is at the peak of working order at all times.

Levonian Brothers, Inc. is not only a leader in the meat processing field, but in the community, by contributing financially and with human resources to help those in need. The company has participated in many civic and charitable organizations over the years. These organizations include the United Way, for which they were awarded recognition for achieving 100 percent participation, and working for a special camp for children suffering from cancer, Camp Good Days and Special Times. More recently, Robert Nazarian co-founded Circle of Champs, which creates special activities for children with various childhood illnesses. In addition, Levonian Brothers contributes to area food banks and other groups needing product donations for fund-raising events. Because the company has been based in Troy since 1947 and is family-owned, it stays close to the needs of the community and is respected and valued for that commitment.

America Riviera working on the sausage line.

MARIA COLLEGE

The Maria Mission: Maria College is an independent two-year college offering associate degrees and one-year certificate programs. Its curriculum is grounded in the humanities, seeking to instill in its graduates a respect for the dignity of each person and the ability to transform learned skills into caring service. The ideal of "service to others" is rooted in the Judeo-Christian tradition and the ideals of the Sisters of Mercy who founded the College.

The intent of the College is to deliver these programs with high academic standards, convenient scheduling formats for students of any age who will benefit from small classes and a warm, encouraging environment.

In 1958, the Religious Sisters of Mercy founded Maria College as a sister formation and liberal arts college with a student body of 52 young women. From its founding, the mission of the College has been to educate for service to the Greater Capital Region, to the communities where its graduates live and work, and to the nation beyond.

While implementing the mission began with the education of Sisters of Mercy, the vision soon broadened with the offering in 1964 of the College's first associate degree program, Early Childhood Education, with enrollment open to the community. All degree programs were opened to co-educational enrollment in 1971, and today male students account for more than 20 percent of Maria's student body.

Business-related degrees appeared in 1967 with concentrations in executive, legal, medical, secretarial and administrative skills. Degrees in Management, Accounting, Travel and Tourism, and a one-year Information Processing Specialist Certificate followed. Legal Assistant (paralegalism) was offered both as a degree and a one-year certificate in 1995.

A nursing program was introduced in 1968 with a unique curriculum that

The Maria Medallion is part of the Madonna and Child stained glass window which graces the entrance to Maria's Administration Building. The window was housed in 1885 in the Chapel of the original Sisters of Mercy Motherhouse in Rensselaer, NY.

applied classroom learning in clinical settings at nearby St. Peter's Hospital and other community health agencies. Its graduates are prepared to sit for the National Council Licensing Examination-RN for licensure as registered nurse.

Degrees in Physical Therapy (1971) and Occupational Therapy (1975) were established, and their graduates are prepared to sit for examination and licensure as Physical Therapist and Occupational Therapy Assistants. Most recently, one-year certificates were established in Gerontology (1997), Bereavement Studies (1999), and Complementary Therapy (2000).

In 1998, the College established a state-of-the-art facility for a new Computer Information Systems degree where its graduates will be prepared to work with confidence in the high technology offices of the New Millennium.

Because a Maria College education has from its founding been grounded

in the liberal arts, Maria's degrees qualify for transfer to four-year institutions—a cost-effective benefit that increasing numbers of its graduates elect. Thus, the wide range of associate's degree programs, complete in themselves, are not only preparation for further education, but also are gateways to professional careers.

With the conviction that the opportunity to learn should embrace the serious student, Maria College established innovative, flexible scheduling formats to serve all students—from recent high school graduates and working professionals seeking to advance or change careers, to older students returning to school. In 1971, Maria established an active evening division which offers degrees in a three-year sequence, and in 1981 announced the first Weekend College in northeastern New York and one of the few in the nation. The unique Weekend College format, which schedules classes only every other weekend, makes it possible to earn associate degrees in two-years. Weekend College, while serving all, serves best the needs of the mature student who must coordinate family and career responsibilities with educational opportunity.

Sister Laureen Fitzgerald, RSM, the third president of Maria College, 1977-present.

The Learning Resource Center was created in the fall of 1982 and has become a major support service for Maria students. The Center has two goals: to provide tutorials for development/remediation in math computation and concepts, study skills, and language arts; and to provide the general student body with supplemental learning materials. The Center's resources include computers, VCRs, and other audio-video equipment. The Center is staffed and available to students in all divisions. Maria's commitment to the needs of the individual student is in evidence nowhere better than in its academic guidance and counseling programs. Academic guidance through a faculty advisor is assigned to each student; professional counseling through the Counseling Center, is available as needed; and career guidance through the College's Career Planning and Placement Office, a service also available to alumnae/i all serve to strengthen that commitment.

The College's intimate campus gives evidence of an academic atmosphere that embraces both the timeless and the contemporary: timeless in its commitment to humanities-based learning, and contemporary in the modern environment in which these classic convictions of the human spirit can be nurtured.

Maria's Administration Building was constructed in 1959, and today houses classrooms, computer and information processing laboratories, multimedia and learning resource centers, administrative and faculty offices, and a working library of more than 34,000 volumes. In addition, through the Internet, is access to the world of knowledge beyond its bounds. The Campus School—a teaching laboratory for students enrolled in the Early Childhood Education degree program—was established in 1967, and opened to community enrollment of young children. With the addition of a kindergarten in 1985, it was

enlarged and renovated.

The cloistered convent of a Dominican order that abutted the campus became available in 1970, and the College, hard pressed for space by a burgeoning enrollment, purchased it from the Catholic Diocese of Albany and located its health care programs there. In 1984, with the support of alumnae/i and friends, through the Second Mile Campaign—a celebration of the 25th anniversary of Maria's founding—the convent was transformed into a state-of-the-art allied health facility. Renovated to preserve architectural integrity, the convent, renamed Marian Hall, was designated an historic building in 1986 by the Historic Albany Foundation.

Maria College has enjoyed more than four decades of growth due in part to the success its graduates have had in establishing themselves in career fields of choice. But beneath this lies the delicate balance the college has been able to maintain between its commitment to the liberal arts and the highly contemporary career-oriented degrees it offers. In accomplishing this, the College breathes life into an educational commitment that seeks to instill in its graduates respect for the dignity of the individual and the ability to transform

Maria College's historic Marian Hall

learned skills into vehicles of service.

Possibly the greatest advantage to being a Maria student, however, is becoming part of a new community of friends—friends with shared personal goals and professional objectives—friends who have shared the enriching experience of having attended a special college in a special setting.

MCNAMEE, LOCHNER, TITUS & WILLIAMS, P.C.

With time comes the experience to be a leader. Such is the case with McNamee, Lochner, Titus & Williams, P.C., one of the oldest and largest law firms located in the Capital Region of the State of New York.

Today, the firm offers a statewide practice with over forty attorneys and a large and qualified support staff. The McNamee firm has concentrations in several areas of law, including: civil litigation, banking, consumer financial services, business, family law, government relations, real estate, estate planning, environmental law, labor and employment law, energy law, construction law and municipal finance.

Founded in 1863, by Stephen O. Shepherd and George L. Stedman, the firm has grown to be a pacesetter in the legal field; however, it has not outgrown its dedication to its community. Located on State Street in Albany, New York, within a block of its original site, the full-service team continues to demonstrate dedication to their clients as well as to the surrounding area through outreach and support efforts—a philosophy founded early in the firm's history.

Partners and associates have assisted in guiding many of the area's non-profit and civic organizations over the years. They are active board participants in local theatres, museums, hospitals and institutions of higher education. They focus their energy towards worthy causes to better their community and have been recognized for those efforts by organizations such as bar associations, the United Way and the Legal Aid Society. In 2001, the firm received the New York law firm pro bono service award from Chief Judge Judith S. Kaye of the New York State Court of Appeals. Giving back is not seen as an obligation for the firm; it is a way to help support a town it has called home for over 138 years.

Many of the members have served as leaders in business government and professional associations. In fact, two partners, David S. Williams in 1981 and Lorraine Power Tharp in 2002, have been elected to fill the role of president of the New York State Bar Association—a 67,000 member professional group. Partners names can be found on the member lists of such groups as the Defense Research Institute, National Association of Bond Lawyers, Estate Planning Council of Eastern New York, the Capital District Women's Bar Association, Albany City Common Council, the American Institute of Public Accountants, The Best

Colonel Frank A. McNamee (1892-1972).

Lawyers in America and Who's Who in American Law.

The blueprint was laid for the culture of the firm by Colonel Frank A. McNamee (1892-1972), who joined the firm in 1921. The Colonel, as he was referred to by the locals of Albany, understood every citizen's right for freedom and a fair legal system as he was a distinguished veteran of both World Wars I and II.

Colonel McNamee's history is intertwined with the town in which he was raised. He graduated from the Albany Academy in 1911 and then Williams College in 1915.

In the fall of 1915, the Colonel enrolled at Harvard Law School, pursuing his dream to become an attorney. Unfortunately, he could not complete the program as he was called to be a member of the Army Calvary Reserve, which fought Poncho Villa on the Mexican border before World War I. He then joined the European Theater where he stayed for the duration of the war, while rising to the rank of captain.

After the war was through and he had served his country proudly, Colonel McNamee returned to Harvard Law School to continue his pursuit of a degree. He was graduated from the ivy-league institution in 1921 and immediately went to work for the firm, which was then titled Visscher, Whalen, Loucks & Murphy. He returned to military service in 1943.

The Colonel was not the only notable figure in the history of the firm. Charles J. Buchanan, who was added to the firm's moniker in 1880, also fought for freedom and justice. He enlisted as a volunteer for the Union cause in the autumn of 1861, serving in the First Regiment of U.S. (Berdan's) Sharpshooters. He also joined the Army of the Potomac, in which he served with distinguished gallantry for three years, rising to the rank of first lieutenant and acting adjutant.

In 1867, Mr. Buchanan was appointed by President Johnson as a cadet to the U.S. Military Academy at West Point. He resigned his cadetship in October 1870 to study law. He too had the long-time aspiration to serve as a lawyer. He was admitted to the bar in January 1874 and the following year he became a partner in the firm, which then operated as Smith, Bancroft & Moak.

Mr. Buchanan's name was added to the law firm's title in 1880, after the death of Mr. S.G. Bancroft. Mr. Henry Smith passed away in 1884, and the firm became known as Moak & Buchanan. The firm progressed under this new partnership and conducted many important and involved cases.

In 1892, Mr. Nathaniel C. Moak passed away also. However, Mr. Buchanan continued to make the practice a growing viable law firm. His career as a notable and respected attorney evolved as well. Mr. Buchanan served as the second president of the Albany County Bar Association, with a term from 1905 to 1906.

Today, the firm of McNamee, Lochner, Titus & Williams thrives in its rich history, carrying on the pride of its founding partners. They believe in the U.S. Justice System and for all that it stands. They invest in their firm, their profession and their community with the same determination and devotion as Colonel Frank McNamee and Charles J. Buchanan. And they will lead the firm into a future that holds the same great promise as that of the past.

Firm Genealogy

1863	Shepherd & Stedman
1868	Shepherd, Bancroft, Countryman & Moak
1869	Smith, Bancroft & Moak
1880	Smith, Moak & Buchanan
1889	Moak & Buchanan
1894	Charles J. Buchanan
1898	Buchanan & Conway
1899	Buchanan & Lawyer
1909	Buchanan, Lawyer & Whalen
1910	Visscher, Whalen & Austin
1920	Visscher, Whalen, Loucks & Murphy
1924	Whalen, Murphy, McNamee & Creble
1932	Whalen, McNamee, Creble & Nichols
1970	McNamee, Nichols, Lochner & Titus
1972	McNamee, Lochner, Titus & Williams

MOHAWK PAPER MILLS

Mohawk Paper Mills, Inc. is one of North America's leading producers of premium printing papers. Their product line includes coated, uncoated, and a complete line of papers for the new digital presses, such as inkjet, color copy, and laser. Small by paper industry standards, this highly successful company has grown from 900 tons per year on three paper machines (in 1978) to 90,000 tons per year—on the same three machines. The company flourished because of its competitive spirit and its ability to intertwine the craft of traditional papermaking with cutting-edge technology.

The story begins with the Mohawk and Hudson Paper Company, which was established soon after the Civil War at a former axe-handle factory on Kings Canal in Waterford. The enterprise was purchased soon thereafter by Frank Gilbert, one of the founders, and renamed the Frank Gilbert Paper Company. Nathaniel Sylvester, in his 1878 *History of Saratoga County*, de-

The original Cohoes mill of the Frank Gilbert Paper Company—now the location of Mohawk's corporate headquarters

scribes the operation as, "…employing 40 people who produced three tons of printing paper a day, using rags, wood and straw as raw materials." The mill building was purchased in 1881 from Uri Gilbert, a prominent manufacturer of railroad cars.

Frank Gilbert constructed a second paper mill in 1917 in Cohoes, just south of the junction of the Erie and Champlain canals. It manufactured groundwood, bond, mimeo, and wallpaper base stock, until the firm filed for bankruptcy in 1930. It was reorganized as Mohawk Papermakers, Inc. and George E. O'Connor, a Waterford lawyer and father of current CEO Thomas D. O'Connor, was appointed receiver and eventually bought the mill.

At that time the product mix was 80-90 percent converting base stock, box liner and box covering (with very little printing papers). In 1946, Mohawk began to develop its first cover and text line, called Mohawk Superfine. The paper ultimately gave a whole new identity to Mohawk, which began focusing on commercial printing papers. During the 1950s and

'60s Mohawk built a strong presence in the large northeast advertising and printing markets in New York, Boston, Philadelphia, and Washington, D.C. It became known for its quality papers and excellent service.

In 1969, the company was sold to Riegl Paper Co., which was subsequently taken over by Federal Paperboard. Then, in 1972, the company was bought back by Tom O'Connor Sr. and other family members. Thus began the current history of Mohawk Paper Mills, Inc.

In the 1970s and '80s, under Tom O'Connor's direction, Mohawk grew with a series of major capital investments totaling more than $90 million. A new paper machine was installed in Waterford, replacing an old one. The Cohoes machine was essentially rebuilt, with the addition of high speed metering technology, an on-the-machine coater, calendaring equipment, and a state-of-the-art electric drive. The result of these investments was a 20,000 ton capacity boost to 75,000 tons per year, entry into the coated market and the ability to produce a much wider range of grades.

Mohawk Paper Mill, Inc—Waterford Division.

Mohawk also upgraded its environment systems to meet the 1972 federal clean air and clean water standards. One of the outcomes of this upgrade was a shift to cationic dyes. New to the U.S. paper industry, these dyes were safer for employees to handle. They also allowed for the production of acid-free colored papers, which are more permanent than traditional acid-based papers. In fact, Mohawk was an innovator in the manufacture of alkaline papers (which had made it a favorite of fine book publishers around the world). In 1990, Mohawk also pioneered the first post consumer recycled coated paper—Mohawk 50/10—and in 1993, the company received its first Green Seal Certification.

Thomas D. O'Connor, Sr., CEO and chairman, has been with the company for over 50 years, starting with summer employment while in school and interrupted only by a tour in the military. In an interview in the early '90s, he took time to survey the company's accomplishments and look forward to some of its future challenges. "We have spent millions on new technology and equipment in recent years. Today our priority is to provide management and employees with the training and business tools

they need to efficiently manage and operate with our new technology." With this in mind, his vision for the '90s was to build the "people" side of Mohawk, by investing heavily in training and systems that would allow the company to anticipate customer needs and provide them more efficiently.

The decade that followed was a challenging one for Mohawk, as it was for many enterprises. A major recession, combined with technology-driven shifts in the graphic arts industry, completely changed Mohawk's marketing environment. Production of printed materials, once highly concentrated in major industrial markets had become decentralized, with the largest growth in areas where Mohawk had little representation: the South, Midwest, West, and Asia. Plus, a wave of industry consolidations was creating billion-dollar competitors—offering a dizzying array of new products for this small, but lucrative, premium paper market.

Mohawk responded aggressively, and by 1995 had essentially re-invented itself. The company turned its small size to an advantage, moving quickly to capitalize on new opportunities. In 1995 the mill introduced the first of its revolutionary Inxwell® papers, Mohawk Options. Inxwell is a patented paper treatment developed

by Mohawk. It provides uncoated papers with demonstrably better print quality and much higher opacity than was previously possible. Mohawk's Inxwell papers gained immediate market acceptance and have been chosen for many Fortune 500 annual reports. But the pace of change did not stop there. In 1998, Mohawk introduced a new line of digital papers, designed to make the most of new digital printing presses just being launched by Xerox, Heidelberg, and Xeikon. Also in 1998 the company began shipping paper from its Western Regional Distribution Center in Reno, Nevada—dramatically improving service and deliveries to its western customers.

Today, a third generation of the O'Connor family leads a dynamic, experienced young management team. Tom O'Connor, Jr. is president and COO. Joe O'Connor is senior vice president, sales administration, and John O'Connor is senior vice president, international sales and customer service. Together they oversee a highly successful operation, with over 350 employees, manufacturing in excess of 275 tons of premium printing paper per day. Mohawk papers are now distributed across North America and in all major international markets, including Australia, Japan, China, Indonesia, Europe and South America.

PAULSEN DEVELOPMENT COMPANY

"Schuster, bleib bei Deinem heisten," or "Shoemaker, stay with your trade" —whether in German or English, the personal motto of Karl Paulsen, founder of the Paulsen Development Company of Albany, has proven successful for three generations of Paulsens and their satisfied customers. With $400 in 1933, German immigrant Karl Paulsen and his wife Bertha began the business of installing porch enclosures that has grown into one of the most profitable full-service real estate companies in the Capital Region.

Born and raised in the small city of Marne in northwestern Germany, Karl began his apprenticeship as a carpenter in 1926 at the age of 15. He remembers those three years of learning the building trade as some of the best years of his life, although he earned only two dollars a week the first year, three dollars a week the second year, and five dollars a week his last year. His family had survived the war years and the difficult economic times that followed, but young Karl was convinced that immigrating to the United States was the best course of action. "I felt the future for a young man in Germany was not very promising."

He arrived in New York City on May 19, 1930 and, with the help of an uncle and friends from Marne, on May 20 began working for Paramount Home Improvements of Ridgefield, New Jersey, installing porches. Karl met his wife Bertha Dittman in 1931. In 1932, Paramount expanded its territory to Albany and asked Karl to head the branch. Karl left Paramount in 1933 to start a business enclosing porches with two other former Paramount employees. "Those early years were tough," recalls Karl, "Bertha was raising three boys (Carl, Bill and Rudy) and painting the millwork for the porches."

Although things had become a little easier for the Paulsens by the late 1930s, with U.S. entry into World

Karl, Rudy and Rich Paulsen, 1998 at Sand Creek Meadows.

War II in 1941, materials for building became scarce. They kept the porch business going, but in 1943 Karl became supervisor of the Embossing Company that manufactured gun stocks for the U.S. Army. When the war ended, Karl went into the house-building business but had some tough luck there, too. "My father first built a few houses in 1946 and 1947 along Western Avenue, but the experience didn't go as well as he had hoped," stated Rudy. With exceptionally cold weather and an extended winter, the cellar walls buckled, and two of the houses had to be rebuilt.

In 1948, Karl kept busy with repair and renovation work due to fire damage to several area businesses. As he was finishing a job in Troy, he got word

that his own shop and home on Central Avenue were on fire. The shop was badly damaged and the house was smoke-damaged. In typical Paulsen fashion, the family decided to pool its resources, including paper route money from the three boys, and build a new house on the lot next to the shop. That weekend, more than 20 men from the German American Club arrived to help repair the shop and start work on the new house. In two weeks the shop was operating again, and the Paulsens moved into their new house in the spring of 1949.

With son Bill, and Rudy joining the next year, Karl opened the Paulsen Lumber Company in 1953. According to Karl, "We had some materials on hand, some accounts receivable and $7,000 in the bank. If anybody thinks this is what is needed to start a lumber business, forget it, we found out the hard way!" But the Paulsens persevered and eventually prospered despite supply problems and unfair practices from local competitors. Sales in 1953 were $90,000; by 1956 sales had grown to $566,000 with five additional employees. The company became incorporated in October of that year.

By 1959, Paulsen Lumber was the biggest supplier in town and had bought out City Lumber Company, one of its competitors. Becoming cramped for space, the Paulsens moved the lumber company to Railroad Avenue in 1963. "The '60s were good," recalls Karl, who also served as president of the Colonie Chamber of Commerce in 1962-63. "We expanded fast, and we were the first lumberyard in the Albany area to build roof trusses, manufacture pre-hung doors and distribute Pease Doors." With more than 50 employees, the Paulsens also continued to build windows, stairs and other millwork products.

The Paulsens ventured into building again in 1965 with the completion of more than 40 duplexes, at Sandcreek, Commodore Street in Colonie, in Albany and New Turnpike Road. In

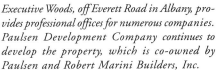

Karl and Bertha Paulsen at the grand opening of Karl A. Paulsen & Sons Lumber Company, Railroad Avenue, 1962.

1968, they built Rose Garden Court Apartments in Latham and Robert Gardens North in Glen Falls, which are still owned and managed by Rudy. Paulsen Lumber acquired a garage-manufacturing business in 1971, Woodcraft Homes. Renamed as Green Island Homes, the division became a profitable branch of Paulsen Lumber over the next ten years, with production of 200-250 garages each year. The lumber company continued to grow and by 1973 sales were $9,000,000; by 1977, the Paulsen Lumber Company employed 90 people.

With the sale of the lumber company and Green Island Homes in 1981, Karl Paulsen "retired" and turned over the day-to-day leadership of the company to Rudy. In 1983, the company changed its name from Karl A. Paulsen and Sons Millwork and

Executive Woods, off Everett Road in Albany, provides professional offices for numerous companies. Paulsen Development Company continues to develop the property, which is co-owned by Paulsen and Robert Marini Builders, Inc.

Lumber Incorporated to Paulsen and Sons, Inc. Throughout the 1980s, the company concentrated on real estate investment and land development, often in conjunction with some of the region's better homebuilders. During this period, Rudy also ventured into commercial development in partnership with Robert Marini, Sr. to build Executive Woods, an attractive professional-offices building on Palisades Drive in Albany, which now headquarters Paulsen Development Company.

Rudy and his son, Rich, began to build single-family homes in 1996. They bought a promising development in Malta, acquired a parcel for development in Clifton Park, and fulfilled plans for a long-held site in Colonie. Rudy and Rich agree that the future of Paulsen Development is in home building. The company has plans to develop a site in Saratoga County and also start a custom home division as well as expand commercial construction and management work. With a master's degree in real estate finance, Rich, who is also a CPA, now manages the company's day-to-day affairs. "We are truly full-service in real estate. We have commercial interests, residential and the apartments...but we will follow Opa's (grandfather's) motto: "Schuster, bleib bei Deinem heisten.""

PIONEER SAVINGS BANK

Pioneer Savings Bank developed from modest beginnings, like many other important institutions in the Hudson-Mohawk Gateway area. Now over a century old, the bank was founded as a building-loan and savings association in March 1889.

Troy at that time had no bank where a resident could make small deposits, so it was difficult for the average wage earner to acquire enough money to build or buy a home of his own. The printers at the *Troy Daily Press* were thus prompted to seek the advice of their publisher, Henry O'Reilly Tucker, in the matter of starting a suitable cooperative.

Impressed by their ambition and sincerity, Tucker "with rare liberality and as an expression of good will to his workmen, engaged at his own expense the services of a lecturer and organizer, who labored here for some time perfecting the preliminaries." What was probably just as helpful to the savings association was the fact that Tucker "opened the columns of his paper to the movement," gaining the support of large and small investors in Troy and surrounding communities.

In its initial articles, the association's purpose was clearly stated: "making loans to shareholders whereby they may be enabled to purchase real estate, to build or provide dwelling houses, to remove encumbrances there from and to accumulate a fund to be returned to the members who do not obtain advances." The organization prospered and was able to survive a financial panic in 1893-1894, the Great Depression, as well as the more modern financial industry crisis during the 1980s wherein a large number of thrift organizations like Pioneer became insolvent and were closed or sold as a result.

Until 1964, the directors, the governing body representatives of the time, met every Tuesday. Now, the governing body representatives are

From 1915-1950, Pioneer's building at 30 Second Street in Troy.

trustees and they meet on the first and third Tuesdays of each month. Tuesday played another important part in the bank's early days. It was the only day of the week when the thrifty members made their deposits of a minimum of twenty-five cents. In 1914 money began to be received on Monday evenings as well, and in 1916 the institution opened daily for transactions. Beginning in 1973, with the opening of the bank's branch in Rotterdam, Pioneer introduced the somewhat unconventional practice of extended full service branch banking hours wherein all branches opened thereafter had a minimum weekly operational schedule of 56 hours per week.

Originally quartered in a structure on River Street near what is now Riverfront Park, the association, after twenty-seven years and three moves, purchased its first building at 30 Second Street. In May 1950, it moved to its present facility at 21 Second Street where the Main Office still exists. The bank additionally opened a non-retail operations center facility in the Hendrick Hudson building at the corner of Second Street and Broadway in 1998.

On July 1, 1972, the Pioneer Building-Loan and Savings Association became Pioneer Savings Bank, under the leadership of Allen L. Gillett. This step allowed the institution to adopt a more extensive branching posture while still maintaining its thrift institution character. Gillett was succeeded as president and CEO in 1973 by Edward H. Nash, who guided the organization until his retirement in 1997. The current president and CEO is John M. Scarchilli, a life long Capital District resident and community leader.

The first branch office, in nearby Latham, was opened in June 1958 in a converted residential home just west of the Latham Traffic Circle on Route 7. In 1978, the branch moved into its current location in the Latham Circle Mall. The Watervliet office was established in 1972, when the savings association became a savings bank, in a converted gas station building at the corner of Second Avenue and 19th Street. The branch quickly outgrew the location and a new building was constructed in 1976, slightly north of the original facility. A fourth office was subsequently opened in Rotterdam in 1973.

Another surge of Capital District branching is currently underway at Pioneer, with four new branch offices having been opened since 1996 in Clifton Park, Malta, Wynantskill and Brunswick. Pioneer operates exclusively in the Hudson-Mohawk Gateway region and has plans to further enhance its presence in the region with additional branches in the future.

It has been a source of satisfaction to the trustees, officers and staff that Pioneer Savings Bank, through many years and many changes, remains a local community bank focused on the financial needs of local residents, still true to the aims of its founders over 110 years ago.

Above: The computer room in the '50s.

Below: One of the famous Tuesday nights of an earlier day.

PRICE CHOPPER/GOLUB CORPORATION

In 1932, in the midst of the Great Depression, the idea of opening a new kind of food market in Schenectady, New York would not have seemed like a very good idea. But, that is exactly what the brothers Golub, Ben & Bill, did. And it proved to be a very good idea, indeed.

The new "one stop shopping" concept was called the Public Service Market and offered groceries, meat, fresh produce, clothing, dry goods, home appliances, shoe repair shop, antique dealer, book shop, jeweler and cafeteria—all in an old warehouse without windows. The next year, as thousands of banks failed across the country and unemployment reached more than 13 million, the one-stop shopping idea took root and the first store carrying the Central Market name opened.

It was soon followed by other stores in Watervliet, North Troy, and Glens Falls. As the chain grew, it became known as a trendsetter among the area's grocery businesses.

Central Markets was one of the first supermarkets in the country to introduce S&H Green stamps in 1951—a great boon to the business.

Above: 1933–The first Central Market opened in Schenectady, New York.

Below: Innovation has always been at the core of the Golub Corporation. In 1999, the company opened its own bakery school in Schenectady, to address the industry-wide shortage of bakers.

Their leadership in the fast growing supermarket industry led them, in 1937, to help organize a national association, the Supermarket Institute, which is now known as the Food Marketing Institute (FMI).

Central Markets continued to innovate, launching new ideas and developing creative approaches that were setting the standard for the industry. In 1951, it was one of the first chains to issue S&H Trading Stamps. Saving stamps became almost as exciting as saving money and resulted in a tremendous increase in business for the company. S&H Trading Stamps soon became a national household word.

In that same year Central Markets began a program which gave a big boost to the local agricultural industry. Working with Cornell University and the NY State Department of Agriculture, Central Markets started the Empire State Red Label Egg Program that ensured customers they would get fresh Grade A and Grade AA eggs from local farmers instead of weeks old eggs from the midwest.

A second boost to the New York State farm industry was Central Markets' guarantee that it would purchase farmers' crops at fair market prices. The "Grower-Producer Program" helped many small family farms stay in business by helping local farmers develop modern business methods and new farming techniques. Later, William Golub instituted a program that offered free seeds to 4-H youngsters with the agreement that the company would buy back the best of the young

Above: A modern-day Price Chopper.

farmers' crops for sale at Central Market stores.

By the late '50s there were 25 Central Markets in upstate New York and one in Massachusetts. Seven new stores were opened in 1963 and four in 1965. Throughout the 1960s supermarkets became the focal point of suburban shopping centers and malls. Central Markets kept pace with this suburban boon.

During a difficult economic climate in the early '70s, Central Markets eliminated stamps and slashed prices and adopted a new name to reflect this pricing policy: Price Chopper. Quickly Price Chopper became the area's low price, high quality operator. New stores were opened in rapid succession in New York, Massachusetts, and Pennsylvania. In 1990, 13 stores in Vermont were acquired followed by the purchase of a 12-store chain in the Worcester, MA area. Today, there are almost 100 Price Chopper supermarkets in New York, Vermont, Connecticut, Pennsylvania, Massachusetts and New Hampshire.

Throughout its history, the Golub Corporation has earned a reputation for community involvement, giving back to the localities it serves. This effort includes such diverse program as senior citizen busing, printing tickets for worthy causes, scholarships, charitable donations, and the encour-

agement of all associates to become involved in volunteer activities.

Since the day it started, the Golub Corporation has embodied a cooperative and friendly working relationship with its associates. It has never lost a single day to either labor disputes or strikes. Today, its more than 19,000 associates own 47 percentof the company.

In the 1980s, the leadership of the company passed to Ben and Bill's sons, Lewis and Neil. In 1982, Lewis Golub became chief executive officer and Neil, president. In 2000, Neil Golub was named chief executive officer and Lewis Golub continued to retain the title of chairman of the board, remaining active in the company. Three next generation Golubs are involved in the business and are assuming leadership positions.

The future of the Golub Corporation remains bright thanks to its dedicated workforce, its loyal customers and its commitment to service.

Below: Price Chopper operates stores in six northeastern states.

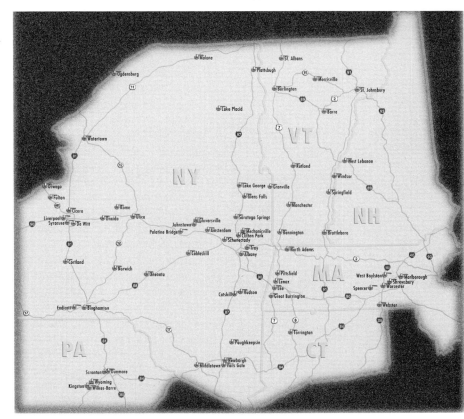

RENSSELAER POLYTECHNIC INSTITUTE

In its commitment to top-quality education concentrating on science and technology, Rensselaer Polytechnic Institute has grown from the Rensselaer School, which pioneered engineering education, to an internationally renowned technological university.

Founded in 1824 by Stephen Van Rensselaer, for instructing students "in the application of science to the common purposes of life," the school developed during the massive transformations of America's Industrial Revolution. Informed scientists were needed to teach the public about science, and imaginative civil engineers were needed to construct the Erie Canal, bridges, railroads, factories, tunnels, dams, and other industrial works.

Today the Institute has not departed from Van Rensselaer's original vision for the school in its stated mission: "Rensselaer educates the leaders of tomorrow for technologically based careers. We celebrate discovery, and the responsible application of technology, to create knowledge and global prosperity."

Rensselaer's Hunt Archway welcomes students from all 50 states and more than 80 countries.

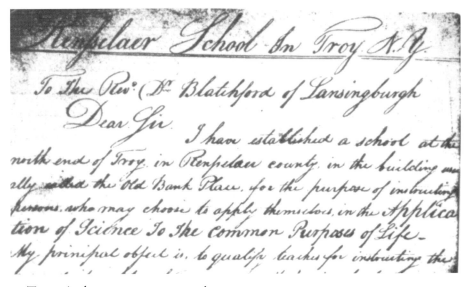

Stephen Van Rensselaer founded what is now known as Rensselaer Polytechnic Institute in 1824.

Twentieth-century expansion broadened the engineering and science curriculum with management, architecture, and humanities. A revolution in communications technologies inspired the creation of degree-granting programs in information technology. Rensselaer now is home to five schools—Architecture, Engineering, Humanities and Social Sciences, the Lally School of Management and Technology, and Science.

Rensselaer enrolls undergraduates, graduate students, and working professionals from all 50 states and more than 80 countries at campuses in Troy, New York, and Hartford, Connecticut, and through distance learning opportunities around the world.

Excellence in education inspired the founders of Rensselaer, and innovative pedagogy remains a core value of the Institute. The university's faculty-driven initiatives in creating an inventive undergraduate curriculum have been recognized with national awards. Its pioneering studio classroom format, enhanced by state-of-the-art educational technology, fosters student-centered, hands-on learning based on teamwork and a mentoring relationship with faculty.

The Rensselaer faculty is known for its dual strength in teaching and research, which enriches the student experience and creates an exciting environment of discovery. The creation of new knowledge is critical to a stimulating learning environment. Cutting-edge research enables faculty to include students as partners in discovery and open their minds to inquiry.

As a world-class research university, Rensselaer has built an outstanding faculty, including members of the National Academy of Sciences and the National Academy of Engineering, National Science Foundation Presidential Faculty Fellows, a Nobel laureate, and other eminent professionals. Rensselaer faculty are recognized leaders, receiving peer recognition and funding, defining the discourse in their fields, and setting scholarly and professional agendas in national and international arenas.

Rensselaer has excelled in pioneering research, and has achieved international distinction in many fields. Interdisciplinary research with strong industrial participation has been a hallmark, involving focused research programs in biotechnology and bioinformatics, information technology, advanced materials, nanotechnologies, microelectronics, scientific computation, polymer synthesis, image processing, electronic media, lighting, freshwater science, and entrepreneurship. These programs integrate basic and applied research with industrial needs, and have developed a base of support from complementary federal, state, and industry sources.

The Institute is especially well known for its success in the transfer of technology from the laboratory to the marketplace so that new discoveries and inventions benefit human life, protect the environment, and strengthen economic development. Since the days when Alexander Holley brought the Bessemer process to America, the Gurley brothers made significant innovations in precision instruments, and Sanford Cluett perfected "sanforization," faculty, students, and alumni have successfully developed technologies, created innovations, and formed business ventures to bring ideas into practice to create value.

Since 1980 Rensselaer has encouraged technology partnerships and dissemination through a flourishing technology

Pioneering research is a hallmark of Rensselaer. Its Class 100 Clean Room supports critical work in microelectronics.

park and an internationally recognized incubator center, which spawns high-tech start-up companies. Serving as national models, the Rensselaer Incubator Center, with facilities on campus and in downtown Troy, and the Rensselaer Technology Park, on 1,200 acres in nearby Defreestville, benefit by ready access to and interaction with Rensselaer faculty and students.

The Tech Park and Incubator are vibrant examples of the contributions Rensselaer makes to the vitality of the Hudson Valley. The university's research centers, by serving as a surrogate R&D arm for small and mid-sized local companies, also influence the creation and retention of high-value technology-based jobs in the Capital Region.

To foster close and mutually beneficial relationships with the surrounding community, Rensselaer offers faculty resources and research skills to assist in community development projects. New collaborations and longstanding alliances with industry, government, and institutions (i.e., Albany Medical College, the University at Albany, Hudson Valley Community College, the Sage Colleges, Albany Law and the Wadsworth Center of the New York State Department of Health) increase Rensselaer's impact on the region's economic future.

Because Rensselaer students are educated in an environment of leading-edge research and innovation, they

The Mueller Center, Rensselaer's state-of-the-art fitness center.

are highly prized by the institutions that hire them, where they have an immediate impact and step up to leadership roles in technology-based careers.

Through productive and accomplished alumni, Rensselaer's reach has extended throughout the world for nearly two centuries. Rensselaer alumni are active and influential in all facets of society. They are engineers, scientists, physicians, attorneys, architects, writers, inventors, and entrepreneurs. Rensselaer alumni are responsible for the hand-held calculator and the television tube. They built the nation's canals, highways, railroads, and bridges, and they put men on the moon. They head multinational corporations, serve in Congress, sit on the federal bench, direct many of the country's leading laboratories, and teach at virtually all of the nation's top colleges and universities.

Rensselaer's graduates are testimony to the enduring quality of education they have received at one of the nation's top-ranked research universities. While standing firm in its founder's original vision, Rensselaer has continually driven advances in technology and renewed its educational model to inspire and challenge each new generation of students.

ADAM ROSS CUT STONE CO., INC.

Adam Ross, the founder of Adam Ross Cut Stone, was born in 1839 in Prestonpons, Dunbartonshire, Scotland. In 1854, at the age of 15, he left Scotland on a sailing ship and, after a six week voyage, arrived in New York City with scarcely a dollar in his pocket. His desire was to become a stonecutter and master carver. Traveling up the Hudson River, he began to ply his trade and went into business for a time with Robert Connell, brother of his wife-to-be. Many markers in Oakwood Cemetery in Troy, New York soon said "Connell and Ross" in small carved letters on the base.

Several years later, Robert Connell left for Iowa. In 1865, Adam married Agnes Connell. After their marriage, Agnes saved up so Adam could go into business for himself. At first he worked by himself accepting only very small jobs. As time went by he hired two or three stonecutters to help him. At that time the principal tools of the trade were hammers and chisels. Cut stone was delivered by horse-drawn wagons.

First year in Albany, 1906.

A stonecutter worked ten hours a day for five days and eight hours on Saturday, allowing some time for family shopping on Saturday evening. His pay might reach as much as $12.00 per week.

In 1889, Adam's sons, John, Adam, Jr. and Charles, began working for their father. As a result, the business began to expand and Adam Ross & Son was founded on Sixth Avenue in Troy, New York. From here the business grew, moving to its present location at 999-1003 Broadway in Albany, New York in 1906, while still maintaining an office in Troy.

Adam Ross & Son's Troy location merged with the Albany business in 1911 and became incorporated as Adam Ross Cut Stone Company, Inc. Adam Ross, the founder, died prior to World War I and his son, Charles Ross, Sr. took control and continued to operate the business until the time his death in 1951. He was helped by his three sons, Donald, Kenneth, Charles, Jr. and one daughter, Bertha. In the years following, sons Donald, Charles, Jr. and later grandson, Robert E. Ross and great-grandson, David C. Ross have headed the business. Currently, David C. Ross and Randall R. Ross (sons of Robert E. Ross), George E. Mallette (grandson of Charles Ross, Sr.) and June B. Ross (wife of David C. Ross) are running the business. Thus, five generations of the Ross family have continued to operate the stone business since its inception in 1889.

There have been some difficult times over the years in the stone industry. During World War I (1917-18) there was no demand for stone. However, Charles Ross, Sr. was aware that stone planers could be used to roughly plane iron and steel, for

Albany parade, 1924.

which there was a demand. Through his contacts with others in the stone industry, he was able to buy stone planers that were then idle and sell them to those in the iron finishing industry and thus were able to survive during the lean war years. Later, the Depression years from 1929-36 were extremely difficult. During World War II (1940-45) the stone business came to a screeching halt. At this time they went into warehousing in transit mainly for General Electric products (transformers, motors, etc.). These items awaited the availability of a ship leaving from New York City. When a ship became available, items from the Ross warehousing operation would be loaded on railroad cars and shipped to New York City.

Over the years there have been many changes in the tools and machinery used at Adam Ross Cut Stone. Some of the major changes were:
 • Trucks replaced horse-drawn wagons;
 • Use of shot instead of sand on the gang saw making cutting of stone much easier;
 • Wooden lean-to buildings were replaced by brick buildings in 1927;
 • Introduction of overhead crane instead of hand-operated derricks;
 • Compressed air which made pneumatic tools possible instead of hammer and chisel;
 • Introduction of diamond saw blades to replace the old carborundum blades;
 • Introduction of diamonds for finishing and polishing;
 • Use of thinner pieces of stone (panels) for exterior of commercial buildings;
 • Use of stone for interior use in homes and businesses;
 • Introduction of computer controlled saws and routers.

Over the years the business has increased from less than $5,000 to over $2,000,000 a year in sales and, at the

Inside new mill, 1927.

same time, the territory served has grown from the Tri-City area to the entire eastern United States. Cut stone is supplied for commercial and institutional use as well as interior and exterior applications to meet every need of homeowners. Shapes and finishes are contingent upon owner's specifications and variety is almost unlimited except for availability and practical consideration of cost. Modern transportation facilities on land, water

and air have bridged the gap from most anywhere in the world to their shop or to the jobsite. Adam Ross Cut Stone Company, Inc. has produced a product which is long-lasting and practically indestructible. Their basic philosophy has been long hours of hard work to produce a quality product. Guiding principles for over 100 years have centered on quality and service.

New mill and office, 1927.

CL KING & ASSOCIATES, INC.
PARADIGM CAPITAL MANAGEMENT, INC

Candace King Weir founded CL King & Associates, Inc., an independent research boutique firm in 1972. It is one of the oldest (if not the oldest) women owned securities firms in the United States. Ms. Weir's goal has and continues to be making investing more efficient and effective for institutional investors of small-cap stocks. Her clients include some of the nation's most respected money management firms, among them Citibank, Fidelity Management & Research Co., Harvard Management, Lazard Freres Asset Management, Merrill Lynch Asset Management, Putnam Companies, and Prudential Equity Management. CL King is headquartered in Albany, New York, and has offices in New York City and Boston.

In the early 1970s, Ms. Weir was immediately faced with the uncertain market of that period. To be effective in marketing to institutions, Ms. Weir placed a premium on developing a discipline and focus that would deliver relatively consistent performance despite these conditions. A commitment to this philosophy, which is now the bedrock of her company, has ensured her survival and continued success in a highly competitive and ever-consolidating industry.

Ms. Weir has built on a long tradition of identifying undervalued, under-represented companies in institutional portfolios. Ms. Weir and her team utilize fundamental research and analysis to evaluate investment opportunities for their institutional clients. In adopting a value-oriented approach, their intent is to uncover attractive investment opportunities in companies with market capitalization ranging from $50 million to $1 billion.

In 1994, Ms. Weir formed Paradigm Capital Management, to provide investment management services to individuals, to pension and profit sharing plans and to corporations seeking long-term asset growth. The superior research provided by CL King to money managers is also used to construct investment portfolios for investors through Paradigm. Since its formation, Paradigm has been one of the country's outstanding small-cap equity investment firms. The key to this superior performance record lies in Ms. Weir's commitment to research and identifying securities poised for growth or undervalued in the market and on a thorough understanding of, and appreciation for, each client's individual needs and attitudes.

Ms. Weir has avoided a philosophy based on short-term market swings, speculation or market timing. She instead relies on adherence to a research-based stock selection process that constantly reviews each company's prospects for future growth in relation to its evaluation and general market conditions.

Today, Paradigm manages $620 million. Investment purchases for client portfolios are typically made with long-term appreciation in mind. Ms. Weir and her staff screen and identify companies that are generally under-followed or out of favor. They focus on knowing the goals, the strategies and competitors of the companies Paradigm researches.

Artist's rendering of CL King & Associates and Paradigm Capital Management offices at Eight and Nine Elk Street in Albany.

ST. MARY'S HOSPITAL-PART OF SETON HEALTH SYSTEM

High on a Troy hillside, St. Mary's Hospital has been a beacon of health and hope for the surrounding neighborhoods for 150 years.

Today, St. Mary's is the heart of Seton Health, an integrated health care system whose neighborhoods embrace three counties of the Capital Region.

St. Mary's Hospital originated when Father Peter Havermans requested the assistance of the Daughters of Charity in caring for sick immigrants in the 1840s. Many of these immigrants had fled the potato famine in Ireland and were suffering from malnutrition and disease. More than 200 of them were quarantined in temporary shelters since Troy had no hospital at the time. This led Father Havermans to work with the Daughters of Charity to build the city's first hospital, which was actually one room in a four-story building. This "hospital," completed in 1850, had a staff of three attending physicians and two consulting physicians.

In the years that followed, the hospital expanded, eventually taking over the entire building (which burned in 1856 and was rebuilt in the same spot). The hospital moved to Fulton and Eighth Streets in 1869 and had grown to 125 beds. It moved to its current location on Massachusetts Avenue in 1914. From the 1950s to the 1980s, considerable expansions and services were added, including an Intensive Care Unit, a Laboratory wing, and a building for medical offices.

In 1995, St. Mary's joined forces with nearby Leonard Hospital (founded in 1893) to become Seton Health System, part of the Daughters of Charity National Health System.

Today, St. Mary's is the anchor of Seton Health. The system's 1,300 employees work from more than 20 sites throughout the region.

Seton Health has grown into one of the largest primary care providers in the Capital Region, and offers a wide range of specialized outpatient programs, emergency and hospital services, and continuing care.

In 1999, the Daughters of Charity Nation Health System merged with the Sisters of St. Joseph Health System to create a new national health ministry—Ascension Health.

Although 150 years have passed, the same values on which St. Mary's Hospital was founded are still relevant today. No matter how much health care delivery and technology change, what patients really want is people caring for them.

Seton Health remains dedicated to caring for body, mind and spirit.

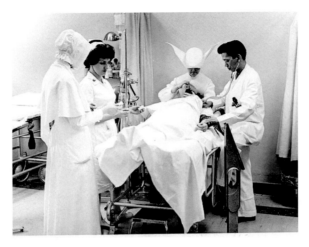

A patient is prepped for surgery in this photo taken in 1959. Notice the traditional "winged" Coronet worn by the Sister administering the anesthesia.

St. Mary's Hospital/Seton Health Timeline:

- 1850–Troy Hospital is founded to serve the growing population of the city, particularly an influx of sickly Irish immigrants. The hospital is at the corner of Washington and Fifth Street and has a medical staff of five.
- 1856–The hospital burns down, but a better-designed hospital is built in the same spot.
- 1860–Operation of the hospital is transferred to the Daughters of Charity.
- 1869–The hospital moves to Eighth Street (in a building now part of the RPI campus).
- 1894–The hospital School of Nursing is established and a Gynecology Department opens.
- 1895–X-ray service established at the hospital.
- 1907–Horse-drawn ambulance services offered at the hospital.
- 1914–The hospital opens at its current location, 1300 Massachusetts Avenue.
- 1935–A Maternity Unit opens at the hospital.
- 1949—The hospital becomes St. Mary's Hospital of Troy.
- 1963—St. Mary's affiliates with Hudson Valley Community College's nursing program.
- 1964–Intensive Care Unit opens.
- 1968–St. Mary's opens its Cardiac Care Unit—the first of its kind in Rensselaer County.
- 1977–Cancer Clinic established.
- 1983–Surgical pavilion opens.
- 1995–St. Mary's and Leonard Hospital merge to form Seton Health System. Leonard is closed and St. Mary's becomes the health system's base.
- 1996–The Massry Center opens just down the road from St. Mary's, providing a convenient, comfortable place for many outpatient services.
- 1998–Medical and dental practices have grown dramatically, with more than 160,000 patient visits this year.
- 1999–The De Paul Building—a three-story addition to the hospital—opens, featuring new Intensive Care and Pediatric units and a state-of-the-art Childbirth Center. Seton Health's national sponsor, the Daughters of Charity National Health System, merges with the Sisters of St. Joseph Health System to form Ascension Health.
- 2000-St. Mary's Hospital celebrates its 150th anniversary.

SIMMONS MACHINE TOOL CORPORATION

Simmons is located in Albany New York, the capital city of the state of New York. Simmons, from its inception until the mid 1960s was widely recognized as the premier Remanufacturer of general-purpose machine tools. Simmons was founded by Charles A. Simmons in 1910. His idea was to not let old machines just fade away but rather to see the potential they have when they are remanufactured. This concept became both crucial and widely used at the dawn of the United States' entry into World War II due to the fast turn around time of equipment. The United States Government touted Charles Simmons' concept of turning "junk" into useful machines and Simmons became a large contributor to the war effort. Simmons received the coveted Army-Navy "E" award for excellence in 1942.

The story goes that Charles Simmons founded this company with just 50 cents in his pocket

Simmons prepares for "E" award and celebration in 1942.

Simmons' CEO, Mr. Hans J. Naumann.

when he received his first order. He went to New York City to meet with a gentleman to convince him of the potential to remanufacture "old" machines. He apparently missed the original meeting due to his train being late, but after some good fortune and a little fate, Mr. Simmons ran into that potential buyer before his return trip to Albany and the beginning of a company that was launched into the next century began.

Charles Simmons grew up on a farm in Oneida, N.Y. but had a love for machines. In the early 1900s he had an idea for a machine holder he had invented, but due to economics, he had to purchase used equipment and rebuild it for his needs. Thus, the legacy began and Charles Simmons would later be known as the machine "doctor", the man who could fix anything.

By November of 1941 the story of the company's ability to take machines out of the graveyards and put them into production became known throughout the United States and Simmons in turn had to significantly increase production. The factory was enlarged and two shifts were worked seven days a week. The whole country would recognize how crucial the concept of remanufacturing would become to the war effort.

Unfortunately, after the war came to an end, the need for high volume remanufactured old machines steadily declined. Charles Simmons in the late 1940s pleaded with the War Assets Administration (WAA) to let Simmons assist in the rebuilding of Western Europe but was unsuccessful.

In 1984, Simmons changed hands to its current owner. Mr. Hans J. Naumann graduated from the University of Hamburg in 1960 with his degree in Mechanical Engineering and moved to the United States to pursue an education at Rochester University, in N.Y., where he graduated in 1965 with his master's degree in Business Administration. Mr. Naumann became familiar with the machine tool industry and its importance to the maintenance and repair within the Rail Industry at the Farrel Corporation, in Rochester N.Y. From there, Mr. Naumann proceeded to Troy, Michigan and the Hegenshcheidt Corporation in 1966 where he became president and part owner. By 1970, he also became chief executive officer and part owner of Hegensheidt GmbH, in West Germany. With Naumann's knowledge of the industry and his strong leadership Hegenscheidt grew to become the largest railway equipment provider in Europe with plants in Johannesburg, South Africa, Sydney, Australia and a licensing agreement in Brazil, India and Japan.

In 1984 Naumann would leave Hegenscheidt to operate his own business and continue being a leader within the railway industry with his acquisition of Simmons Machine Tool Corporation, the home of Niles USA. In addition to offering a remanufactured product line, Simmons purchased the NILES product line in 1964 from the Baldwin, Lima and Hamilton Corporation. The Niles product line originated out of Cincinnati Ohio, in 1833 and was part of Niles Bement Pound. In 1898 the German Niles Works was founded, resulting in Niles-Berlin and Niles-Chemnitz. Niles-Chemnitz was purchased by Mr. Hans Naumann and Mr. John O. Naumann in 1992. The newly acquired company, Niles-Simmons Industrieanlagen GMBH symbolizes the reunification of Niles product lines in the United States and Germany. Hans Naumann did not stop with just the Niles product line but also acquired the

Farrel and Stanray product lines as well. Simmons Machine Tool Corporation has its headquarters in Albany, N.Y. Its affiliated company, Niles-Simmons Indurtrieanlagen is located in Chemnitz, Germany. With the product lines of Niles, Stanray, and Farrel, Simmons became the premier manufacturer within the railway industry with the largest product line worldwide of equipment for the maintenance and repair of railway and transit,

Officers of Simmons Machine Tool Corporation, left to right: Joe Eramo, vice president of sales and marketing; Blaine Salvador, general manager; John O. Naumann, president and COO; and David Simonian, cheif financial officer.

Article in local newspaper demonstrating the importance of Simmons to the war effort.

wheelsets, wheels and axles. Simmons is the only remaining Original Equipment Manufacturer (OEM) in the United States.

Simmons' president and chief operating officer is Mr. John O. Naumann. Mr. Hans J. Naumann is chairman of the board, and to this day Simmons remains one of the largest machine tool builders in the United States. Simmons continues to be a leader within the railway industry with the development of new machines to help maintain the rail industry's rolling stock. In addition to the railroad industry, Simmons has diversified its industry branches to include the automotive industry as well as the general purpose machine tool industry.

Simmons began with the idea that machines could be "re-engineered" and therefore modernized by the process of remanufacturing. This concept is still present in the Simmons of the 21st Century where re-manufacturing its product line is still a large percentage of its business.

STRAIGHT LINE INDUSTRIES, INC.

Straight Line Industries, Inc., a unique business by virtue of the nature of its specialty and its ownership, is actually representative of hundreds of other businesses which thrive in the upstate New York economy. Small businesses are the mainstay of the area, each with unique skills. These businesses have found a niche and help to provide a living for their owners and employees.

Straight Line Industries, Inc. is a pavement marking contractor operating out of facilities in Cohoes, NY, near Albany, the state capital of New York State. The company is owned and operated by its founder, Pilar G. Dexter, and is the only minority/woman-owned striping business in the state. SLI owns 21 vehicles which include crew vehicles, long line traffic painting trucks, epoxy applicators, traffic control attenuator trucks, line erradicators and variable message boards, not to mention numerous hand machines. Two of its line applicators install epoxy lines. These two machines represent approximately 80 nationwide, which are used to install

Above: Ronald Marks, SLI's chief technician, checks spray operation.

Below: "A work of art," I-90 Exit 8 gore areas, painted in epoxy by Richard Fremont, shows the intricate designs which are the safety guides for traveling motorists.

epoxy durable pavement markings to fight off the freeze-thaw cycles so prevalent in the northern climates.

Since its inception, SLI has become adept at installing pavement markings of all kinds at a rate of approximately 25 million linear feet annually. The painting crews utilize a variety of line marking products including various traffic paints, pre-formed plastic markings and epoxy, for both temporary and permanent applications. Typically, SLI runs nine crews daily, which are dispatched to paint highways, parking lots, game fields and running tracks. From time to time they also paint specialty items such as meditation labyrinths at veterans hospitals, indoor warehouse safety lines, runway markings for jet aircraft and intricate corporate and school logos.

Straight Line began in 1993 with one truck and three people and has since evolved into a $5 million company with its own building and a workforce of 30. SLI's territory covers all of New York State, Northern New Jersey, Western Massachusetts and Southern Vermont, and they have also completed projects in Canada, Pennsylvania, Kansas, North Carolina and Maryland.

SLI's founder and owner, Pilar G. Dexter, is as multi-faceted as the company itself. Ms. Dexter grew up in the Upstate Area. Her Mexican mother and German American father instilled in her and her sisters a basic work ethic, which has dominated her professional life. She left the area to go to school in Washington, D.C., worked for a local congressman and later moved to a position at the United Nations Development Programme in New York. While in New York Pilar had the opportunity to work for some highly-entrepreneurial businessmen who were developing a health consulting company. Their entrepreneurial spirit was contagious and Ms. Dexter knew that someday she would be run-

ning her own business. In 1992, she moved back to her hometown in order to raise her family. She found that the local business world was not ready for her. Her frustrations led her to the Dale Carnegie Institute where she met Richard Fremont, the operations manager from the Albany County Airport. He had been running a small striping business and was looking to develop the business into a full size, fulltime enterprise. A friendship ensued, but not a partnership, so Ms. Dexter built on her experiences and formed Straight Line Industries in 1993.

In 1994, Ms. Dexter took advantage of highly-publicized SBA Business loans for women and minorities and purchased the assets of a Syracuse-based striping company from its retiring owners. Armed with equipment and employees she began to bid projects with local general contractors

looking to meet their minority and women goals on federal and state government contracts. Once the general contractors experienced the quality of work and service that SLI could provide, the contractors continued calling. SLI purchased the assets of Pavemark Striping Systems in 1997 and, with Mr. Fremont as director of operations, SLI has become a viable and complete pavement markings contractor.

Straight Line Industries, Inc. now provides meaningful employment for more than 30 employees annually and is active in civic organizations such as the Albany-Colonie Chamber of Commerce and the Rensselaer County Regional Chamber of Commerce. SLI also belongs to the Associated General Contractors of New York, Inc., the National Association of Women in Construction and the American Traffic Safety Services Association. In 1997,

John Williams and Joseph Casale lead their crew in hand painting epoxy symbols on Route 434 in Tioga County.

SLI was presented an award by the Enterprising Women's Leadership Institute followed in 1998 by the SBA Small Business Excellence Award and the "Good News" Award by the Albany-Colonie Chamber of Commerce. Most recently, Ms. Dexter's story was depicted in the *Historical Encyclopedia of American Women Entrepreneurs* published by Greenwood Press.

The New York Capital District is filled with stories of this type—of small companies with big or unique ideas owned by unique individuals who are willing to make the sacrifices necessary to be their own boss. The SBA holds the archives of stories like this one and others, filled with technological mavericks, many of whom call the Capital Region "home."

SAWCHUK, BROWN ASSOCIATES

The Hudson-Mohawk Gateway has been a hub of commerce throughout its history. Communications has been integral to the region's growth and development, and in recent years professional communications has played a significant role in marketing, public affairs, government relations and commercial expansion.

Sawchuk, Brown Associates—specializing in public relations, public affairs and strategic marketing—has been a leader in its field since its founding in 1979. That was the year Pamela Sawchuk left her position as a newspaper editor to launch the firm with a special project for The Picotte Companies.

Today, the project—Corporate Woods—is the region's premier office park, and The Picotte Companies remains a major client of the firm, along with more than 70 others. Sawchuk, Brown Associates is the leading independent public relations/ public affairs firm in Upstate New York.

Entering its third decade, the firm has developed in size and stature, representing an impressive client list. It serves regional, statewide and national clients with counsel and services, including: public relations, public affairs and marketing strategy; media relations; community relations; crisis communications; publications, video and editorial services; marketing support; database communications and research; on-line communications and web site counsel; and government communications. Over the years it has developed expertise in a wide range of areas, including economic development, education, employee relations, entertainment and the arts, environmental issues, financial services, health care, state associations, state and local government relations, technology, telecommunications and travel and tourism.

The firm is an original member of the prestigious Council of Public Relations Firms, which represents the

David Brown, president, and Pamela Sawchuk Brown, founder of the leading independent public relation/public affairs firm in Upstate New York.

leadership of the public relations industry in the United States.

Founded as Pamela Sawchuk Associates, the firm was incorporated as Sawchuk, Brown Associates in 1988, reflecting the principal role of David P. Brown, formerly executive news editor of the Albany *Times Union* and editor of the Sunday *Times Union*. Like his wife, Pamela Sawchuk Brown, Mr. Brown had extensive journalism experience, more than 16 years as a reporter and editor for daily newspapers in New York and Virginia.

Over the years, the firm has built a strong staff of professionals from journalism, business, government and academia, including public relations specialists from national firms, who have served hundreds of clients.

The firm is organized into three core practice groups: health care/ education; corporate/technology and because of its location in the capital of New York state—public affairs.

The communications-focused public affairs operation, which often works with lobbyists and law firms, was established in 1988. It offers public affairs and government relations services, including issues management, legislative and issues research, grassroots lobbying, media relations, speech writing, association communications, prepara-

tion of testimony, coalition building, political assessment/ analysis, access to decision makers, and seminars and legislative functions. The public affairs operation has received national honors from the Public Relations Society of America (PRSA) and *Inside PR* magazine.

The firm has received local, regional and national professional recognition, including "Company of the Year" (under 100 employees) by the *Capital District Business Review*; "Small Business of the Year" by the Albany-Colonie Regional Chamber of Commerce; honors from PRSA, the International Association of Business Communicators (IABC) and the American Marketing Association; and a "Creativity in Public Relations Award" from *Inside PR* magazine. *Inside PR* magazine also named Sawchuk, Brown one of the "12 best managed agencies" in the country.

The firm is the upstate New York associate of Hill and Knowlton (H&K), one of the world's leading public relations/public affairs firms, and often works with H&K on joint projects. Through this relationship, SBA has national and global reach.

Sawchuk, Brown's staff of 30 is actively involved with, and holds leadership positions in professional organizations such as PRSA, Women's Press Club and American Marketing Association and business groups such as the Albany-Colonie Regional Chamber of Commerce, Business Council of New York State and Center for Economic Growth. They are also active in several leading institutions and organizations in the arts, education, health care and social services.

In 2000, Pamela Sawchuk was named one of 100 "Women of Excellence" who have made significant contributions and "pioneered change" in the Capital Region over the last 100 years.

SUNMARK FEDERAL CREDIT UNION®

Sunmark Federal Credit Union® (formerly Turbine) began its operations in 1937 out of the Schenectady General Electric main plant, buckets department. For many years during General Electric's heyday, Sunmark operated out of the home of Arthur Bufe, credit union president, who lived just over the bridge in Scotia, New York. Most of the business was transacted at the plant however, where collection boxes were placed for members to leave deposits and loan payments. Also, there were designated "collectors" throughout the plant who were credit union volunteers. Their job was to sign up new members, promote the credit union, and answer questions.

In the early 1960s, the center of operations was moved to the first professional office on Guilderland Avenue in Rotterdam, New York, where Sunmark operated for over ten years. Sunmark bought property at 1616 Broadway in Schenectady, New York in 1971 and built its first stand-alone office. Carl Damberg, who was the board president from 1963 to 1995, was instrumental in this accomplishment. By 1971, the credit union had grown to $8 million in assets.

Sunmark hired its first professional manager in the early '60s, Warren Hickok, who ran the credit union until he retired in 1986. The credit union experienced much growth under the leadership of Damberg and Hickok. Sunmark also benefited from the consolidation of credit unions during that

Sunmark FCU's (formerly Turbine) first stand-alone office.

Ribbon-cuttong ceremony for Sunmark's first stand-alone office, at 1616 Broadway in Schenectady.

period. At one point in the 1940s, there were 14 different credit unions at the General Electric Main Plant. By 1986, that number had dropped to eight.

Sunmark's board hired Bruce M. Beaudette as its new general manager in 1986. Mr. Beaudette, who is the president/CEO today, made many positive changes to Sunmark's product line by adding credit and ATM cards, home equity loans, mortgages and much more. He teamed up with Mr. Damberg to open the first branch office at the General Electric plant in Building 33 in 1986. An additional branch was added at the plant in Building 5 in 1992, when Northeast Savings Bank vacated its office there.

In 1994, Sunmark opened its most modern facility on Route 50 in Glenville, New York, which had formerly been a Ponderosa Restaurant. The rear portion of this spacious office is now the headquarters for Sunmark Financial Services, LLC, a complete financial services provider and wholly-owned subsidiary of Sunmark Federal Credit Union®.

Berthold (Bud) Sackett retired in

1997 as treasurer of Sunmark, a position he held for many years. In all, Bud was a Sunmark volunteer for more than 52 years!

Mergers became active under Mr. Beaudette's leadership. There were eight in total between 1988 and 2000. Assets grew rapidly to over $180 million by the new millennium. Because of the strong capital position that was built up over the years prior to Mr. Beaudette's tenure, the federal regulators allowed and even promoted Sunmark's rapid expansion. When General Electric began downsizing in the mid-1980s, Sunmark decided to recruit employer groups beyond General Electric. By 2000, Sunmark served more than 230 companies in the Capital District area and many members throughout the world.

Throughout its history, Sunmark's mission has remained constant—to excel in member service and provide technology driven services at a low cost and in a convenient manner.

TEMPER CORPORATION

Unsuspecting visitors, be it friends, job seekers, customers or vendors, are inevitably surprised, indeed astounded, when touring Temper Corporation. Who would think that, tucked into the rolling foot-hilled landscape of the Mohawk River, the Temper facade houses a well-honed, high-tech, precision community that received recognition as New York State Small Business Manufacturer of the Year–2000 !

Temper's founder and CEO, John E. Rode, recognized as a genius in his field, works in a milieu of enthusiastic, professionally-careered staff and equally enthusiastic in-house trained technicians to design, develop, and manufacture products which not only solve customers' problems, but also, due to increased efficiency, add dollars to their bottom line.

John Rode, who stopped counting patents at number 30, founded Tem-

Below: Temper's variety of products includes components vital to the assembly of farm tractors, boat motors, and trucks as well as minimally invasive surgical instruments.

per in Pennsylvania in 1969. In 1971, Temper relocated to its present home in Fonda, five minutes from the Thruway and the Mohawk River. Thirty years have established relationships and partnering with nearly 100 customers, including notables such as Mercury Marine, Pratt and Whitney Aircraft, Sauer-Danfoss, New Holland, and John Deere. Five lines of stainless

Above: John E. Rode, Temper Corporation founder and president with his patented magical magnet rings.

steel products were developed: jet engine seals, surgical scissors, magnet rings, sensor housings, and adjustable spacers. Most are custom-designed in-house and made nowhere else in the world. Temper has acquired a collection of the latest state-of-the-art equipment to design, develop, test and manufacture precision items with tolerances to one thousandth of an inch. Specialized machines for making Temper products are the brainchild of John Rode and his team, and are designed, developed and made at Temper.

The company is located on 99 acres in a country setting. All operations were confined to about 3,500 square feet in a rustic wooden farm building until 1989 when 6,000 square feet were added by renovating two stories of the old dairy barn. The property was permanently zoned for industrial use in 1991 and a 5,000 square foot machine shop was added. That building was expanded with office space and another 6000 square feet of manufacturing space in 2000.

Temper's scissors are used in thousands of minimally invasive surgeries each year. This product was developed for another local company, ConMed Corporation of Utica, New York, to complement their line of medical products.

Temper seals have escaped the gravity of Planet Earth in every space shuttle. The company was originally founded to make high temperature metal spring gaskets for jet engines, but the product emphasis shifted to the newly invented compressible spacers , enabling the company to spread its dependence on a broader industrial marketplace. Development was extremely slow because there was no competing product on the market. Customers had to be convinced that Temper's compressible spacers would survive in all operating environments without failure. Temper adjustable spacers are now responsible for precision bearing fits in many boat motors, forklifts, farm tractors and industrial

Sean Strait, designer, and Peter Karpinski, sales and marketing engineer are the next generation of talent evolving Temper products.

machines. During recent years the company developed heavy-duty ring designs with capacities up to 100 tons. In the meantime, the jet engine seal business developed. Many of today's jetliners now use Temper-seals to prevent leakage between joints in the engine casings: seals that remain flexible at red-hot operating temperatures.

Temper's patented magnet rings and sensor housings are at the heart of the

smart controls in modern day bulldozers, backhoes and street sweeping machines. The magnet ring was invented in response to a customer's request for a secure, flexible, multi-pole magnetic strip that would easily be fitted on a hydraulic pump or motor shaft capable of spinning at speeds up to 7,000 rpm.

Complementing this list of stainless steel products are custom designed smart presses and special gaging which increase cost savings for customers by better utilization of Temper's adjustable spacers in their product assembly. John Rode invented the first smart press to quickly adjust bearing clearances in worm gear speed reducers and delivered the first machine to Winsmith in Buffalo, NY during the blizzard of 1977. That product remains successful today and has produced over a million bearing assemblies. The latest machines are computer controlled for the most efficient production line assemblies.

The company's latest product innovations include a heavy-duty adjustable spacer that is being tested on truck trailer wheels to improve bearing adjustment accuracy, longer life and greater safety.

Temper Corporation proudly displays a United States flag flown over our nation's Capitol in recognition of the company's unique capabilities and accomplishments.

Paul Saltsman roll forming a jet engine seal used in modern aircraft engines.

TOUGHER INDUSTRIES, INC.

The origins of the present corporation of Tougher Industries, Inc. go back to the late 19th century when Robert Moore, an immigrant from Ireland who ran a lumber business in Albany, sent to Ireland for his nephew, Jim Hunter. Jim, who was born on January 4, 1865, in Gilford, County Down, Ireland, came to the United States on March 25, 1883 to work for his uncle receiving lumber from the barges and sailing vessels that plied the Hudson River at that time.

Between 1887 and 1900, Jim Hunter started his own heating business. In 1900, it was located on Church Street in Albany. The business subsequently moved to 207-209 Broadway in 1914 and ultimately to its final location of 65 Liberty Street in 1920.

Jim Hunter, an imposing hulk of an Irishman with a full, bushy mustache, usually sporting a narrow brimmed derby, was a personal friend of Teddy Roosevelt. A pioneer of his day, he championed the use of hot water for central heating, instead of the popular steam heating systems of the time. Among the notable installations by Jim Hunter were the D & H building in the City of Albany. Tougher Industries also provided the ventilation and air conditioning systems for the D & H building renovations in the mid-1970s and for the N.Y. State Education Department Headquarters.

Jim Hunter's nephew, Bob Tougher came from Belfast, Ireland to work for Jim Hunter in about 1926. He subsequently sent for his brothers (John and then Bill), who also worked for Jim Hunter, as pipefitters. After Jim Hunter died in 1944, Bob Tougher and his brother John then started a heating business under their own names. They were joined after the war by brother Bill, who had served in the U.S. Navy.

Tougher's main post-war business was the conversion of residential coal-

Jim Hunter, 1865-1944.

fired systems to modern G.E. oil-fired units. As business prospered, they branched into the commercial industrial market, providing heating systems for many of the area's new public schools and municipal buildings.

By the time Tougher Heating and Plumbing Co. celebrated its 25th anniversary with a gala party in 1969, it had acquired Charles R. Joyce & Son, a major sheet metal contracting firm;

Tougher's main office located on Broadway in Menands.

had become a partner in Tri-City Insulation Co.; and had formed Mid City Supply Co., a wholesaler. Among the company's significant projects at the time were the four agency buildings and the cultural center in what is now the $1 billion Empire State Plaza. It provided mechanical systems in most of the region's major hospitals, educational institutions and state facilities. The company established its reputation as one of the area's leading mechanical contractors. *Fortune Magazine* lists the company among the top 500 plumbing and heating contractors in the United States.

In 1974, the Tougher Brothers decided it was time to turn over the reigns to the third generation of family members and employees. Tougher Industries, Inc. was formed on June 17,

1974. They acquired the assets of the predecessor company and hired its employees. From an initial capital investment of $150,000 in June 1974, Tougher Industries increased its net worth to over $6 million and its volume to over $50 million annually, and expanded its territory to a 300-mile radius of Albany. Since 1984, Tougher Industries has been listed by *Domestic Engineering, Engineering News Record,* and *Contractor and Service Reporter,* all national publications, as among the top 100 mechanical contracting firms in the United States. Its chief executive officer Donald A. McKay, served as president of the Mechanical Contractors Association of

America, commencing its 100th anniversary convention in Orlando, Florida in February 1989. He was the first resident of Albany to hold that office.

Tougher Industries acquired Mechanical Construction Corp. of Poughkeepsie, New York in 1994. The former owners of Mechanical, Henry and Raymond Meagher, had started MCC in 1910. The company currently operates both a construction and service division.

In January 2000, Tougher Industries was acquired by PSEG Energy Technologies. PSEG-ET is a subsidiary of Public Service Enterprise Group Incorporated (PSEG), a company with more than $17 billion in assets and nearly a century of experience in the energy business.

THE TROY SAVINGS BANK

The Troy Savings Bank, founded in 1823, is the oldest state-chartered bank in New York. In the spring of 1823, 11 prominent Troy businessmen met at the establishment of innkeeper Platt Titus and drew up a petition to the state legislature requesting to form a mutual savings bank "for the purpose of receiving on deposit such sums of money as might be deposited by tradesmen, mechanics, laborers, minors, servants and others" and investing the money to the advantage of its depositors.

The legislature passed the act of incorporation on April 23, and named nine of the 11 incorporators and 10 other prominent residents as trustees for the new venture. The appointed trustees were permitted at that time to make arrangements with either of Troy's two commercial banks, The Farmers Bank or the Bank of Troy, to receive deposits from the new savings bank. The Troy Savings Bank opened for business the last Saturday evening of August 1823, with monies placed

Prior to its 1950 remodeling, The Troy Savings Bank utilized only the south side of the main level for its own business. The rest of the space was rented out to other businesses and organizations.

Innkeeper Platt Titus, whose hostelry was on First Street near the junction with River Street, was one of the 19 founders of The Troy Savings Bank. The board of managers signed the papers of incorporation at his inn in April 1823.

on deposit every Monday into Farmers Bank.

Following six years of meeting at Platt Titus' Troy house, the trustees hired an attorney, Jacob L. Lane, to receive deposits and soon their meetings were moved to his office. Several of the original and many of the later trustees were also associated with other banks in Troy. All were prominent in business and civic circles and most remained board members.

The Troy Savings Bank grew and in 1844 purchased land on First Street just south of Troy House on which to construct a new building. By the early 1870s, the Bank's continued growth necessitated even more space and the Bank's present main office, designed by architect George B. Post, was constructed in 1875.

The Board of Trustees held its initial meeting in the new building on April 19, 1875. An inaugural concert was held the same evening in The Troy Savings Bank Music Hall, which sits atop the building and has long since become recognized as one of the finest acoustical concert halls in the world. The Music Hall was a "gift" to the people of Troy from the Trustees in appreciation of their support of the Bank.

The Troy Savings Bank continued to grow through the years in assets, services for its clients and in branch locations. When the Bank celebrated its 175th anniversary in 1998, it had 14 locations serving six counties in the Greater Capital District Area: Rensselaer, Albany, Schenectady, Saratoga, Warren and Washington.

The Troy Savings Bank converted from a mutual to a publicly owned savings bank on March 31, 1999 and The Troy Financial Corporation (NASDAQ: TRYF) headquartered in Troy became the holding company of the Bank. Troy Financial Corporation created The Troy Commercial Bank in August of 2000, primarily to accept municipal deposits. Savings banks were permitted to lend funds to municipalities but were precluded by law from taking deposits. The Troy Savings Bank completed the acquisition of The Catskill Savings Bank in November of 2000, with seven offices primarily in Schoharie and Greene Counties. The Bank now has 21 offices serving eight counties with total assets of $1.3 billion.

The Troy Savings Bank now operates as a full-service financial

institution for both individuals and businesses and its future growth and development look extremely bright. The year 2000 also marked the 150th anniversary of the Bank's main office and the Music Hall, both of which are listed as historical landmarks.

Since its founding in 1823, The Troy Savings Bank has had only 15 presidents in 177 years: Townsend McCoun (1823-1834); Richard P. Hart (1834-1839); Stephen Warren (1839-1847); Gurdon Corning (1847-1850); Jared S. Weed (1850-1870); Charles B. Russell (18701887); Derick Lane (1887-1892); Charles Hanaman (1893-1916); William H. Shields (1916-1933); Henry Colvin (1933-1936); Barnard Townsend (1936-1948); John I. Millet (1948-1969); Herbert J. Fadeley, Jr. (1969-1982); and J.Barker Houle (1982-1985). The current President and Chief Executive Officer, Daniel J. Hogarty, Jr., was elected president and a trustee in 1985 and chief executive officer in 1987. He is also chairman, president and chief executive officer of Troy Financial Corporation.

Above: The Troy Savings Bank Music Hall, regarded as one of the finest acoustical concert halls in the world, sits atop the Bank's main office in downtown Troy. Many of the finest classical, jazz and contemporary musicians have "played" the hall—Jose Iturbi, Myra Hess, Vladimir Horowitz, Yehudi Menuhin, Arthur Rubenstein, Yo Yo Ma, Isaac Stern, Ella Fitzgerald, Sara Vaughn, Dave Brubeck, Wynton Marsalis, Chet Atkins, Burl Ives, Pete Seeger, Benny Goodman, and Gordon Lightfoot—among others. The Hall seats 1250 people and was a "gift" from the Bank's trustees to the people of Troy for their support of the Bank.

Right: The Troy Savings Bank's Main Office at Second and State Streets in Downtown Troy—designed by respected New York City architect George B. Post—was completed in 1875. Both the Bank and the Troy Savings Music Hall, which sits atop the building, celebrated their 125th anniversary in 2000. The Bank observed its 175th anniversary in 1998.

ZWACK, INC.

Founded in 1970, Zwack, Inc. today enjoys a strong reputation as an innovative manufacturer of special machinery and equipment for industry, municipalities and a variety of other customers. This second generation, family-owned business enjoys a long term business relationship with small, large, and Fortune 500 customers, including General Electric Power Systems, Intermagnetics, Instron, Albany International, Taconic, MIT, Newark Paper Group, Encore Paper, and municipalities in the surrounding four state area.

Zwack, Inc. began as a specialty manufacturer for one primary customer and today employs more than 60 people to provide clients worldwide with engineering, design, and manufacturing options, ranging in size and complexity from products such as highway sand and salt spreaders, firefighting equipment, transformer core winding machines, generator stator frames, paper mill frames, large magnet winding machines, computer controlled core stacking machines, a proprietary cold fusion process for manufacture of copper, aluminum transition pieces, to...whatever machinery or other need a customer may ask to have built. The products manufactured by Zwack, Inc., in use throughout the United States, Canada, Europe and

A new automated generator core stacking machine.

Asia, attest to Zwack's commitment to providing each customer with solid craftsmanship, economic value, and successful adaption of ever changing technology.

This family owned business is located in a picturesque valley between the Taconic and Berkshire Hills, in Rensselaer County, New York. The surrounding communities are home to a number of colleges and universities, as well as many diversified businesses that provide products and services to this world-wide supplier of specialty machine products. A sponsor of the Hudson Valley Community College Machinist Apprentice Program and its Capstone Project, Zwack, Inc. also affords industry experience and opportunity to grad students in the RPI

CAT program and RPI's Senior Mechanical Design Group, as well as to local high school students in a JOBS program.

Zwack, Inc. continues a long tradition of support and involvement in church, community and civic organizations, and actively encourages employee participation in volunteer fire and emergency medical services, as well as membership in the State National Guard. Members of the Zwack family are involved in numerous community activities and local government, including school board, volunteer fire company, local fire district, library board, and cemetery board. Zwack, Inc. remains firmly committed to the community in which it began and is today located. Stephentown and Rensselaer County provide Zwack, Inc. with the right location for expanding its business opportunities, whether they be just around the corner or around the world.

One of Zwack, Inc.'s paper making machines.

A TIMELINE OF HUDSON MOHAWK GATEWAY'S HISTORY

10,500 B.C. – Paleo-Indians populate the valleys now known as Hudson and Mohawk.

1609 – Henry Hudson sails the *Half Moon* up the river that now bears his name to a point south of present-day Albany. Lucrative fur trade inspires the creation of the Dutch West India Company.

1630 – Dutch merchant Killiaen Van Rensselaer, patroon of Rensselaerwyck, purchases Indian land.

1634 – Lubbertsland, now Troy, is named after early settler Lubbert Gijsbertsz.

1658 – Wynant Gerritse van der Poel begins milling in present-day South Troy on the Wynantskill, or Wynant's Channel.

1707 – Derick Van der Heyden rents 497 acres along the Hudson from the Poesten Kill to the Piscawen Kill for three and three-quarter bushels of wheat and two fat hens.

1735 – The Van Schaick House is built on Van Schaick Island, opposite present-day Lansingburgh. General Schuyler will quarter his staff there in 1777.

1763 – Abraham Jacob Lansing purchases Stone Arabia Patent (Lansingburgh).

1771 – A map of New City (Lansingburgh) is filed to distinguish it from Old City (Albany). Lansingburgh merchants prosper, supplying customers in Vermont, in Lake George, and along the Hudson.

1786 – Van der Heyden's land is owned by great-grandsons Jacob I. Van der Heyden (north patroon), Jacob David Van der Heyden (middle patroon), and Matthias Van der Heyden (south patroon). New City's growth pressures the patroons to sell lots to settle the area around Ashley's Ferry, where the stagecoach line between New City and Old City crosses the Hudson. This will become the core of downtown Troy.

1787 – Flores Bancker plans a village on Jacob David Van der Heyden's farm in the style of Philadelphia, with

MATHIAS VAN DER HEYDEN'S HOUSE
1752.
Stephen Ashley's Tavern, 1786

Inside this tavern in 1789, Troy got its name from a small band of visionary residents. From History of the City of Troy, *by Weise, 1876*

regular squares and rectangular streets. Early settlers include physician Samuel Gale and merchants Benjamin Thurber, Colonel Albert Pawling, Colonel Abraham Ten Eyck, and Benjamin Covell.

1789 – Van der Heyden's settlement is named Troy at a meeting at Ashley's Tavern. New Hampshire brothers Samuel and Ebenezer Wilson arrive in Troy, establishing a brick manufactory at Ferry Street and Sixth Avenue.

1792 – Mahlon Taylor purchases an old mill site on the Poestenkill Gorge, rebuilds the dam, and constructs the first paper mill in northern New York.

1795 – The first bridge across the Mohawk, a toll bridge, connects Cohoes and Waterford.

1804 – The first bridge over the Hudson River north of New York City, a Burr Arch Truss, built by the Union Bridge Company, connects Lansingburgh and Waterford.

1807 – The success of the *North River Steamboat of Clermont* wins Robert Fulton and Robert R. Livingston a monopoly over steamboat operations in New York.

1808 – Connecticut native Benjamin Hanks and son Julius open a bronze foundry in Gibbonsville (now Watervliet), beginning a world famous

bell industry involving four different but related firms.

1809 – Troy Iron and Nail Factory opens on the south side of Wynantskill's upper falls; 13 years later, engineer Henry Burden will become superintendent and, after inventing machines to make horseshoes and railroad spikes, will assume full ownership in 1848.

1812 – To provide ammunition and supplies for the War of 1812, Congress purchases property from James Gibbons, at Gibbonsville (now Watervliet), to build an arsenal. Meatpacker Samuel Wilson, nicknamed Uncle Sam, supplies meat packed in barrels stamped "US" to the army encampment near Greenbush.

1820 – Orsamus Eaton opens a Troy coach factory. In 1831, apprentice Uri Gilbert becomes a partner as focus gradually shifts to the manufacture of railroad passenger cars. After a fire in 1852, the firm moves to Green Island.

1820 – Lansingburgh Academy opens with Reverend Samuel Blatchford (RPI's first President) as principal, and students include author Herman Melville

A statue of Emma Willard now stands in front of the site in downtown Troy where she relocated her female seminary in 1821. Photo by Sloane Bullough

and future US President Chester A. Arthur.

1821 – Struggling educator Emma Willard relocates her Female Seminary from Waterford to Troy's Moulton Coffeehouse on Second Street. In 1910, Emma Willard School will move to Pawling Avenue.

1821 – Charles and Nathaniel Starbuck and Ephraim Gurley initiate area stove manufacturing. Thirty years later, seven Troy foundries will operate, the most popular stove—Philo P. Stewart's.

1823 – The first state dam and lock on the Hudson, between Troy and Green Island, opens Lansingburgh to seasonal sloop navigation.

1823 – The *Troy Sentinel* becomes the world's first publisher of "A Visit From Saint Nicholas."

1824 – Stephen Van Rensselaer III, patroon of Rensselaerwyck, founds the Rensselaer School, now Rensselaer Polytechnic Institute, in the Farmers Bank Building at 703 River Street, Troy.

1824 – Chief Justice Marshall declares the Livingston/Fulton steamboat monopoly unconstitutional. In gratitude,

the Troy Steamboat Company will later name their first steamboat after him.

1825 – The Erie Canal opens from Buffalo to New York City.

1827 – Hannah Lord Montague invents the detachable collar. The collar industry thrives, earning Troy the nickname "Collar City."

1829 – Deborah Powers inherits her husband William's Lansingburgh floor cloth business, the forerunner of linoleum, after his death in a varnish fire. D. Powers and Sons, Inc., flourishes under her leadership, expanding to Newburgh and New York City.

1831 – Canvass White designs a dam across the Mohawk River above Cohoes Falls, allowing Cohoes and its future Harmony Mills to become nationally significant in textile manufacturing.

1838 – *Moby Dick* author Herman Melville moves to Lansingburgh, where he writes *Typee* and *Omoo*.

1838 – The Burden Water Wheel is built at Burden's iron works in South Troy. Sixty feet high, it is known as the "Niagara of Waterwheels," the most powerful vertical water wheel ever made.

1840 – Census data indicates Troy is, per capita, the fourth wealthiest city in the US.

1840 – Benjamin Marshall creates a Troy cotton mill by damming the Poestenkill above Mt. Ida Falls, inspiring additional factories by Kellogg, Manning, Orr, and Smart.

1845 – Trojans William Gurley and Jonas Phelps partner to make precision instruments and eventually will become famous as W. & L.E. Gurley, world's largest manufacturer of surveying instruments.

1845 – George W. Eddy establishes a stove-making foundry, later specializing in valve-making.

1846 – William Manning, Gardner Howland, and Alvin Williams found the Mt. Ida Mill that in 1855 becomes Manning and Peckham and eventually Hammermill Paper Company in Green Island in 1962.

1848 – The Troy Gas Light Company is formed. In the 1870s, it will build its famous Gasholder House.

1849 – Erastus Corning's Albany Iron Works builds the first steam-powered

The historic DeFreest House, now the headquarters of the Rensselaer Technology Park, provides an excellent example of the marriage of the past and the future in the historic Gateway region. Photo by Denise Scammell

For nine years, Herman Melville made his home in Lansingburgh as he began his career as a novelist. Photo by Sloane Bullough

rolling mill near today's Menands Bridge.

1854 – The Troy Union Railroad Company opens the Sixth Avenue Union depot.

1856 – Names of African-American citizens are no longer italicized in the Troy *City Directory*, but oppression continues.

1860 – Charles Nalle, fugitive slave, escapes authorities amid an angry mob on First and State streets in Troy with Harriet Tubman's assistance. Uri Gilbert, Nalle's employer, raises $650 to buy his freedom.

1861 – Designed by John Ericsson, the *U.S.S. Monitor* is constructed, with armor hull plates forged at the Corning, Winslow & Co. With the financial backing of John A. Griswold, the contract is signed in a small room now preserved in the present-day Franklin Plaza in downtown Troy.

1862 – Henry Burden builds his Lower Works along the Hudson above the Wynantskill.

1862 – A spark from an engine crossing the Troy-Green Island Railroad Bridge ignites the wooden roof, destroying 75 acres of Troy's downtown.

1863 – Draft and anti-black riots occur in response to the war. A mob trying to burn down the black Liberty St. Presbyterian Church is discour-

aged by Rev. Peter Havermans, pastor of Troy's first Catholic parish. Burden iron workers protest the Troy *Daily Times* editorial's support of $300 payments to escape conscription.

1864 – Labor activist Kate Mullaney organizes the first truly all-female labor union in the country, the Troy Collar Laundry Union.

1865 – Rev. Henry Highland Garnet, escaped slave and former pastor of Troy's Liberty Street Presbyterian Church, offers an anti-slavery prayer before the House of Representatives, the first person of African-American descent to do so.

1865 – John A. Griswold introduces the Bessemer process to the US, converting pig iron into steel, at Rensselaer Steel and Iron Works.

1875 – Railroads, taking 11 hours compared to 10 days by canal to transport goods from Buffalo to New York City, now handle the bulk of commercial traffic.

1875 – Troy Music Hall opens and becomes famous for its superb acoustics.

1880s – Labor organizations protest

working conditions, and stove manufacturers begin to leave Troy.

1886 – Prosperous breweries in Troy produce over 175,000 barrels.

1890-1891 – The Soldiers and Sailors Monument is erected in Washington Square (now Monument Square) in Troy to honor local soldiers.

1890 – The Gardner Earl Chapel and Crematorium at Oakwood Cemetery is built in memory of the son of collar manufacturers. Its costly architectural splendor complements the cemetery's many monuments and mausoleums.

1890 – The Burden Water Wheel ceases operation, and in 1896 the Upper Burden Iron Works are abandoned. The wheel is in all likelihood the inspiration for the world's first Ferris Wheel in 1893, designed by RPI graduate George Washington Gale Ferris, Jr.

1893 – Troy's Ross Valve moves to

Downtown Troy stands devastated following the great fire of 10 May 1862. From Harper's Weekly, 24 May 1862, based upon a photograph by Schoonmaker

Oakwood Avenue and eventually becomes world famous.

1897 – Troy Public Library moves to the William Howard Hart Memorial Building, home to one of Troy's many famous Tiffany windows, donated by Mary E. Hart.

1897 – Wealthy dry goods merchant William H. Frear opens the new Troy Cash Bazaar in the Frear Building.

1900 – Troy's Chamber of Commerce is formed.

1900 – Area trolley car workers begin a series of strikes that lasts 30 years.

1901 – Lansingburgh consolidates with Troy, retaining separate school districts.

1903 – Troy purchases the Warren and Vail properties on Congress Street, at which site Garnett D. Baltimore, RPI's first black graduate, designs Prospect Park.

1907 – The Approach is built where RPI's main building was destroyed by fire in 1904, linking downtown with RPI.

1909 – Cluett Peabody and Company of Troy builds a bleachery at Peebles Island, the first place to use the Sanforization process invented by

Above: Smith's Restaurant in Cohoes continues its long and colorful history of providing good food and drink to area residents. The 50 foot Victorian bar, purportedly from Tammany Hall in New York City, was purchased by former owner "Big Mike" Smith in the 1930s. Photo by Robert Thayer.

Sanford Cluett. It later will become a facility of the New York State Office of Parks, Recreation, and Historic Preservation.

1914 – The Burden Water Wheel collapses. Remnants will be sold for scrap in the 1940s.

1916 – Russell Sage College for Women opens on the former Emma Willard campus.

1916 – The new Federal Lock and Dam is completed at the foot of Bond Street.

1918 – The Waterford locks are built and the New York State Barge Canal system is completed.

1932 – Trolley car service ends in Troy.

1934 – Troy Airport opens south of Campbell Avenue on the Williams family property, later becoming an industrial park.

1938 – Burden Iron Company ceases operations.

1940 – Republic Steel purchases the Burden Iron Company's Lower Works property.

1941 – Troy Cash Bazaar closes and is sold to investors.

1948 – The North/South Arterial is proposed from the Menands Bridge to the Waterford Bridge. It will be suc-

The majestic elegance of this detail of the Frear staircase, once the centerpiece of one of the leading department stores in upstate New York, is typical of the abundant ornamental ironwork that attracts tourists to downtown Troy. Photo by Sloane Bullough

cessfully blocked by the Lansingburgh Third Avenue Association, and will later be built on the Watervliet side of the Hudson.

1951 – The last bell foundry in the region closes, area foundries having cast over 100,000 bells including the Liberty Bell's replacement in 1876. The most famous are the bells of the two Meneely foundries.

1955 – Union Depot closes, ending passenger train service in Troy.

1966 – The Troy Urban Renewal Agency begins to demolish the central downtown business area.

1967 – Troy Plaza opens on Hoosick Street, siphoning retail business from downtown.

1972 – The Preservation Committee of the Rensselaer County Historical Society spins off the Hudson Mohawk Industrial Gateway.

1974 – The Gateway buys the Burden Office property at the foot of Polk Street from Republic Steel for $10

after having successfully nominated it to the National Register of Historic Places.

1977 – The Green Island Bridge collapses when a pier from the 1834-era bridge is weakened by high waters. It will be rebuilt in 1981.

1977 – Carl Grimm purchases the Frear Building, hoping to resurrect downtown Troy.

1979 – The Hudson-Mohawk Urban Cultural Park is established. The Uncle Sam Atrium opens in the Frear building. Denby's and Carl's become short-lived anchor stores.

1980 – The Collar City Bridge opens, completing the link with Interstate 787.

1980 – In the new Uncle Sam Atrium, Carl Grimm opens Troy's first new movie theater in 45 years.

1981 – Rensselaer Technology Park is planned on 1,200 acres on Route 4 at Jordan Road, incorporating the historic Philip DeFreest farmhouse as an administration building.

1982 – Railroad tracks from Green Island to Waterford are removed and Matton Shipyard in Cohoes closes. The

Arrow Shirt Factory moves 200 jobs out of Troy.

1990 – Hedley Park Place office complex opens in the former Cluett building in Troy.

1999 – The refurbished Approach reunites downtown with RPI at the Winslow Building, the Junior Museum's new location.

2000 – The Arts Center of the Capital Region moves from Washington Park's Uri Gilbert House to renovated buildings on River Street, helping to revitalize downtown Troy.

From about 70,000 half a century ago, Troy's population has declined. The recent interest of New Urbanists has not reversed that trend, but it may have slowed it slightly. Data from U.S. Bureau of the Census, chart by P. Thomas Carroll

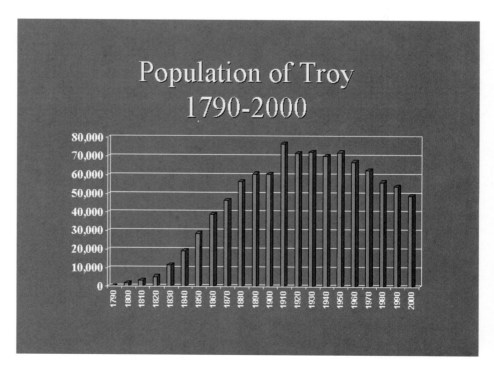

An artist's rendering of the new bicycle path slowly taking shape all along Troy's Hudson River waterfront. Drawing by Christopher Chadbourne & Associates.

BIBLIOGRAPHY

These are some of the most important works used in the preparation of this book. Other sources include city directories, newspapers, maps and atlases, company documents, historic research papers done by the principal author's students, the files of the Rensselaer County Historical Society, and the files of the Hudson Mohawk Industrial Gateway. For additional sources, consult www.hudsonmohawkgateway.org and www.troyvisitorcenter.org.

Adams, Samuel Hopkins, *Sunrise to Sunset*. New York: Random House, 1950.

Anderson, George Baker, *Landmarks of Rensselaer County, New York*. Syracuse: D. Mason & Co., 1897.

Bliven, Rachel, Robert N. Anderson, G. Steven Draper, Eva and Hughes Gemmill, Joseph A. Parker, and Helen M. Upton, *A Resourceful People: A Pictorial History of Rensselaer County, New York*. Norfolk, Va.: The Donning Company, Publishers, 1987.

Broderick, Frances D., *The Burial Grounds of Lansingburgh, Rensselaer County, New York*. Published by the author, 1965.

Broderick, Warren, ed., *Brunswick— A Pictorial History*. Troy: Walter Snyder Printer, Inc., 1978.

Carroll, P. Thomas, "Designing Modern America in the Silicon Valley of the Nineteenth Century," *Rensselaer* (March 1999).

Cohoes Centennial Committee, *Cohoes Centennial, 1870-1970*. Cohoes, 1970.

Crisman, Kevin J., and Arthur B. Cohn, *When Horses Walked on Water: Horse-Powered Ferries in Nineteenth-Century America*. Washington and London: Smithsonian Institution Press, 1998.

Crowl, John R., and Kathryn A. Youngs, *Harmony Mills Historic District*. Troy: Hudson Mohawk Industrial Gateway, 1978.

Dunn, Shirley W., *The Mohican World, 1680-1750*. Fleischmans, N.Y.: Purple Mountain Press, 2000.

_____, *The Mohicans and Their Land, 1690-1730*. Fleischmans, N.Y.: Purple Mountain Press, 1994.

Funk, Robert E., *Recent Contributions to Hudson Valley Prehistory*. New York State Museum, Memoir 22. Albany: University of the State of New York, State Education Department, 1976.

Goddard, Abba A., ed., *The Trojan Sketch Book*. Troy: Young & Hart, 1846.

Gordon, Robert B., *American Iron, 1607-1900*. Baltimore and London: The Johns Hopkins University Press, 1996.

Hammersley, Sydney Ernest, *The History of Waterford, New York*. Published by the author, 1957.

Hayner, Rutherford, *Troy and Rensselaer County, New York*. 3 vols. New York and Chicago: Lewis Historical Publishing Co., Inc., 1925.

Holmes, Oliver W., and Peter T. Rohrbach, *Stagecoach East*. Washington, D.C.: Smithsonian Institution Press, 1983.

Hutchinson, Samuel, *et al.*, *Green Island Heritage and the Bicentennial*. Green Island, 1976.

Kalm, Peter, *The America of 1750: Travels in North America*. 2 vols. New York: Dover Publications, 1966.

Kammen, Michael, *Colonial New York: A History*. New York: Oxford University Press, 1996.

Lord, Jane S., ed., *Lansingburgh, New York, 1771-1971*. Troy: Lansingburgh Historical Society, 1971.

Marcou, O'Leary and Associates, Inc., and Rensselaer Polytechnic Institute, *Historic Cohoes, New York: A Survey of Historic Resources*. [Troy]: [Rensselaer Polytechnic Institute, Center for Architectural Research], 1971.

Masten, Arthur H., *The History of Cohoes, New York*. Albany: Joel Munsell, 1877.

McHugh, Jeanne, *Alexander Holley and the Makers of Steel*. Baltimore: The Johns Hopkins University Press, 1980.

Moore, H. Irving, *A Pictorial Reminiscence and Brief History of Lansingburgh, Rensselaer County, N.Y., Founded in 1770*. Published by the author, 1957.

Murray, James V., and John Swantek, eds., *The Watervliet Arsenal: A Chronology of the Nation's Oldest Arsenal*. Watervliet: Watervliet Arsenal, 1997.

Myer, James T., *History of the City of Watervliet, N.Y., 1630 to 1910*. Troy, 1910.

Parker, Amasor J., *Landmarks of Albany County, N.Y.* Syracuse: D. Mason and Co., 1897.

Parker, Joseph A., *Looking Back: A History of Troy and Rensselaer County, 1925-1980*. Published by the author, 1982.

Pearson, Jonathan, *Early Records of the City and County of Albany and Colony of Rensselaerwyck*. Albany: The University of the State of New York, 1916, 1918, and 1919.

_____, *Contributions for the Genealogies of the First Settlers of the Ancient County of Albany, 1630-1800*. Baltimore: Genealogical Publishing Co., Inc., 1976.

Phelan, Thomas, D. Michael Ross, and Carl A. Westerdahl, *Rensselaer, Where Imagination Achieves the Impossible: An Illustrated History of Rensselaer*

Polytechnic Institute. Troy: Rensselaer Polytechnic Institute, in association with Mount Ida Press, 1995.

Proudfit, Margaret Burden, *Henry Burden, His Life and a History of His Inventions Compiled from the Public Press.* Troy: Pafraets Press, 1904.

Rezneck, Samuel, *Profiles Out of the Past of Troy, New York, since 1789.* Troy: Chamber of Commerce, 1970.

Ritchie, William A., *The Archaeology of New York State.* Garden City, N.J.: The Natural History Press, 1969.

_____, *An Introduction to Hudson Valley Pre-History.* Bulletin 367. Albany: New York State Museum and Science Service, 1958.

Rittner, Don, *Images of America: Lansingburgh.* Charleston, S.C.: Arcadia Publishing, 1999.

_____, *Images of America: Troy.* Charleston, S.C.: Arcadia Publishing, 1998.

Robertson, Constance, *The Unterrified.* New York: Henry Holt & Co., 1946.

Ross, James A., *A Martyr of Today: The Life of Robert Ross.* Boston: James H. Earle, 1894.

Sarnoff, Paul, *Russell Sage, the Money King.* New York: Ivan Obolensky, Inc., 1965.

Selzer, Richard, *Down from Troy: A Doctor Comes of Age.* New York: William Morrow and Company, Inc., 1992.

Sheriff, Carol, *The Artificial River: The Erie Canal and the Paradox of Progress, 1817-1862.* New York: Hill and Wang, 1996.

Sylvester, Nathaniel Bartlett, *History of Rensselaer Co., New York.* Philadelphia: Everts & Peek, 1880.

Turbin, Carole, *Working Women of Collar City: Gender, Class, and Community in Troy, New York, 1864-1886.* Urbana: University of Illinois Press, 1992.

United States Bicentennial Commission of Cohoes, Inc., *Cohoes in '76.* Cohoes, 1976.

Vogel, Robert M., ed., *A Report of the Mohawk-Hudson Area Survey.* Washington, D.C.: Smithsonian Institution Press, 1973.

Waite, Diana S., *Ornamental Ironwork: Two Centuries of Craftsmanship in Albany and Troy, New York.* Albany: Mount Ida Press, 1990.

_____, *The Troy Light Company Gas Holder House.* Troy: Hudson Mohawk Industrial Gateway, 1977.

Waite, Diana S. and John G., *Industrial Archaeology in Troy, Waterford, Cohoes, Green Island, and Watervliet.* Troy: Hudson Mohawk Industrial Gateway, 1973, revised 1984.

John G. Waite Associates, Architects, PLLC, *The Marble House in Second Street: Biography of a Town House and Its Occupants, 1825-2000.* Troy: Rensselaer County Historical Society, 2000.

Walkowitz, Daniel J., *Worker City, Company Town.* Urbana: University of Illinois Press, 1978.

Waterford Historical Museum and Cultural Center, Inc., *The Waterford Flight.* Waterford, 1965.

_____, *The White Homestead on Wheels.* Waterford, 1976.

Watervliet Arsenal, *Quarters One: A Place in History.* Watervliet: Watervliet Arsenal, 1978.

Weise, Arthur James, *City of Troy and Its Vicinity.* Troy: Edward Green, 1886.

_____, *The Firemen and Fire Departments of Troy, N.Y.* Albany: Weed-Parsons Printing Co., 1895.

_____, *History of the City of Troy.* Troy: William H. Young, 1876.

_____, *Troy's One Hundred Years.* Troy: William H. Young, 1891.

Wertheimer, Barbara Mayer, *We Were There.* New York: Pantheon Books, 1977.

Woodworth, John, *Reminiscences of Troy: From Its Settlement in 1790 to 1807.* Albany: Munsell, 1860.

INDEX